'I found *Takeover* well researched, interesting and entertaining . . . [it] communicates the excitement and the adrenaline of a takeover battle.'
John M Allen, Chief Executive, Ocean Group plc

'A really enjoyable read.'
Eric Anstee, Group Finance Director, Old Mutual plc

'A gripping tale of intrigue and passions involved in a hostile takeover. Surely, compulsory reading for those fascinated by how the City goes about bringing unwilling parties to the table.'
Sir Malcolm Bates, Chairman, Pearl Group plc

'An enthralling novel on the shenanigans in the business world of today. A book every business person should read.'
John Cowling, Managing Director, Casio Electronics Co. Ltd

'*Takeover* is training in the value of emotions within work and enjoying the experience. An excellent book by Peter Waine and Mike Walker in the art of handling oneself and each other.'
Kami Farhadi, CEO, Portmeirion Potteries

'This is an excellent portrayal of the takeover game, a deadly serious affair, portrayed with driving passion and intrigue by the characters in this book. The business people and advisers show their true colours as the hunter and hunted. The deadly countdown to completion of the takeover heightens the excitement and parallels real life all too closely. This is a book that is hard to put down.'
Richard Holland, CEO, Boosey & Hawkes Group plc

'At last, a "business" book written in proper English and free of jargon. Business people will enjoy finding out if fiction is stranger than truth.'
Richard Jewson, Chairman, Savills plc

'The authors have captured the atmosphere with great accuracy. Those who have survived the process will recognise the key players instantly. For newcomers *Takeover* is a useful guide to the conventions of the "game without rules".'
Neil Johnson, NED, Hornby

'An entertaining read with valuable governance warnings for all.'
Brook Land, Partner, Nabarro Nathanson

'*Takeover* is first of all a very good story which moves with pace, bringing to life all the greed, excitement, ambition, personal agenda and pain of a city takeover battle. Whilst being gripping, topical and warm hearted, it is also packed with information on the realities of business today.'

Geoffrey Maddrell, Chairman, Glenmorangie

'Think takeover, think of the jungle. There are many characters here that I recognise. The authors have caught the mood and attributes of an imperfect system that reflects the real world.'

John Matthews, Chairman, Crest Nicholson

'A wonderful parable – congratulations to Peter and Mike in making a serious business issue into a readable story. I enjoyed it immensely.'

Gordon Owen, Chairman, Energis Communications Ltd

'A most entertaining view of the human dimensions of takeovers combined with clear lessons for the appropriate composition of company boards.'

Martin Packman, MD Corporate Finance, Société Génerale

'Paints as large as life the struggles, pressures and moments of exhilaration experienced by those who play in larger than life roles the cut and thrust of an acquisition. These are pressures that extend into the home and family and the consequences of the contest are often unforeseeable and sometimes extreme. Even experienced practitioners can absorb both entertainment and almost a case study in this lively book.'

C.M. Stuart, Chairman, Scottish Power plc

'A management book with a difference: an unfolding story illustrates the decisions we face in our business and the impact our private lives can have on the outcome. A compelling read.'

Dr Julia Walsh, NED, British Energy plc

'Beyond the drama [there is] a penetrating insight into the boardroom dilemmas that this [situation] creates.'

Peter Warry, former CEO, Nuclear Energy

TAKEOVER

TAKEOVER

Peter Waine & Mike Walker

JOHN WILEY & SONS, LTD
Chichester · New York · Weinheim · Brisbane · Singapore · Toronto

Published in 2000 by John Wiley & Sons Ltd,
Baffins Lane, Chichester,
West Sussex PO19 1UD, England
National 01243 779777
International (+44) 1243 779777

e-mail (for orders and customer service enquiries): cs-books@wiley.co.uk
Visit our Home Page on http://www.wiley.co.uk
or http://www.wiley.com

Other Wiley Editorial Offices
John Wiley & Sons, Inc., 605 Third Avenue,
New York, NY 10158-0012, USA

Wiley-VCH Verlag GmbH, Pappelallee 3,
D-69469 Weinheim, Germany

Jacaranda Wiley Ltd, 33 Park Road, Milton,
Queensland 4064, Australia

John Wiley & Sons (Asia) Pte Ltd, 2 Clementi Loop #02-01,
Jin Xing Distripark, Singapore 129809

John Wiley & Sons (Canada) Ltd, 22 Worcester Road,
Rexdale, Ontario M9W 1L1, Canada

British Library Cataloguing in Publication Data
A catalogue record for this book is available from the British Library

ISBN 0-471-49222-1

Typeset in 10/13.5pt Melior by Hewer Text Ltd, Edinburgh
Printed and bound in Great Britain by
Biddles Ltd, Guildford and King's Lynn

This book is printed on acid-free paper responsibly manufactured from
sustainable forestry, in which at least two trees are planted for each one used
for paper production.

PW:
STEFANIE and PHILIPPA

MW:
MY MOTHER

Contents

Part One

The River

Businessmen aren't fools. They can see as clearly as the next person the right way to do something. After all, no one sets out to do it wrong! But have you ever thought how rarely anyone ever gets it right? And I think this is because you can't make decisions about business in a vacuum. Nothing lives in a vacuum – all it does is keep tea hot. Decisions are made in the world, they are always a compromise between a few things that are about business and a thousand other things that aren't. The baby is teething, your neighbour's just bought a better car than you, the cat was sick on the carpet, who was that gorgeous girl standing next to you in the lift? Are you going to put your mother in a nursing home? These are the stuff of business decisions just as much as balance sheets and sales forecasts.

Jim Crawford, interview in
the *Guardian*, Oct. 1999

LONDON'S DOCKLANDS WERE, for centuries, the receiving bay of the British Empire. Ships from all over the world travelled up the Thames to the Pool of London where they were berthed by highly skilled pilots at any one of a dozen great docks. Here an army of lightermen and stevedores unloaded and ferried the cargoes to the railheads or canals where steam and horsepower waited to transport them across the country to the great manufacturing centres. There were thousands of men with hundreds of different skills, often passed on through generations of the same family. And of all the trades and occupations practised on the docks, the one most enthusiastically followed was larceny.

Every dock had its feared and despised police force who checked the men in, when they gathered first thing in the morning to be picked by the ganger for the day's work, and who, more assiduously, checked them out at night, searching under coats, down boots, everywhere a man's natural ingenuity might lead him to hide a bolt of silk from the Far East or a few thousand cigarettes from the United States.

Time and change, however, wither all things, and as the world and Britain's place in it began to alter after the Second World War, the torrent of goods turned first to a stream, then a trickle and finally dried up altogether. The docks lay empty and silent: the old trades, the riverside cries and the chants of the local wild boys lived only in the memories of an ageing population.

But what goes around comes around, and after years of

5

neglect, new life began to grow out of old soil. The wharves were converted to luxury flats with eye-wateringly expensive river views; the docks became marinas and towers sprang up everywhere, serviced by automatic trains that delivered a new workforce with new skills: financial services, information technology, the electronic and print media; and, Jim Crawford was wont to say, of all the skills exercised in Docklands, the most enthusiastically followed was still larceny – only now it was legal and it was called business!

Admittedly, Crawford was joking when he made the remark to a journalist at one of the parties he liked to hold in his penthouse flat at Tower Bridge but, like many of his more perceptive remarks, it did have a basis in truth. There were, he knew, many people in the business world who would like to see him locked up behind the once-forbidding but now tourist-friendly walls of the Tower of London, just across the river from his balcony. He'd once overheard a member of his main board compare him to Sir Walter Raleigh, public adventurer and private pirate, and suggest that a few years with Crawford out of circulation might make all their lives a little easier. He'd been tempted to butt in and ask why life or business should ever be easy; only, for once, caution had intervened.

Not that he'd been displeased with the comparison. He *was* a pirate, he took chances that others feared, he ventured where they were afraid to go and he came back, if not always with treasure, at least with a hefty reward for himself and, more to the point, a good dividend for his shareholders. In today's business world, a company is competitive or dead!

As far as he was concerned, the entrepreneur was king – it was his flair and the guts to go right to the wire time after time that was the real engine of the British economy – not the pussy-footing of the young investment bankers and the rocket scientists in their offices and on the trading floors of the City. It was dirt under the nails, it was sheer chutzpah, it was a quality he loved to illustrate with a tale from the old days on the docks, of a legendary stevedore noted for his larceny and cunning. And this story, perhaps more than anything else he ever said in public, gives a clue about the man, his fundamental attitude towards business and the events he was shortly to set in progress.

'This docker, his name was Jack Fletcher, was active back in the days when they still used horses to pull the larger loads and, one evening, he arrived at the dock gate, where his perennial enemies the dock police waited, with a barrowload of horse manure. "For the roses," he said. The police, of course, believed not a word of it and sent out for a fork and carefully examined every inch of the odorous load. Finally, they had to admit: it was manure and only manure. They let Jack go home. The next evening he arrives at the gate with another load of manure. They check this – nothing there – and let him go. The next evening the same. The policeman says: "Blimey, Jack, how many roses have you got?"

'Jack shrugs and says, "I got roses, I got friends who've got roses. Any law against taking a load of horse manure home, you find it and I'll stop. But until you do . . ." And, with a smile, he goes off whistling.

'Now, as you can imagine, this really rubs the coppers up the wrong way and they are absolutely determined to discover what it is that Jack is sneaking out in these loads of manure. So, every night after that, they go through the pile with a fine-tooth comb, getting themselves thoroughly . . . manured in the process. Well, this goes on for a couple of weeks and then one evening, no more manure. "That's it," Jack says, and off he goes, as cool as a January night.'

At this point, Crawford would wait until one of his listeners finally twigged, 'He was stealing wheelbarrows!'

And then he would laugh and say, 'Oh, a lot more than that. Yes, he was stealing a barrow every day, but he was also getting his revenge on the dock police; not only making them look stupid, in their own and everyone else's eyes, but forcing them into a position where they actually covered *themselves* in shit!'

Takeover

Jim Crawford might have reflected that you can only steal so many wheelbarrows before even the dumbest dock-gate policeman gets the point, but he was not a man given to reflection and, as the Indian summer of 1999 drew to its glowing close, he was ready to make his move and dump the first barrowload of manure.

monday 4th oct.

butler's wharf, london

CRAWFORD LEANED ON THE BALCONY RAIL of his flat and breathed in the smell of the river and the scent of garlic and hot olive oil rising from *Le Pont de La Tour* restaurant which occupied the lower floor of the converted wharf. He wondered if he and Andrea might pop down for a little lunch later. A table could usually be found for them; *Le Pont* was, in a way, his local . . .

His train of thought was broken by the sound of the phone ringing in the room behind him. He'd been waiting for the call all morning but even so, he walked back inside slowly; it wouldn't do to betray any sense of impatience to his caller.

'Yes?' He didn't waste time with pleasantries.

'Are you ready to go?' The voice was anonymously middle class, saying nothing about itself one way or the other.

'You know damn well I am.' Crawford's bark still bore the accent of his Berkshire childhood – it was something he'd never even tried to lose; part of his public personality.

'Have you spoken to your people yet?'

'I've been waiting for you.'

'Really, how thoughtful.' There was no affection in the tone, only cynical amusement. 'In that case, I think you could start the ball rolling.'

'That's what I've been waiting to hear.' Crawford's voice was full of barely suppressed excitement. 'You are absolutely sure about this? The timing here is vital. If I'm hanging my balls out over a river, I want to be sure there aren't any hungry alligators lurking!'

'I thought *you* were the alligator.' This time the caller chuckled.

'Not me, I'm the alligator hunter.'

'Then just remember, old man, I'm handing you a loaded gun but it doesn't mean a thing if you don't have the guts to pull the trigger.'

This time Crawford laughed out loud. 'Tell your wife to expect an alligator handbag for Christmas.'

He put the phone down without saying goodbye – it wasn't that kind of call – and walked back out onto the balcony.

Overhead a short-haul airliner banked in towards the City airport beyond Silvertown, the sun catching its body in a blaze of light. Crawford breathed in deeply, feeling, as he was to say months later, after the events he was about to start had run their course: 'all the excitement of not knowing. I suppose it's part of being a gambler; you set everything up, you make your pre-parations, you think you know the odds, the chances, you have the resolve to make your play and put your money down, but you can't ever know how the game will come out. Not that I want to say that corporate life is anything like a casino.'

These were afterthoughts; reflections made when, as a jour-nalist put it: 'The bodies had been buried, the wounded carried off to hospital and the blood wiped off the floor.' On that Monday morning Jim Crawford was as sure as he'd ever been that he was about to make the right play.

He picked up the phone again and punched out a number, idly tapping the receiver while he waited to be connected. It was a direct line – he wasn't the kind of man who expected to be kept waiting by secretaries – and the moment it was picked up, he barked, 'Celia? Jim Crawford. I need to see you. Tomorrow at 11.00 would be fine.'

Day

tuesday 5th oct. 23:14

waymouth, paternoster, docklands

CELIA HART, A YOUNG, SHARP (and very attractive, though Crawford would not have alluded to that in these PC times) analyst, had acted for his company, Ayot, for the past two years. No doubt she'd be moving on soon, the good ones always did (one of his private maxims ran: if nobody is after my best people, then they're not my best people any more). For now she was one of his soldiers, or in fact one of his mercenaries, since she was employed by the investment bank to cover the whole electronics sector and merely lent, as a gun for hire, to Crawford. Still, she was a very good gun and the two of them, despite the difference in age and position, got on well.

They met at her office – Crawford didn't want to start any hares by having her come to him – and over a cup of coffee, he said: 'Byfield plc.'

Celia shrugged: 'Middle-sized British company; used to be called Sheetrock – the American word for what we'd call plasterboard, I believe.' She wore very red lipstick and wore it well – her smile was dazzling and dangerous! Watch the smile, miss the mind at work. 'Some sharpie obviously persuaded the Chairman that he needed a name more in tune with the times – something people would remember. They have an electronics components company based in Swindon.'

'With a subsidiary in Fort William,' Crawford added, glad to have caught her out for once.

'Just outside Fort William, actually. Speen Bridge. Also a company providing aggregates for the building trade, a small papermaking and, I think, card-publishing firm in . . . somewhere in the Midlands and . . . something else, I can't be sure. I think it's a construction and development outfit. A bit of a mess, actually.' She pushed the silver coffee tray across the brilliantly polished desk top. 'More?'

'I drink too much as it is.'

'You probably only think you do,' she scooted her chair back to her bookcase and pulled out a reference book. As she took the volume's considerable weight, Crawford noticed the muscle firming under her sleeve. She was obviously still working out. Lucky boyfriend, he thought, and recalled that the current candidate was some kind of financial journalist. However, he knew Celia would be discreet: analysts who blabbed were not analysts for long. On the other hand, they didn't seem to be anything for long in this day and age – Celia was no more than 25 and already earning the kind of yearly bonuses that put Crawford's (official) salary into the shade. 'Let's see, shall we . . .' There was a blur as she fanned the pages, then came to a stop. 'I assume you know all this but you'd better let me catch up.'

'Why?'

'Why catch up?' She ran her finger down a column.

'No, why do I think I drink too much coffee?'

'Byfield plc. Sector: Electronic and electrical. Building and retail. Activities: Research, development, engineering, manufacturing and marketing of . . . It's a diuretic.'

'Sorry?' he said.

'Coffee. Makes you pee more, James. Turnover 350 million. Market capital 136 million. Annual profits, 23 million.' She paused and looked up at him across the desk. If eyes could be shrewd, hers were.

'How did you know?' Crawford asked.

'I didn't, but now I'm reading it . . .'

'That I'm peeing more. I haven't even told my doctor.'

'You hide things from your doctor, James. Next time he asks you how much you're drinking nowadays and you tell him, "half a bottle of wine with dinner," look what he puts down. He'll double it. Don't feel bad, all men hide things from their doctors, from their wives, they even cheat when they have their waists measured for a pair of trousers.'

'You're very philosophical today, Celia.' He'd wondered often and often if she would, if he offered, if he took the chance, would she? But they were friends – beyond business – and friends are better than lovers; they last longer – though the betrayal, when it comes, is often sharper.

'And you're wool-gathering, James, which is equally unlike you. Are you feeling old?'

'I'm 47. I'm young.' Looking around him at the City today, he had an uneasy feeling that in fact, yes, he *was* old.

'It's not your age, it's your appetite.'

'Oh, I'm still as hungry as I was when I was your age, Celia. That's why I'm here.'

'So stop worrying about your prostate, be happy that you pee a lot, it's better for you, and have another cup of bloody coffee since you know you want it.'

'Thank you. I will.' As he poured, she carried on summarising Byfield's entry: 'On a turnover of 350 million, you'd be looking for an annual profit of 8 to 10 per cent, which is what?' As she concentrated, her forehead wrinkled charmingly just at the top of her nose, '32 million. And what they've got is 23. That's interesting. Head and Reg. office: Goldhawk Mews, SW. Executive Directors: John Parker, Chairman; Angus Howerd, Sales and Marketing; E.J. Stewart, Financial. I know Beth Stewart. She's good.'

'How long has she been with them?'

'Not long. Nine months, maybe. She was Financial Controller at Riechman-Harvester.'

'How do you know her?'

'Women in Business; we meet up, exchange news and views. She was looking for a position on a main board and Parker took her on. One of his better decisions, I suspect.'

'So do I,' Crawford said, 'but it does mean she hasn't got that much direct contact with the City.'

'She's a fast learner. Let's see: W.H. Harper, Chief Executive Officer. Don't know much about him, I'm afraid. Non-executive directors: only one and I don't recognise the name. I suspect that Parker hasn't really taken on the idea of using non-execs properly.'

'Absolutely – Cadbury recommends three,' Crawford said.

'And you have?' Celia asked.

'Three. Top people in their field and recent too.'

'That's a point in your favour as far as the City will see it. Good.' She returned her attention to the list of Byfield directors. 'Most of this lot don't light any fires. Anybody with any spark has either left or just arrived, like Beth Stewart. Let's see what they pay themselves.'

'I can tell you, Celia. Too much. Too little to the shareholders.'

'Who are,' she said, as she went on down the entry, 'Vulcan Asset, 7.5 per cent; Norwich Union, 3.5 per cent; the Corporate Bank 8 per cent; United Funds, 7.6 per cent; H.F. Parker 14.5 per cent. A considerable holding of family shares then. Would that be a grandfather, an uncle? We'd need to find out. You've not thought of buying any shares yourself?'

'No, it would only push the price up as soon as some sharp-eyed trader noticed.'

Celia tapped the edge of her coffee cup with a beautifully manicured fingernail. 'Basically this is a conglomerate, with all the advantages and disadvantages that implies.'

Crawford raised his eyebrows, waiting for her to go on, interested in how she would respond.

'Whatever the industrial weather, they can hedge their bets. One or two of their companies will always be doing reasonably well so they can balance out the overall results . . .'

'And hide a mediocre performance,' Crawford put in.

'Particularly of the core business, which is where their expertise *should* lie. And where they should be mustering all their biggest guns to wipe out the competition. OK, I see that. There's nothing on the table, of course?'

'Not yet. There will be if the wind is blowing in the right direction. You know the electronics sector – how does it feel?'

She closed the book, sat back in her chair and tented her fingers in front of her, rather as if she were praying.

'It isn't performing as well as it should, or could. I seem to recall that last year their CEO forecast growth of 12 per cent. I'd have to check the exact figure but that's close enough. They didn't perform to anywhere near that level, so something is wrong with the direction of the company. They probably think they're an active management, whereas they're just reacting to events.'

'Far too common,' Crawford said. 'It goes back to the main board. They're being swept along and they're looking down at the ground rushing past their feet rather than trying to predict where they might end up.'

'I don't quite see how they've been missed by other . . .' she paused a second and peeked at him over her fingers, 'other predators. I likewise don't see how they got through the eighties without sharpening up their act.'

She was referring to the changes introduced by a number of companies in the eighties, when they feared that large conglomerates might spot them lumbering temptingly through the undergrowth and come and gobble them up. Slimming down and becoming more efficient *before* they were attacked, not only saved them from takeover but also made them more effective. As an American chairman had once said of his own company: 'Let's look at who wants us, what they'll pay for us and what we can do about it!'

'I think they've stayed in the clear because, I suspect, the City would think almost anything offered for them would be too expensive.'

'I thought that depended on who was buying and who was selling?'

'To an extent, yes. I think there's also a feeling that companies in trouble attract predators – the wounded animal at the rear of the herd – and Byfield doesn't have any obvious signs of financial ill-health. Also, it's difficult to buy well-run companies at a competitive price and, unless you look quite closely, Byfield does give the impression of being, if not well run, at least not badly run. In the main, it's the corporate identity, the way this man Parker manages to make it appear that things are OK.'

'And would I be correct, James, in surmising from your tone that you don't very much like Mr Parker?'

'You would.'

'Want to tell me about it?'

'Some things even you have to wait for, Celia.'

'All right, go on.'

'It's a public company but it's still, somehow, got that stamp of family and tradition; they're decent people who . . .' he sucked air in through the gap in his front teeth as he searched for the word, 'still believe in loyalty.'

'Dinosaurs, in other words.'

'I've nothing against loyalty, Celia. I think it's very important.'

'In its place, James?' When he didn't answer, she went on: 'OK, I'm an analyst, I don't run companies. I merely sit and observe but I would guess that they've got their strategy right in not diversifying into unknown corporate territory – they've stuck with what they know, even if they are overextended with electronics and papermaking and building. On the other hand, it looks to me as if they're standing still. We both know, companies go *up* or they go *down*! They have a number of institutional shareholders who would certainly listen to any proposals we might put on the table; they have a sleepy board and individual shareholders who aren't getting the return they should. And we both know that the City puts pressure on companies to pay dividends which, sometimes, haven't actually been earned, so they must be feeling some heat from that direction. We also know that the City loves harmony so a new board might look good from the Stock Exchange.'

'And I don't think that anyone on their main board, with the possible exception of your friend Stewart, has the slightest idea or experience of keeping the City happy.'

'Good point, James. They were less than accurate with their financial forecasts, and that isn't going to earn them any brownie points, once the rumours and the gossip starts.'

'Intelligence is vital, Celia. It's how the City operates.'

'Granted. But let's keep our sights on Byfield, shall we? There is a considerable family shareholding still, which probably means that board members aren't being offered any decent equity, though what that says about their loyalty or fighting spirit, I don't know.'

'So, what's your feeling?'

She looked at him: 'It walks like a duck, it quacks like a duck, it looks like a duck. Let's call it.'

'It's a duck.'

'And a bit of a lame one, too. Only remember one thing, James.'

'Just one?'

'This isn't business, just as a friend.'

'Go on.'

'Ducks have a notoriously unstable digestive system. There's a story about Errol Flynn feeding a piece of fatty pork on a string to a whole load of ducks; it went right through each one, the next one gobbled it down, and so on. They ended up threaded, the whole flock of them.'

'What's the point of the story, Celia?'

'The point is, James, the ducks never learnt. They just couldn't resist gobbling up that fatty pork. Be careful, that's all.'

With a thud she shut the reference volume and pushed her chair back to the bookshelf, allowing her skirt to ride a couple of inches further up her long, long legs as she reached out to slide the book into its place.

'Careful wins no prizes, Celia.'

'Yeah, well, I don't want to trade pithy sayings with you, James, not before lunch at any rate. You want my feeling, my feeling is good. But I can't get rid of one question . . .'

He looked at her. 'Go on.'

'What do you get out of it?'

'They have some good development people. Young, innovative. They're being held back at the moment but give them their heads and they'll turn the operation round in a year.'

'So why not hire them away – isn't that rather more in your style? Start with what you've got, not what you might – and note that "might" – make out of it somewhere down the line. Look at the company and ask, why hasn't someone snapped it up already? Could it be, because it isn't worth it?'

'It's worth it to me, Celia. And you'll get your fees. Unless you want to pass on this one?'

'Not a chance, James. I trust your instincts – I sure as hell don't understand them, but up to now you've been right 75 per cent of the time, which is well ahead of the odds – so I guess I'll sit down at the table and take a chance with you.'

Crawford got to his feet and grinned, 'I never take chances, not those kind of chances, anyhow. No, don't get up, I'll see myself out.' He paused by the door and looked back at her. She hadn't moved – and the appraising expression was still on her face. 'Relax,' he said. 'Trust me, everything will be fine. We'll have some fun and make some money – what could be better than that?'

Day −26

wednesday 6th oct. 20:15

regent palace hotel, london

'I JUST DON'T KNOW HOW THEY DO IT!' Andrea had to raise her voice against the hubbub of conversation which filled the function suite of the West End hotel. She was referring to a line of waiters, perhaps 30 people long, which issued from double doors carrying the evening's main course, sweeping through the room like a snake. Winding and rewinding around the 75 or so round tables that dotted the floor, they deftly placed the inevitable chicken supreme or vegetarian alternative before the diners, circled 10 to a table, before slipping away to pick up another two servings. Crawford looked down at his chicken with a certain amount of suspicion – having started out supplying frozen foods to the hotel business, he knew that what went through was sometimes best disguised with a good thick sauce but you can't hide inside knowledge with a sauce or anything else. Still, what the eye didn't see. He grinned at Andrea, sitting beside him with her stuffed aubergine and Persian rice.

'They do it because they're waiters,' he said. 'That's what waiters do! Simple.'

She laughed back, the lights catching the diamonds in her necklace as she moved her head. She was, at 38, a damned fine-looking woman, Crawford thought, her skin still as smooth as it had been when they'd first met 18 years before, just when his life had entered its darkest period. He had loved and desired her at first sight and still did so today, at what must have been the millionth sight.

'What are you thinking?' she asked.

He leaned close and whispered into her ear: 'That I would love to take you out of here right now, get in the lift and shag the arse off you!'

She gurgled with shocked and delighted laughter. Her neighbour turned and raised an enquiring – though polite, this was after all a celebration of business achievement – eyebrow; perhaps he hoped to pick up another Crawford anecdote for his next board meeting. Crawford nodded to him and said, 'These bloody occasions, like giving one to the wife on Saturday night – you don't really want to do it but you feel better when it's over.'

The neighbour – he was from some kind of retail outfit – grinned weakly. Perhaps the woman sitting next to him *was* his wife; in which case, Crawford thought, the sentiment was apposite indeed. Andrea, adept at managing the embarrassment Crawford customarily caused whenever, as she put it, he was let out, leaned forward and said: 'I was talking about the waiters, wondering how on earth they manage to get everything to table so quickly.'

Crawford sat back and let the conversation go on its polite and trivial way around him. Andrea was far better than he was at handling these kinds of occasion. Business Forward or some such thing it was tonight. Awards to those who had, in some way or another, come to the notice of the business press and managed not to blot their copybooks in this age of New Labour correctness. Craning his neck, he could just make out the Chancellor of the Exchequer sitting at a table right under the dais where, later in the evening, some rent-a-celeb would present plastic prizes to the good boys and girls. Or maybe he was wrong, and this was Internet Awareness, with prizes for . . . but he didn't really care. He had to be here because if he wasn't, it would have been noticed, and the last thing he wanted right now was to attract any notice. The hacks from the financial pages were always alert to a change of habit and could grow the

wildest of rumours from the most unpromising of soils. He cut
into his chicken and forked a lump of meat into his mouth. At
least it was well cooked.

'Jim . . .' He felt a hand on his shoulder and turned to see an
old acquaintance, Paolo Matteo, the Chairman of the Regent
Palace Hotel Group. They had first met years before, when
Crawford had approached the young Matteo about supplying
frozen meat to the motorway motel chain he was managing.
They had both been young men on the make and had engineered
a deal profitable to both – if not always to the diners who sat
down to their meals after a long drive. They had kept in touch, as
both their careers had prospered, and saw each other every few
years, generally at functions like this.

Crawford excused himself to Andrea and his neighbours and
slipped out of his chair, taking both of Matteo's hands and
shaking them warmly. 'Paolo, you're looking well.'

'You mean I'm looking fat, eh?' It was true, Paolo had become
as sleek and well-padded as a seal over the years. Crawford
himself was no longer the skinny kid looking for a deal he'd
once been, but his waistline had kept well within his age –
Paolo, at 45, was ahead of his.

'Well, a thin hotelier is like a sick doctor, Paolo. Who trusts
him? Are you here as giver or guest?'

'A bit of both. I'm presenting one of the awards – for tourism –
and, obviously, with all you influential folk around, it makes
sense to show my face.'

Crawford nodded towards the dais. 'That's where the influence is today, Paolo. The Iron Chancellor, aren't they calling
him?'

'I think that's what the Prime Minister calls him – have you
met? If you'd like to I could take you over.'

'Why not? Chancellors are useful friends to have. When he
retires, maybe I could offer him a directorship!'

Paolo laughed. 'I doubt it – I think he'll go back to Scotland
and start preaching hellfire sermons. I've always felt there's

something . . .' he sucked his teeth for a moment as he steered Crawford along the winding path to the top table, 'something a little too puritanical about the man. You remember the character in Stevenson's *Dr Jekyll and Mr Hyde*, the lawyer Utterson who loves fine wine but, to mortify himself, drinks only cold gin . . . Ah, Chancellor, may I introduce my old friend Jim Crawford?'

The politician set down his fork and, as if he had been waiting for Crawford all evening, turned, smiled and shook his hand.

'Mr Crawford, a pleasure. I think we've inhabited some of the same seminars before now but we've never had the chance of a few words. As you know, I'm very keen on encouraging the middle-sized businessman, the entrepreneur . . .'

They talked for several minutes, both men secretly pleased they had an excuse not to eat their dinner though, as Crawford reflected when he made his way back to his table, for the Scottish Chancellor it was probably a greater sin than it was for Crawford. Still, he thought, the man had undoubted talent and a real commitment to smaller and middle-sized businesses. He also had that quality – Crawford sometimes characterised it as the ability to shine – which being in the centre of public attention gives to a person. A certain larger-than-lifeness. It was something he had experienced himself, in the early years of his success, when his DIY chain had taken off with a series of adverts on TV featuring Crawford himself as Mr DIY coming to the aid of Everyman and -woman at their hours of greatest home-improvement need. For a while his had been one of those faces that, somehow, were more real than everyday life. A smart young thing in black at the ad agency had told him this was because 'Television *is* better than life for most people.' Crawford had been tempted to hit the little sod, who can't have been much more than 22 but, on reflection, he wasn't sure that the statement wasn't true after all.

'Excuse me!'

Crawford came back to himself with a jerk. He had inadvertently bumped into someone getting up from their seat. In his fifties, going to stoutness, wearing a dinner suit that was just a little too old and a little too tight but wearing it with a confidence that didn't even, for one moment, think that anything at all could be wrong with something John Parker had chosen to put on.

Crawford stepped back and a smile spread across his face. He held out his hand . . . 'John, how are you? It's been a long time.'

Parker looked at him, looked down at his extended hand, looked as if he were about to turn away and then shrugged and put out his own hand. 'Oh, pretty chipper, Jim. And you?'

'Busy, you know how it is.'

'Absolutely. Can't let the grass grow . . . and all that.'

'Still playing golf, John?'

'When I can.' Neither man had loosened his handshake – they stood facing each other for a long moment until a speaker crackled and the voice of the President of the CBI erupted from the air around them.

'Good evening, ladies and gentlemen, welcome to the Business Innovations Awards 1999.'

'Ah, innovations,' Crawford said. 'I thought it was Internet. How about you, John? Are you on the Internet down at Byfield?'

'Naturally. Now, if you'll excuse me, I have to get back . . .'

'Heather here, is she? Give her my best. Oh, and your son, how's he getting on?'

'Fine, thank you, Jim.' Parker relaxed his grip first. It was only a fraction of a second but Crawford noticed and smiled as he opened his hand.

'Nice to see you again, John.' The two men turned away from each other and headed back towards their separate tables.

Crawford found his pudding – something with a raspberry sauce and pastry dusted with icing sugar – waiting for him. Andrea looked across as he sat down.

'Well, was it useful?'

'The Chancellor? Certainly. Never know when you might need a friend in high places.'

'You're looking very pleased with yourself, Jim.'

He spooned up a piece of crisp pastry with a little bit of pear inside. Combined with the raspberry sauce it was actually quite pleasant. He held up his spoon in a gesture of 'later!' as the CBI man introduced, 'John Bellamy, tonight's innovative keynote speaker.'

The speech included all that such speeches are meant to: a self-deprecating joke, a serious bit, a poignant anecdote, a slightly risqué story, something about the environment, the Internet, Tony Blair, another joke, another serious bit and the wrap-up, introducing television's lovely, talented, impossibly – and Crawford thought, probably dangerously – slim front-woman from some show that only those who had the afternoon free ever watched. Prizes were announced, follow-spots tracked bemused and tipsy winners to the podium where their speeches were expertly cut short and they were sent back to their tables. It was no different from a thousand other such events and every-one there was quite happy because this was what they had sat through a hundred times before, watching other lucky buggers get the plastic and brass awards and – now it was their turn – they wanted to enjoy exactly the same thing for themselves!

These were the thoughts Crawford shared with Andrea in the hired car that ferried them home. 'So why,' he finished up, 'innovate when what they really want is more of the same?'

Andrea yawned. 'Don't we all work better for being thrown the odd banana? A bit of well-deserved praise?'

'Maybe. I suppose it doesn't do any harm. Gives them some-thing to put in the boardroom.'

'I thought Bellamy was rather good.'

'He was. He knows his stuff and he believes in it, passionately. It always shows – that kind of commitment. You can't fake it.'

They were approaching the river and the lights of Tower Bridge. The car slid into the cobbled streets of Butler's Wharf and stopped at the glass-fronted entry-hall where a bank of key-operated lifts waited for their affluent ascenders. Crawford nodded to the driver. He didn't tip the man – the company paid and paid well, there was no point in over-egging the cake.

As the lift purred up towards the penthouse suite, Andrea said: 'So, what's been making you smile all night?'

'Nothing, just feeling relaxed, that's all.'

The lift stopped and the doors opened with the faintest of sounds, depositing them on their exclusive landing. They could have arranged things so that they arrived within the flat but Andrea had preferred at least one lockable door between her and the rest of the world. She walked ahead and unlocked the door. 'Are you going to stand there all night?'

As she went through, he thought, as he had many times in his life, how much he loved the shape of women. The way they, so physically perfectly, *were*; the way they moved, the way they wore their clothes and took them off.

He closed the door and joined her by the balcony windows. She hadn't switched the lights on and was standing close to the glass watching the whole illuminated scene: the river, the bridge, the Tower and the traffic. She spoke without turning.

'So, come on, Jimmy, what's the secret? What's up?'

He stood behind her and put his arms around her waist, pulling her to him, cradling her bottom against his groin. She spluttered with laughter.

'Oh, that's up – but what else?'

He kissed the back of her neck and felt her shiver. 'I can't tell you now,' he mumbled, kissing along the tender edge of her jaw line, breathing in the smell of her hair, her scent.

'Well, it must be something pretty big,' she wriggled herself against him deliciously, 'because it's made you randier than you have been for months. Not that I'm complaining, mind you.'

She turned around and, as a police launch hooted raucously on the Thames, they kissed and moved towards the bedroom.

Day −24

friday 8th oct. 10:45

waymouth, paternoster, city of london

UNLIKE THEIR ANALYSTS AND TRADERS, housed in fashionable Docklands, the investment banking arm of Waymouth, Paternoster inhabited a slightly shabby building on the southern edge of the City of London where – so far at least – the developers had yet to bring their improvements, or depredations, depending on how you looked at it. Crawford had no particular opinion in the matter. His own company headquarters was part of a new development that towered over the Euston area of London and, from his top-floor office, he could watch mainline trains in and out of Euston Station if he chose. From the window of the meeting room at Waymouth, Paternoster he could see little more than the walls of the building opposite and the street below.

The room was perfectly pleasant: maybe five by seven metres, a table in the centre with chairs placed round it, a panoramic window with net curtains and vertically slatted blinds, a print of something bland and modern on the wall. It said that this place was about business. It said nothing about tradition, the past, faded glories. Most of the people who worked in this building didn't even remember the eighties – for them, the early nineties were history. The key to their future lay across the Atlantic, on Wall Street, where the investment bank had its corporate HQ and where the elect laboured every waking hour and a trader who didn't earn a bar, or a million bonus in a year was a failure.

On his way in today, Crawford had wondered: are people

26

really getting younger or is it me? It wasn't him – the kids, the rocket scientists who grappled with the complexities of modern investment banking and broking were old by the time they hit 30 – they were also, a lot of them, seriously rich. Not that this made them, in Crawford's eyes, either sympathetic to deal with or easy to understand. They lived, he thought, in a world of their own, drinking (but only after working hours) in their own bars, buying their own (vastly expensive) cars, eating in their own restaurants. They gloried in their toughness: working long hours without coffee or lunch breaks; they talked the talk and walked the walk and if they no longer admitted to being masters of the universe (or even remembered, or had read, Tom Wolfe's novel) they believed that they made the world go round that made the world go round.

In many ways they were newly minted, interested in only one thing: money in all its endless guises and variations. They talked of retiring early, of finding something else but, for them, *something else* didn't exist any more and so here they were, partners, associates, directors, making deals and making money.

Owen Powys, Crawford's banker, was 29. His hair was cut very short; his suit was very expensive but slightly creased, as if the cost didn't really matter; he wore a coloured shirt and loafers and still spoke with a slight Welsh twang to his voice. He looked like a street market trader and had earned his stripes as a derivatives market trader before jumping across into the slightly more respectable world of investment banking. He was, Crawford knew from past experience, something of a hard man who delighted in giving way to apoplectic temper tantrums when juniors were around. He did it to keep them sharp, he used to say. He also had a reputation as a practical joker who had caused, more than once, younger colleagues to leave the floor in tears. But as he had said, when you find yourself, as Powys had as a graduate trainee, working on a $1 billion deal, there's no time for dicking around and no place for tears.

Privately, Crawford thought that Owen Powys was an arrogant

little shit but then, he was a very good arrogant little shit and who needed politeness anyway?

The door slammed open – one of Powys' specialities – and the banker hurried into the room, slapping down a pile of papers on the table.

'So, you want to hit me with it, Jim?'

Nowadays, it was quite unusual for a businessman to approach his merchant or investment bank on matters of acquisition; the banks had become far more proactive and the work of their analysts and brokers would be combined with the expertise of men like Powys to produce pitch books, collections of companies they saw as ripe for acquisition which they would hawk around potential predators. Crawford, however, was aware that Ayot was not in that kind of league; not yet, anyway.

'Owen, I have a mind to acquire the Byfield Group.'

'Why?' No beating around the bush – *time is money* was truer here than anywhere else in the world. There was already a slightly predatory gleam in Powys' eyes.

'I think that together we can claim a larger market share of the electronics sector. Also, they have some talented but underused research and development people and their peripheral businesses can either be sold or, in the case of the aggregates and building firm, they'll work in very well with our hydraulic systems division.'

Powys said, 'I've never been that happy about the earth moving for you.' He grinned. 'JCB are the only real players in that field.'

'I know. I keep in touch with what my competitors are doing and I reckon this might give me an advantage – we nip around the back, provide a more inclusive service. OK, it's not going to light any fires internationally, it's strictly a home market, like DIY, but it is a growing one. Look at the recent report on house building in the south-east.'

'Have your development people checked it out?'

'We commissioned a report, or at least the MD of that division did and it looks promising. There is a big share of the market which is coming up for grabs. It'll make money, real cash money and you know what you people are always saying, Owen: whether you're an individual or a company, cash gives you choice.'

'True, but it might not bring lasting happiness.'

'Come on, we both know companies get into trouble when they run out of cash, not when they make a loss – not that Ayot makes a loss, or ever has or ever will while I'm in charge.' Crawford added, 'So, there we have it. Byfield. And I'd like you to act for me in this.'

Though it would be Crawford's group, Ayot, which would acquire Byfield, the actual bid would be made by the bank, who would have to ensure that everything was done correctly, answering for their overall behaviour to the Takeover Panel.

Once a company is listed on the Stock Exchange and is involved in a merger or an acquisition, either friendly or hostile, the whole process comes under the eye of the panel, composed of full-time officials and experts seconded from various City institutions who consider, wisely it is hoped, questions of business practice and ethics placed before them, taking their guidelines from the Takeover Code.

This, in a peculiarly British way, is a set of suggestions as to the protocols that should be followed during a takeover; suggestions only, since nothing in the code has the force of law behind it, merely the rather more far-reaching power of opinion and practice in the City. If anyone does breach the code, they'll find themselves out on a very thin branch above a rather messy creek. They'll be ostracised and, in an interdependent system like the City, that means effectively they'll be finished. So a predator must tread very carefully since no one can bend the rules where there are no rules, only suggestions. It appears to some as a rather amateur, shambolic system; and yet it works reasonably well, adapting to change with a dynamic denied the rigid US system of legally backed controls.

There are, of course, disadvantages. Sometimes a CEO or chairman will have an inflated reputation in the City that is quite undeserved; the same can be said of badmouthing. The City rumour mills are as prone to gossip as any supermarket-till queue and, just as it is hard to avoid rules that are not rules, so it is almost impossible to alter or live down an opinion that has no more substance that a few words over a designer beer at a Bishopsgate bar.

Owen said, 'You're an old client, Jim, so certainly we'll take a very close look at this and, provided there aren't any obvious – or less than obvious – disadvantages . . .'

'Have I ever brought you anything that was rubbish?' Crawford cut in.

'No. On the other hand, will running this new company, supposing we pull it off, be any closer to your style?'

'I'm ready for a change, Owen. Want to try something different.' Crawford shrugged, as if to say: believe it or don't! Powys was on top of the subject – obviously had been since Celia Hart had briefed him.

'You're not considering a joint venture or merger?'

'No point,' Crawford said. 'Two mediocre companies trying to kick-start their businesses and become one big mediocre company. Besides, someone always ends up in charge so it's more efficient to start out that way. Too many managers are like too many cooks, Owen. Let's keep it simple.'

'Is that for the shareholders' benefit or yours?'

'They're the same thing, aren't they?'

'Are they?'

Crawford looked at him, his face blank, and shrugged. After a pause, Powys asked, 'This will be a friendly acquisition?' By this, he meant a takeover that the target company and their bankers would be happy to recommend to the shareholders. These happen all the time as industries grow and change and rarely do they excite any comment, unless the Monopolies Board is called in.

'Not friendly, Owen. Their Chairman, John Parker – I had a word with him last night, at the Innovations Awards. He's totally set against it.'

'Why?'

'Why not. Well, not quite. He doesn't like my style of management or Ayot's way of doing business. He wants to keep the culture of the group unchanged. He thinks they can continue serving their customers . . . Basically, it's his company and he doesn't want to lose it.'

'He may have to. What about the board?'

'I don't want to buy the board, I want the company. On the whole, their future is not bright.'

'And the shareholders,' Powys said. 'Presumably a few funds?'

'Funds, individuals, some family holdings.'

'What are they trading at?'

'88p,' Crawford said. 'I can certainly offer an attractive deal but there's no point in pushing the boat out too far at the beginning.'

'No, no, quite. It's the hostile nature of the bid that makes it interesting.'

So it should, Crawford thought. Takeover advisers were making record profits for their banks so far this year, and record profits would mean record bonuses. He said, 'What are you driving at the moment, Owen?'

The banker grinned; 'Not what I'll be driving in the new year. It could be fun, Jim, I grant you that.'

'Why bother with it otherwise?'

Powys pulled a note-pad from the centre of his documents. Crawford noticed a loose-leaf binder containing the Takeover Code on the top of the pile. 'OK, you want us to take a look at this?'

'I do.'

'It does mean – the fact that right from the start this is going to be a hostile bid – information is not going to be freely given. It'll be harder work to root it out.'

'I accept that,' Crawford said, 'and I've no doubt it will be reflected in your initial fee?' Powys nodded with a slight grin. Crawford went on: 'I'm happy, that's no problem. In fact, the quieter you can keep this, before we go live, the better. I don't want to alert anyone else if I can avoid it.'

'The moment we start the process, the Chinese walls go up. Inside the building or out, I can promise you, nothing will get out. Of course, when it's on the table, we might consult any in-house fund managers holding equity in Byfield as to their feeling.'

'It's preannouncement I'm concerned about. I want to hit the ground running with the offer. I want it to be a surprise, I want them in confusion.'

'It won't be that much of a surprise if you've already approached John Parker.'

'He thinks he's seen me off. He won't suspect.'

'You seem very sure of that. Do you two know each other?'

'We've met up on the odd occasion. Nothing else.'

'So we'll do a SWOT analysis, look at the figures, look at the management, do a bit of basic number-crunching and get back to you.'

'Fine, Owen, but I do want to move on this. Let's not waste time.'

'We never waste time at Waymouth, Paternoster,' Powys said. 'Better let me see you out, Jim. This place is so security-conscious now – get stuck inside myself sometimes. You know, I get Christmas cards with Strictly Confidential on the envelope. God knows what my secretary thinks I'm sending away for; contact magazines, I guess. *Business swinger, wants to meet same for dirty money fun.* He stood up. The meeting was over. 'Oh, one thing,' he paused by the open door. 'If you want to keep this quiet until we've something on the table, we'd better not meet here. Anyone seeing Jim Crawford arrive more than once in a couple of weeks is bound to smell something.'

'Give me a call, then. We'll do a restaurant. Somewhere on the outside, right?'

'Right.'

Day

crawford house, euston road, london

MARK SINGH CHIMA, COMPANY SECRETARY of the Ayot Group, was not a happy man. This had very little to do with his job – he was, as the CEO had told him on more than one occasion, first class – it was everything to do with . . . everything else. With who he was or who he wasn't. At 38 he had achieved almost all his parents had hoped for when they insisted he did his homework and stayed in on Saturday afternoons to revise. They were proud of him. Many of his friends, particularly in the Sikh community, were proud of him; he had a position, he had gravitas and respect; he had been a local councillor, he had a wife and two children, both of whom worked hard and did their homework and would, when the time came, stay in on Saturday afternoons to revise. They would probably even attend a university close to home, as Mark had done. Or, rather, as Ranjit had done, since that was his name. Mark . . . Mark was the one single moment in his life when he had rebelled.

The first week at university. He was as confused and lost as every other fresher; looking at the various societies, visiting the student bar but not drinking; trying to familiarise himself with so much that was new. And a girl had asked him what his name was and he'd said, 'Mark Chima'. In no way, not for one second, was this a repudiation of who he was, of his Sikh heritage; it was something else entirely and he hadn't even begun to understand what or why until he'd left with a first-class degree, gone into business and got married. Not to the girl who'd asked his name but to a girl his family had . . . not *exactly* chosen. After all, he and Manjit had known each other since they were kids and it was accepted that they would marry, and they did, after she had finished university and got her first-class degree in physics. And he liked her very much, and every time he thought of her *not* pursuing a career in science but looking after the family, he felt a twinge of guilt. But still, he had known her all his life and it was like marrying your sister. It was boring. He was boring. Even his one attempt to escape from the suffocating blanket of his extended family was boring. Mark. Well, that's some rebellion. Calling yourself Mark. And going home to Manjit, who was putting on more weight and looking more like everyone's mother and not at all like Diane Ellroy, who was almost ten years older than Manjit and looked a good, a very good ten years younger!

Mark Singh Chima sighed and returned his attention to Companies Form 403a, declaration of satisfaction in full or in part of mortgage or charge, pursuant to section 403(1) of the Companies Act 1986. He picked it up and began to read, but before his frankly bored mind could grasp anything of meaning, his office door burst open and in strode the CEO.

'Mark, how goes it?'

No one else in the group would crash in like this – no one else could get away with it but somehow the CEO made every room, every corridor in Crawford House his own. Mark would not have been surprised to see him burst into one of the stalls in the gents' toilet with exactly the same cheery greeting.

'Fine, Jim, fine. Just checking over the completion of . . .'

'Never mind that stuff, Mark. I don't want to know unless there's a problem.'

'There's no problem.'

'Of course there isn't. That's why I pay you. You're the best.'

'Oh, I wouldn't go that far,' Mark demurred. Crawford came round the desk and placed one hand on Mark's shoulder, almost forcing him to look his CEO right in the eyes.

'If you say you won't go *that far*, Mark, then you surely won't. And you're a guy with bags of talent. So you should go a long way. Right?' He let go and Mark gave a silent sigh of relief. He always hated these up-close-and-personal moments with the CEO. It just wasn't his style.

'Right, absolutely. Yes. Right!' He cleared his throat and an embarrassed grin settled on his face. 'Uhm, was there something you wanted, in particular?'

'Board meeting, Mark.'

'November's?'

'No, this month, the 27th. Shall we say eleven in the morning? I want everyone there, the whole board. Right?'

This was interesting. Board meetings weren't called just like that, not at Ayot, for sure, where the CEO liked to keep a tight grip on everything. In fact, any director or the chairman can ask the company secretary to call a board meeting at any time but that had never happened to Mark so far in his career.

'Any particular measures I should take; specific figures or business forecasts you're going to need?'

Crawford grinned. 'Nothing, Mark. Just make sure they're all present.' And then he was gone, slamming the door behind him.

Hastily finishing Form 403a, Mark left his office and hurried along the corridor. If he was quick he might just catch her before she left. She wasn't, however, in her office, though her secretary said she'd only just gone. He rang down to reception, telling the night man, who had just arrived, to ask Ms Ellroy to wait a moment. Then he ran back to his office, locked away his papers, grabbed his jacket and ran for the lifts.

Reception at Crawford House was all glass and steel and the kind of lights you couldn't look at without blinding yourself. As he stepped from the lift, Mark saw Diane Ellroy standing in the waiting area casually flicking through the pages of a magazine and – as always when he saw her again, even after five minutes – his heart gave a little leap. A small woman, maybe five foot four, she somehow commanded the attention; whether it was her impeccable sense of dress (he didn't have the nerve to ask if it was designer label or not, though she certainly wore it as if it were) or her slim figure, the bob of blacker-than-black hair or the eyes, sleepy somehow and casual, always looking at you as though she had just come from or was just going to somewhere terribly exclusive and rather amusing. A New Yorker who really had, it sometimes seemed, gone to all those exclusive places sometime in her 45 years, she made Mark feel like a schoolboy – a schoolboy who was head over heels in love with his friend's sexy mother.

'Diane,' he called. 'Sorry to keep you. I mean . . . not . . .' He cleared his throat and tried again. 'I just wondered if you have a moment. Something rather odd just came up.'

'Sure, Mark, I'm not in any hurry.' She smiled and her face lit up. 'What did you have in mind, dinner at Chez Nico?'

He felt himself blushing. 'No, no, I mean it was . . .'

'Relax,' she said, 'I'm not going to take you away from the joys of home and hearth.'

I wish you would, he thought. 'The CEO just asked me to call a board meeting for the 27th of the month.'

'Oh, that *is* interesting. What do you reckon?'

'He didn't tell me. Only he was acting pretty hyped up.' In spite of himself, Mark couldn't help flicking a look up at one of the CCTV cameras that dotted the building.

'Don't worry,' Diane said, 'the old bastard can't read lips, not yet anyhow.'

Diane Ellroy was on the board of Ayot as Development Director and, over the two years since she'd joined the company, transferring from the London office of an Anglo-American con-glomerate, she and Mark Chima had discovered a mutual suspi-cion of the CEO's style of leadership – or as Diane styled it: dictatorship. She was, in Mark's eyes, prejudiced though she was one of the most innovative members of Crawford's board. She listened to people – to the right people – and, as far as her own team was concerned, chose her staff well and allowed them to run as far as their enthusiasm and talent would take them, while giving them a clear idea of what she and the company situation expected. Unfortunately, Crawford didn't always listen to her and, over the course of a number of board meetings, she and Mark had begun to build up an ad-hoc analysis of the CEO. Their feelings had got no further than a slight distaste for Crawford's style of corporate governance, though Mark had a suspicion that if he'd pushed things just a little, then their mutual suspicion and their friendship might have progressed a good deal further.

Diane said, 'Something's going down, that much I do know. The Chairman has been acting even more bemused than usual and I saw Cousteau,' this was one of the non-executive directors, 'smirking around the corridors the other day.'

'Crawford wants everyone present,' Mark said.

'Probably got one of his successes to report. He does love an audience, particularly when they all love him. He also likes to let some people in on the deal and exclude others. Keeps us all off balance.'

'He brings home the bacon – or at least the profits, Diane, you have to give him that.'

'Oh, I'll give him all that and more. Because I don't like the guy's style, doesn't mean I don't admire his results. I just have the feeling that what goes up like a rocket might come down like one too. And who wants to be underneath!'

'Or pick up the pieces?'

'Now that might be a different matter. Maybe rearrange the pieces. Only that's the future. Our problems are right here and now, with Peter Allbury.'

Allbury was the Chairman of the group and generally regarded as being a decent, straight sort of guy but one who was unable to counter Crawford's cavalier influence. The fact that the Chairman had an office – the second best in the building, just along from his Chief Executive, who had the best – did not mean that his calming influence changed or even ameliorated any of Crawford's decisions. Allbury never had the space to operate freely or the time to implement decisions before Crawford stuck in his, admittedly effective, oar. Mark and Diane were both aware that ideally a chairman should lead the board but should also be capable of being part of the management team if it became necessary. For the last year Diane had been trying, subtly, to build an alliance with the Chairman but he had continually fought shy of committing himself to any plan of action which might result in a boardroom revolt.

'Well, Peter's as decent as they come,' Mark said. 'No way is he ever going to risk letting the wife and kids down.'

'Not to mention the bantams, the pygmy goats, the kune kune pigs and that damned Studebaker he's been rebuilding ever since I've known him. He's really in the wrong company, he should go and join someone nice like the John Lewis Partnership.'

Mark laughed; Diane's picture of the sober Allbury was unerringly correct. There was seldom a day when he didn't have some new story about the animals or the car. Mark had long ago given him up as a bad job but Diane still had hopes. She had once said, 'There's a rebel in every man, no matter how deeply buried. You only have to have the persistence to dig it out.' Mark wondered if there was a rebel in him – and if one day Diane would tempt him out enough to declare himself.

'So what do you think about next week, the meeting?' he said, returning, with an accountant's instinct, to the matter in hand.

'A good board should have a good early-warning system. We don't have a great board but we don't have a bad one either – without You-know-who we might have a real chance of doing something interesting – but leaving that aside, I do think we'd pick up any obvious signs of trouble and I also think that Allbury would share any concerns he had about the business, and he didn't say anything at the last meeting, right?'

'No, I've been through the minutes. There's nothing, not even a hint.'

'He who keeps the minutes controls the meeting,' she said. 'So we wait and see, Mark. And when we see – then . . .' she looked at her watch, 'you sure you don't want a drink? It's the kind of night that makes me feel like finding a bar where they can build a really good martini and sitting there and downing a few.'

Mark shrugged, 'Sorry, I'd love to but I have to take Manjit shopping.'

'Please yourself. And keep your ears skinned, isn't that what you Brits say?'

'*Ear* to the ground, it's your eyes you keep skinned.'

'Sure it is. Night, Mark.'

With a waft of perfume – he wondered if he could find out what it was and buy some for Manjit but that would be too like betrayal – she turned and walked smartly to the revolving door where she was lost in the reflections for a moment before emerging on the other side to hail a taxi, which, of course, she got immediately. Mark screwed his eyes shut and shouted at himself inside his head: Bloody fool, why didn't you say yes? What have you got instead? An hour and a half in Waitrose. The TV. Manjit poring over the *New Scientist* with resentment in every plane of the back she turned on him. He hated his life sometimes and wished that something, anything, *something* would happen.

friday 15th oct. 13:00

river café, london

THE YOUNG WAITER GRINNED and squatted by the table, resting a forearm along its edge. 'So, decided yet?'

In any other restaurant in London such behaviour would have been beyond the pale but here at the River Café, amidst the functional beauty of Richard Rogers' design, near the wood-fired open oven, surrounded by a roomful of above-the-line celebs, the casual style was absolutely right – friendly without being either pushy or obsequious.

Crawford and Owen Powys looked at Celia Hart – as indeed did the waiter, in his case with open admiration – waiting for her to order first.

'The roasted peppers and aubergines and then the salad.'

Both men followed Celia's example in the starter and Powys also ordered the salad while Crawford went for turbot. Celia and Powys drank water in order to keep a clear head for the afternoon's work but ordered a top of the line Pino Alto for Crawford. For the guest, the boat would be pushed out as far and expensively as necessary. After all, as Powys might have said but didn't, whose money were they spending?

'Great.' The waiter smiled at Celia and loped off to the long metal-topped bar that ran down one whole wall of the dining-room.

'What is it with waiters and women?' Powys asked. 'I mean, is it some kind of skill you're born with, Celia?'

41

'It's just something that happens, Owen. You could probably do it by waving money at them.'

There was a rumour of a run-in between Celia and Powys, when she had been a graduate trainee; nobody still around knew the details but it was clear the two did not really like each other. It was no secret, either, that Celia was desperate to get to the New York HQ and become a broker; like most of her peers she was intensely focused upon her career objectives and knew that, right now, she needed Powys. Things had changed since the mid-nineties, when a young derivatives trader had, unsupervised, run up millions in losses and bankrupted his employers. Back then, in the City, there had been a strict ladder of precedence between analysts, traders, brokers and the lordly bankers at the top. Because of this, those on the lower rungs were often unsupervised or their work not properly understood, with disastrous consequences. Things had changed smartly after the *affaire Leeson*. Investment banks still worked in a departmentalised way but the head always made sure it knew exactly what the hands or the feet were up to. Celia needed Powys' patronage right now – later, if he slowed down, she might well be doing his job. At their wage levels, performance was all, no one was safe. It was a situation of which both were well aware and that gave Jim Crawford not a little amusement by the by.

'This is getting a mite philosophical,' Crawford said, sipping from his apéritif. 'Waiters are waiters so they flirt with young women. Even gay waiters flirt with young women. I was saying something of the kind to Andrea the other night.'

'How is she?' Celia asked. 'Give her my best. We ought to meet up sometime, do some shopping.'

Powys said, 'I never really thought of you as a shopper, Celia.'

'To shop is to live, Owen.' She turned back to Crawford, 'Tell her I'll give her a call sometime.'

'Will do. So . . .' he pushed his chair back the very few inches allowed by the placing of the next table, 'here we are.'

'Discreet enough for you, I hope?' Powys asked. 'We felt, Celia and I, that this was better than Nico or Marco or any of that lot. Too many bankers there.' As if reminded by his own words, he checked his messages – obviously hating to be away from the office for any length of time.

Celia said, 'Too many journalists on expense accounts.' And checked *her* messages.

Crawford said, 'Does that include your boyfriend? Mead, is it?'

'Hugh Mead. You should meet him sometime, you'd like him. He's your kind of man, James. Totally dedicated to himself.'

Powys cut off Crawford's delighted chortle; even at lunch, time was not to be wasted. 'We've had a look at the numbers and the board feels that we should go with you.'

'Great, I knew you would,' Crawford beamed. 'You won't regret it.'

'Of course we won't,' Powys said. 'We're investment bankers, we always come out with a profit.' It was impossible to be sure if Powys was being ironic or just ballsy.

Crawford said, 'As long as our interests coincide, right?'

'Right, James,' Celia held up a warning hand as the waiter approached. The buzz of conversation in the room around them would prevent anyone at a nearby table overhearing, but waiters, like taxi-drivers, receptionists and maintenance technicians all have ears and – in London anyway – a fine sense of the value of information.

The roast peppers and aubergines were placed deftly before them, the wine was poured for Crawford to taste and the diners were left alone again.

'You want us to put together an offer document?' Powys asked.

'Certainly. I'll get anything you need on Ayot over to you. What about Byfield – how do you see it going?'

'Celia . . .' Powys nodded across the table, and the analyst, after sipping her carbonated water appreciatively, said: 'We still can't quite understand why you want them, James. One of the reasons they've survived, I suspect, is that they're nothing very much. Not going up, not going down, not really innovative, despite what you say about their young designers. It seems to me that any spark there might have been a few years ago has been put out by complacency. OK, their building and aggregates division is doing well but nothing special, despite what you say about a house-building boom in the next few years. The core business of electronics, as we established, is . . .'

She looked at Powys and he took up the monologue: 'Adequate. Could be better but there are bigger players in the field who already have a foothold in new markets. Why not go after one of them? We could easily put a pitch together for you.'

'Later. Maybe. But right now, I want . . .'

'Byfield. Fine. Then if you're happy and we feel that there's not going to be any backing out for tactical reasons halfway through?'

'I don't have anything like that in mind, Owen.'

'As you know, the Takeover Code is quite clear that we must have given, and I quote, the most careful and responsible consideration to the offer before we make it and that we have every reason to believe we can and will be able to implement the offer. And that goes for us as well as you.'

Crawford wiped a lump of grainy bread in the sauce that remained on the bottom of his plate. 'Owen, I know I have a reputation as a bit of a pirate . . .'

Celia said, 'A *bit*? You're the Blackbeard of pirates! If that isn't a tautology?'

Rubbing his clean-shaven chin, Crawford went on: 'OK, but this offer is, as far as I am able to tell right now, absolutely genuine. I want Parker's company. I will follow through the bid all the way to the bitter end. Satisfied, both of you?'

Celia and Powys nodded, but only after giving the thought a moment's consideration, during which the plates were whipped away.

Crawford raised his glass: 'So let's drink to it.'

Three glasses touched with a silvery note that was instantly lost in the general burble of conversation. They each said, 'Cheers, good luck,' and drank the toast; and as he tasted the sharp complexity of the wine on his tongue, Crawford thought: *That's it now – no turning back, whatever happens. Payback time!*

They sat silent, each perhaps contemplating the days and weeks ahead, until their main course arrived. Then Powys said: 'We'll start due diligence, put a financial package together for you, look at clearances and any competition, though, obviously that will all be speculative, since who knows which way the spot market might respond or what other companies might feel about the whole deal. We'll want to bring in a PR company as soon as possible. Perry King at King Associates is a good man.'

'Not according to his wife,' Celia said, ' or ex-wife. She left him and started up on her own. Queensway Consulting.'

'Well, I don't think we'll drop him because he dropped his wife,' Owen said. 'Besides, he's got a good instinct about how much to let out to the media. He doesn't over-egg the cake, which is a common mistake when companies start to present themselves to City analysts. I'll give him a call – you don't need to see him yet, Jim, unless there's anything specific you want to push out?'

'It's in your hands,' Crawford said, and he was speaking no more than the truth. From the moment the three of them had decided to go ahead, the investment bank would act for Crawford right across the board. It would be they who put the offer together, who made the offer to Byfield's shareholders; it would be they who briefed the lawyers, the PR company and anyone else they might need. It was Powys' job to know the right people and the right time to contact them to make the news look good. And if the news is, or appears to be, good, the City will take notice. It loves a surprise; it hates a shock: Mozart rather than Birtwhistle, though it is quite happy, on occasion, to sponsor both!

Across the restaurant there was a small commotion. All three diners looked over to see Richard Rogers himself enter the room. He was wearing a loose shirt and slacks of linen.

Celia said: 'Eyeew! That material, you can almost smell the flax!'

Rogers went along the bar, shaking hands with various of the waiters and bar people, then, discreetly, swept his eyes around the room, nodding to acquaintances and perhaps – since the River Café had started out as the staff canteen for his architectural practice – at the odd employee. He raised a hand when he saw Crawford and came across.

'Jim, good to see you!' The two men shook hands warmly. Rogers was tanned in that subtle way that only the very rich and the very talented ever quite manage to achieve. 'So, when are you going to give me a job?'

'You don't look too hard-up right now. Besides, I can't afford you. Not after eating here.'

Rogers laughed, 'Should have taken the chance when you had it.' He slapped Crawford's shoulder, nodded amiably to Powys and Celia and went on to another table.

'I didn't know you knew Richard Rogers,' Powys said.

'He knows everybody,' Celia said, 'don't you, James?'

'Did you really once have the chance of using him?'

'A few years ago, when I was putting up Crawford House. It's one of the very few things I regret turning down. Still, what's past is past, we have the future in front of us and, you know what . . .?' He waited until Celia and Powys were both looking at him. 'I think we're going to have some fun!'

Day (−15)

bbc canteen, broadcasting house

'AH, YES!' HUGH MEAD STRETCHED and relaxed, pushing his feet under the table. Angela Daniels, his producer, placed a Styrofoam cup of muddy coffee in front of him. The two of them had been working for the last six hours in a cramped editing channel, trying to put together a report.

'Ah, no!' Hugh peered into the murky surface. 'Didn't I ask for tea?'

Angela slid into the seat opposite. 'You asked for beer actually, though you should know by now they won't sell you booze without a meal.'

'Ah, privatisation.'

'I thought you were in favour?'

'I'm a financial hack, for God's sake. I don't have ideas.'

'Or ideals,' she laughed, unscrewing the top of her bottled water with a barely audible hiss.

'Hugh, laddie, nice show! You too, Angela. I thought you caught the whole thing very well.' It was CR4, a wiry Scot who had revolutionised the network. He was the ultimate arbiter of their fate, and his flattering reference to a long report which had aired the week before, could only do them good; though since he was due to leave soon, how *much* good was a moot point

'Thanks, James . . .' They both nodded and smiled as he passed on.

'I didn't think he knew who I was,' Hugh said, 'let alone my name.'

47

'They know everything,' Angela said. 'Still, he was right, it was good. It made people sit up, the Sundays gave more space to a business show than they've done in ages . . .'

'And not just on the financial pages,' Hugh interrupted. 'We've achieved crossover. Ordinary people listened.'

'What's more important is that ordinary people understood for the first time what's been happening on the boards of the big utilities. The stuff on Midland Water needing to expand beyond supplies and sewerage and choosing . . .'

The pair of them grinned as they recalled the interview Hugh had got with one of the utilities' directors. It was already being talked of as a classic pratfall: the man actually denying a rumour which was confirmed by a press release from his own office! A release that Hugh had produced after the director had dug himself into a hole up to his waist, at which point, rather than take Denis Healey's classic advice to stop digging, he had managed to bury himself completely.

'These people are helpless once you get them away from their advisers,' Hugh said. 'There ought to be compulsory media awareness training for anyone who gets a place on a company board. Look at most of them: you'll find accountants and ex-accountants, maybe engineers but look for human resources and even marketing, you won't find half so many. And as for someone, anyone, who can deal with us – virtually zilch.'

'Just as well,' Angela said. 'It would put people like us out of business.'

'Don't you believe it – there's always a story under the story and OK, sometimes it's hard to dig out, but it's there. That's what is so fascinating about this biz: some guy . . .'

'. . . or girl,' Angela cut in. 'Let's not be sexist about this.'

. . . but more likely guy – let's be realist about this – is pootling around in the back of nowhere. Norwich, say . . .'

'Somebody once asked me for a dirty weekend in Norwich,' Angela said.

'Did they? Somebody in this place? Somebody I know?'

'Would you know the kind of person who wanted to have a "dirty weekend"?'

'Not really. It must have been a suit.'

'That would be telling.'

'What did you say?'

'I told *her*, let's not be sexist about this, that we couldn't possibly have an affair in Norwich, it would be too ridiculous.'

Hugh snorted and swallowed coffee at the same time. When he'd recovered, wiped his eyes, mopped up the spill and laid a napkin across the crutch of his jeans to soak up some of the rapidly cooling liquid, he said: 'Point taken. As I was saying: this director thinks she's just on the board of Doggybrek PLC in Far Norwich, pootling . . .'

'You already said that, and a good hack doesn't repeat himself.'

'Look, the point is that nowadays anyone in management can find themselves in the media eye. Business is in our faces and Norwich or Doncaster or wherever, the financial hacks can appear out of the woodwork at any time – and most of these people simply aren't trained to deal with the situation.'

'So that's your next story?'

'No, I might do it but it isn't big enough to build on the utilities programme. If we can get three or four really hot issues then we'll be a damn sight safer than we are now.'

'Nobody's safe, Hugh.'

'I know that. I said saf-er. Look, I want to raise my profile. I need to get more exposure: do a series, a book of the series, get invited to write for the *Guardian*, whatever, I don't know.'

'What have you got in mind?' Angela was no fool, she was a top editor and had an instinct for what would make a splash. She'd already got a couple of Sony awards under her belt and the only place she was going was up – or across into TV. At 27 she was the right age – if you didn't make it over there by the time you were 30, you didn't make it at all. Hugh was 29, had been for three years now and reckoned he could keep it going for one more at the most.

'My lady . . .'

'Celia Hart?'

'You know she does stuff for Jim Crawford?'

'I think you said something.'

'They're friends. He talks to her.'

'So?'

'He was talking to her last week.'

'And?'

'And nothing.'

'If I may repeat myself, Hugh: So?'

'So we talk, me and her.'

'Is that it?'

'We talk as well, Angela.'

'Where is this leading?'

'If she sees Jim Crawford and *doesn't* mention, in conversation, what they chatted about, if she says nothing, if she doesn't even mention the meeting . . .'

'Then how . . .'

'I check her appointment book. She leaves it lying around.'

'Hugh, you utter, cynical . . .'

'. . . hack. Exactly. The dog in the night.'

'Come on, Sherlock.'

'Crawford is a publicity hound. He didn't bark. Significant? Celia likes to talk about her work. She didn't. Ergo . . .'

'They're keeping quiet about something?'

'I think so. I want to follow it up.'

'Any reason in particular?'

'Crawford has news potential. He's an entrepreneur; he's also a gambler who, up until now, has won consistently in business and in the casino. All my instincts tell me that he's going on a spree, and that it can't last. I want to be there when it goes wrong.'

'He might pull it off, whatever "it" happens to be.'

'Right, and that would be just as fascinating. The man himself is interesting, whatever he does. All that scandal over his mistress.'

50

'Did you ever meet her?'

'Yeah, at dinner with Celia. She's a nice woman. Supports him, that's what he needs; like a lot of these guys, there's a whole load of insecurities somewhere down there in the dark. You know he actually went back to his old school in Reading.'

'Why not? People do,' Angela said.

'A secondary modern? Well, it's a comprehensive now, and a pretty tough one too. He bought them a gym or something. It was kind of touching.'

'Not a word most people would connect with Crawford.'

'Exactly! It's the sort of story that could really make it happen for us, Angie. If we follow it right from the start, before the other hacks get their beaks in there. Full profile: *The Soul of an Entrepreneur.* Imagine being on the inside at Maxwell House when Captain Bob was going down.'

'I always knew you were a liver-and-lights man, Hugh. But Crawford isn't a Maxwell, he's just got a bit of a public persona from those old DIY ads he used to do.'

'Yeah, and how many businessmen have got that? Out there in the big wide world, they . . . they don't know one from another. It's a secret society to those on the outside. If we want to run a story that's going to escape from the business page, we need a strong character to hang it on. Crawford. Ordinary people know the face, the voice. Imagine if Bernard Matthews had been involved in an acquisition battle at the height of his exposure. Great headlines: "Not so bootiful for Bernie!" Same thing with Crawford.'

'That's always assuming that there *is* going to be a story to tell.'

'So far his Ayot group has been just below the parapet. The City isn't really interested in companies with his kind of turn-over; but if he sets out to acquire somebody, even somebody smaller than himself, he's going to find himself a good head taller and all those rifle-sights are going to start swinging in his direction.'

'Hold on,' Angela looked down at the half-inch of liquid left in her cup and rejected it, 'this is all speculation.'

'Call it instinct, Angie.'

'Call it bullshit, Hugh. On the other hand, it could be a story . . .' She pursed her lips as she thought. 'OK, we'll take a punt. But only part time, right. Let's do something on media training just to cover for next month's show. After all, you can't be sure, even if you are a vulture.'

Hugh grinned evilly, flapped his arms and croaked, 'I want carrion – giiiive me carrion.'

'I'll give you a month,' Angela said. 'And now I suggest you buy me a drink before we all go home.'

Day (−13)

waymouth, paternoster, city of london

' "WE'RE GOING TO HAVE SOME FUN." He was sitting there with a glass of wine in his hand and a great big shit-eating grin on his face and he said it.'

'He obviously thinks a lot of himself but then all these guys do; back under Thatcher they were told the sun truly shone out of their arses and they've gone on believing it ever since. And if you want my opinion, Owen, we probably won't have a lot of fun. What we will have is a lot of bother and a piddling little bit of profit at the end of it.'

Owen Powys was speaking to a fellow director, Chris 'Chip' Carpenter. They were in Carpenter's office with a preliminary draft of the offering circular lying on the desk between them. Carpenter flipped to the last section.

'I don't even think he's that efficient. Year-on-year profits are OK but not spectacular and as for this building idea, merging his machinery with Byfield's builders . . . What is it, in a global sense? Pennies, that's all.'

'It is cash, year-on-year, dependable,' Powys said.

'Nothing's dependable, Owen. Not in the long run. What does he want? Have you asked yourself that?'

'He told me: he wants Byfield.'

'I wonder. What does he really want? You know him . . .'

'Not as well as Celia Hart.'

'What's her take?'

53

'He's ready to move into the big league. He wants to be a player.'

'So please tell me why, Owen, he's pissing around with this . . . *nothing* company.'

'The logical answer to that has to be, because he knows something we don't. That sooner or later Byfield is no longer going to be a nothing company but a something company and if he controls it, then he'll be a something businessman.'

'He wouldn't screw with the code, would he? If something came out . . . it'd be worse than insider dealing.'

They looked at each other. The spectre of an employee of a merchant bank buying shares in a company one of their clients was intent on taking over, and profiting as a result, was an ever-present chiller. The compliance department of the bank was there to police the daily running in order to ensure that no one, even if they gave in to temptation, could actually get through the various Chinese walls built around sensitive locations. Even so, it happened – and the concept of becoming involved in a scandal, even if it was advanced and price-sensitive information involved instead of shares, made both men pucker up. Not that there was any great ethical concern – they just knew it would totally finish their careers.

'He gave his word, Chip. It's straight.'

But where there is money there is greed – and where there is greed there is crime and though the City does its best to police itself, its best isn't always good enough.

'Do you believe him, Owen?'

'He's honest, at least he's never given me any cause to think otherwise.'

'You believe him because he's never given you any reason not to – it isn't very strong, is it? Still, you have to trust people, unless they're called Gomez and they arrive with a sack of US dollars and a scattering of white powder.'

'It's small potatoes. The kind of thing that we normally wouldn't touch – unless an old client was involved.'

'And unless the Chancellor was asking why banks weren't supporting entrepreneurs with more vigour. Good luck with it, anyway. Keep the board informed and if anything starts smelling bad . . . I do know a couple of companies who might be interested in parts of Crawford. If it comes to a break-up. We might put together a pitch, just in case.'

'Just in case. I'll tell Celia to keep a weather eye on things from her end.'

'Yeah, do that . . . and what exactly was it between you two guys – what did you do to her, Owen?'

Powys shrugged. 'Life is long, memory is short – thank goodness.'

Day

basement flat, 77 keeble street, victoria, london

ON THE SCREEN, A HOUSE, one of a row of terraces. Outside, a car, a 1979 Ford Escort. The house has net curtains at the windows. A boy, about 10, rides along the road on a bike. The camera stays still, looking at the front of the house. The colour is slightly bleached in that way so characteristic of old footage. After a pause, we hear a wild yell come from the house. Then silence, then another yell. The door opens and a woman comes rushing out, pulling a couple of kids. The camera still doesn't move. There is another yell, wilder even than the first. The door opens and a cat and a dog come rushing out, followed, after a pause, by a budgie, two guinea-pigs and a rabbit. From screen left a figure enters the frame. He wears a boiler suit, has a flat cap and carries an impossibly large toolbox with CAN DIY IT written on it in big letters. Another yell rings out from the house and the figure stops. We zoom in on his face. He shakes his head and says, 'Looks like someone needs a hand!' Cut to the doorbell as his finger presses it and we hear those chimes: Bing-bing-bong-bing-bong! Crash cut into a series of freeze-frames as Mr DIY puts the house to rights in seconds. The final freeze-frame shows the family and the pets at the door. Coming home. Cut.

On the screen, a young couple in their bathroom. It's a tragedy: the walls are damp; the tiles broken, half of them missing; the bath is scratched and paint spattered; the toilet suite beyond contemplation; the taps pitted and leaking; the lino, yes the lino cracked with those little stringy bits sticking out. The young man shakes his head. The young woman, later to become the star of a police procedural show, dabs a tear from her eye. She says, 'We never should have bought the place, Tim. What on earth are we going to do?' And he says, 'We really need a hand.' Downstairs the doorbell rings: Bing-bing-bong-bing-bong! Crash cut to freeze-frames as the bathroom blooms under the helping hand of – you guessed it – Mr DIY and his big box of tools.

On the screen, a lighthouse amidst a stormy sea. Cut to interior: the lighthouse keeper is trying to mend the door hinge. Water keeps flooding through, not surprisingly since the door doesn't fit the doorway. Behind him in the lighthouse the rat family appears with their suitcases and life-jackets. The keeper throws down his obviously inadequate tools in exasperation and joins the rat family as they leave. But hold on, what's this, the HMS *CAN DIY IT* approaches, its hooter hooting the familiar notes: Hee-hee-hoo-hee-hoo and there on the bridge, Captain DIY himself with his . . .

'What on earth are you looking at?'

'Friend at the ad agency found them for me. Regarded as something of a classic campaign now, though they'd got a bit surreal by this time,' Hugh said. 'It didn't really matter what they showed as long as they got in the bing-bing-bong-bing-bong and Mr DIY did his stuff.'

Celia slumped down on the sofa beside him. 'Crawford. I don't believe it. Rewind.'

Hugh did so and Captain DIY ripped off the SureFast insulation and Draftout floor strip, slipped about 200 tools back into the big box and scuttled – as it were – backwards up the gang plank, froze and started down again at a less frantic but still zooming pace. Hugh turned the sound down.

'He's what, late twenties there?' Celia asked.

'This one is from 1980, so I guess he was about 30, 28. Looks pretty much the same, I guess.'

'Not easy to tell under the white whiskers.'

'He's clean-shaven in most of the others. As I said, they were getting a bit wacky by the end – still, he was a national figure and those bloody bongs, remember them . . .?'

Flicking the sound up, Hugh caught the moment and the flat reverberated to the tones that had irritated, exasperated and delighted Britain for a few years at the end of the seventies and the beginning of the eighties, when even St Winifrid's School Choir had included them in their unforgettable Number One Xmas hit, 'No one quite like Grandma'.

'Yeah, that was . . . I remember it, that was truly . . . unforgettable,' Celia groaned. 'Can we look at something else now?'

Hugh turned the set off. 'You want a drink, some tea, coffee, food? I've got some fresh pasta and some pretty good pesto. Bit of salad?'

'Fine, yeah. Why don't you do that and I'll . . . sort of look around the floor at all this stuff . . . cuttings about Jim Crawford you just happen to have scattered by chance . . . Hugh?'

His voice came through from the kitchen. 'Wine?'

'No need to shout.' She leaned against the door while he poured a glass of Italian red. 'So, give. What's the deal with Crawford?'

'I'm doing a profile, that's all. For the show. We thought it might be appropriate.'

'Why?'

'He's interesting. I mean people are interested in him.' He squatted down at a cupboard and pulled out a packet of fresh linguini. 'Will you boil some water?'

Celia filled the kettle and flipped it on. Hugh was pulling salad stuff out of the fridge drawer: rocket, watercress, spinach leaves. She seemed to be eating a lot of Italian lately, and seeing and hearing a lot about Crawford too. 'Do you want tomatoes in this?' Hugh asked.

'No, they're never very good at this time of the year. What about rocket and parmesan?'

'Great.'

'And what about telling the truth.'

'About . . . Crawford, you mean?'

'Yes.' Celia could be a woman of remarkably few words when she chose.

'OK, now I haven't snooped at all but I do have ears and . . .' Celia grabbed the kettle, which had started steaming, and carried it to the pan where she tipped it in, refilled it and flicked it on again. 'Go on.'

'Something is going on. Not one Crawford story have you brought back from at least a couple of meetings. And last week you called Owen Powys to set up lunch at the River Café. Now would I be right in assuming that the unnamed third party at that lunch was . . . Jim Crawford? And would I be right in assuming – and I'm still not asking you to breach any confidences – that he is contemplating some kind of business move? What? A share issue? Hardly something secret. Retirement? Not likely. A change of career? Again, unlikely. Probably a merger or an acquisition, otherwise you would have fessed up.' He began to shave thin slices from the edge of a block of parmesan, letting them fall on a bed of rocket.

Celia sipped her wine. 'That's what you think, is it?'

'I think he's worth a profile at any time. Looking back at his career, at least the public phase of it, I think he's still ambitious and I think that the more chances you take, or I take, the more likely I am to hit it lucky.'

'Well, I'm not going to confirm or deny anything you've said – but have you been looking at his company, Ayot?'

'Yup. Will you pass the kettle?'

She did so and he added the water to the pot. 'Just another half, I think, and we're ready to go.' He held the kettle under the tap for a moment, then passed it back to her. 'The commercial results are good but corporate governance is poor. The City doesn't seem to mind particularly, after all returns are positive but . . . I think . . .'

'Yes, what do you think?'

'That Crawford needs a battle to keep himself sharp. He loses interest once things settle down. He can't run a company on a day-to-day basis and at the same time, he can't keep his mouth shut and go along for the ride. He's the worst kind of back-seat driver. That's an ad-hoc view. I know you like the guy and . . . More wine?'

'I do like him, yes. But I wouldn't want to have to outguess him.'

'Is that a possibility?'

'No, I'm just an adviser, an analyst.' She held out her glass. 'Jim Crawford is something of a law unto himself. Look, Hugh, do you mind if we don't talk any more about it right now? If and as soon as there's anything to say, then I'll tell you but until then, you carry on with your profile and I'll . . . get the balsamic vinegar and olive oil. *Capiche?*'

'*Capiche*! And cheers!'

'Oh, and I nipped into Second Skin during lunch – so don't drink too much, you know how difficult you find all that lacing when you're tipsy.'

'Hey, that was only once.'

'Believe me, Hugh, when it's a question of being trapped inside a rubber catsuit for six hours, once is enough!'

They looked at each other over their wine glasses and laughed.

Day −5

wednesday 27th oct. 11:00

boardroom, crawford house, euston road, london

TRADITIONALLY, THE COMPANY SECRETARY worked with the chairman or the CEO to run board meetings in the smoothest and most efficient manner. This was not Crawford's way, Mark Chima reflected; he preferred a certain edginess to prevail, which left his directors (and he definitely thought of them as *his*) vulnerable to the kind of rabbit-out-of-a-hat flourish in which the man delighted.

Mark had managed to catch a few words with Diane Ellroy before the meeting but neither of them had discovered anything further about the CEO's plans, and anyway, the question was now academic, since the *lapin* would soon be out of the *chapeau*.

The boardroom at Crawford House was, to put it mildly, uncluttered. Two white walls, each with a large abstract painting chosen by a designer, since Crawford's taste in art stopped when the human form lost its form; and two window walls, startlingly clear, looking out over the Euston Road. The glass in these could be dimmed at will, rather as if Crawford had the power to control the sunlight itself. Today, the glass was undimmed, letting in a greyish light that seemed to writhe sluggishly under low clouds and had nothing of the sun about it at all. Below, in the busy streets, traffic crawled and added exhaust fumes to the mix. At one end of the room a pale wood sideboard held tea and coffee pots; the boardroom table was a plain slab of

61

some black material – Mark felt it shared the light-eating qual-
ities of the monolith in Kubrick's *2001* – with pads and pencils
laid out in the directors' places and crystal carafes and glasses
arranged along the centre.

'Dreaming?'

Diane Ellroy had touched him on the shoulder as she passed
and now smiled back at him while she arranged her pile of
papers. He returned her grin and felt a palpable twitch of desire,
followed immediately by a wave of guilt. It was, he thought, that
great old double act: Desire and Guilt. They make you laugh,
they make you cry. They make you think of taking the Development Director's clothes off and nibbling every inch of her
body instead of the business in hand – he blushed and, with a
massive mental effort, pulled his attention back to the table.

Peter Allbury, the Chairman, impeccable as always in char-
coal grey, was sitting at the far end, chatting with Norman
Brown, one of their non-executive directors. He was a merchant
banker of the old school by profession and his task should have
been that of liaising with the City institutions which he knew
well, though only at a high and rather rarefied level nowadays.
In fact, Crawford, as CEO, was as well versed in the labyrinth of
the Square Mile as Brown, and Mark wondered why the man
was kept on the board and what he did to earn his money. It was
all part of the mysterious conundrum surrounding the relationship of Peter Allbury as Chairman and Crawford as CEO. The
natural order had, somehow, been overturned. Granted, the CEO
of any company shouldn't be a shrinking violet; it's his drive
and need to succeed which will ensure the profitability of the
group – but, and this is a very big *but*, the Chairman should
always be there as a court of last resort, as the fail-safe mechan-
ism which, if the CEO ever goes critical, can activate the shut-
down sequence. In short, if the CEO ever gets out of hand, the
chairman may need to sack him. Ultimately, that is his prime
directive. And anyone who knew Peter Allbury, that nice man,
had the greatest doubts that he could ever find the steel within

himself that would, forged in the fires of corporate governance, become the blade that could stab Crawford in the back, the front or any other part of his anatomy.

The relationship between chairman and CEO should be dynamic, moving from mutual suspicion to trust. Diane Ellroy reckoned that on their board it went from mutual suspicion, through total defeat to abject slavery. She would admit, in her mellower moments, that this was a somewhat radical view – but only somewhat. If relationships are the key to corporate success, then Ayot should have been a failure. The fact that it wasn't said a lot about Crawford and the manner in which the rest of his board made do. What it said about the future was – like so much else that awaits us all – as yet unknown.

Jeff Coates, the Financial Director, an accountant who had joined them a few years before, was doodling on his pad. Little sunflowers with faces. He was very much a money man and rarely seemed to offer any opinions outside the counting-house. Sales and marketing's Philip Goodman was the youngest member of the board, in his early thirties, and intensely ambitious, which was good for Ayot. He was also the only member of the board, apart from Diane Ellroy, who had the chutzpah to vote against Crawford on a regular basis. Mark reckoned the Chairman liked to think of himself as encouraging this kind of proactive management but it would surprise no one if Goodman moved on to bigger and better things soon. Colin Burroughs, human resources, appeared to be obsessed with downsizing and would, Mark reckoned, have cut the Ayot workforce by a third, regardless of efficiency, if he were given the chance.

Two of the non-executive directors entered together – something of a study in contrasts. Pierre Cousteau was virtually a stage Frenchman – witty, urbane, impeccably dressed and very sharp. Gavin Clooney was almost equally the caricature of an academic, with a long-serving suit and a sweater that someone should have thrown away years ago. The irony of the situation was that though Pierre looked the part, Gavin Clooney really was it. A generalist, he was able to disassociate himself from the particular and see the long-term strategic aims that executive directors, locked into the day-by-day running of the company, might have missed. He was also able, without causing any offence – and his slightly apologetic, professorial manner helped here – to point out flaws in the reasoning of his fellow board members. Mark knew that Clooney served on a number of other boards and was highly valued for both his practical and theoretical knowledge. He began as an academic, moved into industry where he had been highly successful and now, after a spell in Europe, to which he was devoted, was back teaching part-time. In the course of his non-executive career he had walked away from a couple of boards and, on both occasions, his defection had proved highly perspicacious. On the other hand, rather like a Zen Master, his interventions came seldom and were, for lesser mortals, as hard to comprehend as were his ultimate loyalties.

'Good morning.' Crawford had timed his entrance to the second and now walked along the length of the table, nodding here and there, to the vacant place next to Allbury. He looked down the black rectangle at Mark and nodded to him. He placed a slim black leather folder on the table in front of himself. 'Everybody here – you've all got coffee?' There was general murmur of assent.

'Or tea, if you want it?' And Mark thought: 'Timing', and then, 'Crawford doesn't actually own this company, he just runs it like he does.'

'We're all settled, Jim,' Peter Allbury said. 'I think the board would like to know what you . . . we've called this meeting about.' For all his common sense and decency, Allbury didn't have a relaxed bone in his body; the concept of timing or wit, of saying something just for the hell of it, did not exist in his universe.

Crawford grinned, 'Absolutely, Mr Chairman.'

'Time is money, after all.' Allbury was the only man Mark knew who could bring out a crashing cliché as if he meant it. He was also incapable of pretending that he didn't know what his CEO was about to reveal. Mark wondered who else had been in the secret, whatever it was, and why Diane hadn't been told. And indeed, who else hadn't. And what that might mean in terms of future loyalty. Sometimes Mark felt he was a spectator at a Renaissance court.

Crawford looked round the table, catching every eye, pulling their attention back to himself – not that he needed to. Where else was anyone going to look?

'Ayot is going to acquire the Byfield group of companies. Well, it is if the board decides to back my judgement on this.' He paused, as it were to allow a flock of flying pigs to pass by the windows.

If you back my judgement? Mark thought.

'The offer will be on the table Monday 1 November. I think you'll all agree, once you've seen the figures, that this is not only the right move but that Ayot has the right people and the right skills to make it work. This is a strategic decision – rest assured that the thinking behind it is solid and that the implementation will be every bit as successful. Ayot has never been a company that has surrendered to bureaucracy – we have the will and we have the skill and we'll be in at the kill!'

For a moment, silence. For a longer moment, silence but just beyond it the sound of brains working furiously as they attempted to digest the CEO's statement. Allbury sat back slightly with an expression that said: I knew. Mark looked quickly around the table and noted a number of other faces that betrayed complicity. The rest of the board, those outside the charmed circle, were busy bringing themselves up to speed. He could think of a dozen questions he'd like to ask immediately but it was not the company secretary's place to put them. He noted in his minutes book: The CEO opend m'ting wth stmnt: Takeover Byfield!

'John Parker,' Peter Allbury prompted, to get the ball rolling.

Along the table, Phil Goodman leaned forward: 'Medium-sized electronics. Some other stuff too but I, uh . . . I would have thought that, uhm . . . we should,' he turned directly to Crawford, 'how far, exactly, is this . . . this process along?'

'We'd like to have the offer on the table 1 November. Obviously, it depends on you. The strategy is in place, we have back-up from the banks and our subsidiaries, or we will do when it is necessary, so there's a whole support system working for us if anything should go wrong. Which it won't. Now I don't want you to feel excluded, but there was . . . there is the need for security up to this point. You know what a lot of old women there are around the City.'

Goodman cleared his throat: 'From members of your own board? I mean, if you feel like that about us, maybe we shouldn't be here at all.' He was obviously angry and not troubling to keep it hidden. 'This does concern us, you know.'

'Philip, I know, and I can see just how pissed off you are,' a real Crawford man-of-the-people, I'm-just-one-of-the-boys moment, 'but believe me, there are factors involved here which you will, I promise, be made aware of as soon as . . . as soon as I can do that. And I know that you, particularly, wouldn't want to feel that you were holding back new ideas?'

Goodman nodded, unmollified but holding fire for now; he felt himself to be an innovator and could not, in all conscience, or perhaps vanity, admit to a natural conservatism.

Crawford looked to his left, at Jeff Coates who, as Finance Director, should deliver the first response. 'Jeff?'

'We have been talking about development, right, Diane?'

'Sure we have, Jeff,' Ellroy said. 'We've been specifically, you and I, thinking about expanding beyond the EU. We have foreign markets but no foreign industrial base and I know we both think we should.'

Crawford cut in: 'I am aware of this, Diane, and I think you'll find that Byfield will be useful here. People often talk about the size of a deal but not about its complexity – about what it might do for us . . .'

Goodman said, 'They don't have any overseas links that I'm aware of.'

'That you're aware of at present,' Crawford said. 'Jeff, go on . . .'

'If we're looking to expand, shouldn't we go through the alternatives first? Internal development, for instance. Isn't it better to build than to buy?'

'In certain circumstances, yes,' Crawford said. 'But not always. Internal growth isn't sexy in the eyes of the City. Acquisitions still are. It may be hype but hype can be effective and it can be transmuted into something real.'

'We should at least look at the possibilities. Isn't there the possibility that resources we should be using within the group will go to finance the acquisition? People are people, Jim, they are a vital resource . . .' He flicked a glance at Burroughs – the two had diametrically opposed viewpoints on people – 'If managers feel that we, at board level, are more interested in acquiring other businesses than managing our own, there could be considerable loss of morale.'

Burroughs jumped in before Crawford could reply. 'Jeff, I totally disagree. I feel that the kind of go-ahead can-do management we want, we need to attract, will respond positively to the challenge of a takeover.'

'Maybe,' Coates said, 'but I'm not so sure. And what about integrating new people?'

'Gives us a great choice,' Burroughs said. 'We take the best of the best and get rid of the rest.'

Goodman raised a hand a couple of inches above the table. Mark caught the dull gleam of expensive gold on his wrist. 'From a sales point of view we could be looking at a wider customer base, new technologies . . . self-confidence. Business schools do courses in it – we could get it from this sort of coup. Of course, we could also catch a bad cold or worse.'

'I think you'll find that the initial assessment of a company – of Byfield in this case – is usually correct. There won't be any nasty surprises.'

'And there will be increasing production capacity at a stroke,' put in non-executive Norman Brown.

'OK, OK,' Coates agreed. 'We can see that but . . . it's the local managers who are going to have to handle this influx. Are they prepared to get rid of staff – integrate new staff into the company culture?' Burroughs was about to reply but Coates continued without a gap. 'Jim, you said acquire. Colin said takeover. I mean, is this what you mean? Have you considered say, a joint venture with Byfield or some kind of merger or a licensing agreement? Maybe a minority investment?'

'I have, Jeff. I and my advisers have been through all the alternatives. And we're aware that putting all our eggs into one strategic basket could leave us vulnerable if we lose out. That won't happen. The right strategy, the right people, you and your staff, will ensure success.'

'I thought *we* were supposed to be your advisers, Jim?' Diane Ellroy's ironic tone was unmistakable.

Even Crawford smiled as he replied: 'Of course you are, Diane. And I know that you know me very well. And I know that you know our management style . . .' he meant *his* management style, 'has increased profits year on year for over a decade. And I know that you know it isn't my style, or the Ayot style, to crawl like a snail when we can . . . fly like a bird and crack other juicy snails and eat them. And I know that disagreement is often the precursor of agreement.' He looked around the board with a wide grin. 'It shows that all of you are interested. And interest gives us momentum. And we need to keep up our momentum, otherwise the bike will fall over.'

Pierre Cousteau raised one eyebrow – Mark called it his Spock mode – and murmured: 'Bikes, snails, what next, Jeeem?'

'Increased profits, Pierre. And a vastly increased public presence.'

'You mean publicity?' Diane asked. 'We're going to get a lot of publicity out of this?'

'We are.'

'Which means,' Goodman said, 'that Byfield is going to fight us? This is hostile?'

'This is hostile,' Crawford confirmed. 'I tried the friendly approach and their board made it clear that they would not welcome a merger of any kind. In addition, their advisers want a higher offer price than, frankly, they are worth. Their board is undynamic, stuck in the mud . . .'

'And they don't eat snails,' put in Jeff Coates. 'So why on earth are we . . . sorry, Jim, are you doing this?'

'Because the group itself is healthy, ripe for growth and has terrific potential in markets that we would love to be in. And because I'm a greedy bastard.' The laugh didn't quite give the lie to the remark. And, Mark Chima thought, selfishness isn't leadership – it's just . . . selfishness.

'And due diligence . . . has shown all theees?' asked Cousteau, confirming Mark's suspicion that he was reacting to his cues.

'It is very impressive,' Crawford said, 'as you'll all see when you look at the documents we've prepared for you. Phil, you'll be interested in the sample list of customers we've laid out with addresses and contact numbers. Be subtle in your approach, but I think you'll agree with my conclusions about the potential. Jeff, you'll obviously want to see the management and organisation and I think you'll find scope for, uh . . . your talents there.'

'Uhm . . . if, if I could . . .' Gavin Clooney cleared his throat with a professorial cough. 'Due diligence, Jim. I always rather feel it's a little like a company audit. Internal audit.' He spoke quietly, so that the whole board had to give their attention to the remarks, in case they missed anything. 'We tend to think of these things as financial. And we tend to think of finance as being the be-all and end-all, eh? And sometimes we forget that due diligence should be about culture too. The ambience, so to say, the tone of voice of the organisation we wish to acquire. I mention it merely so that we are aware, when the time comes that, uhm . . . one night does not make a marriage.' He smiled and settled back in his chair.

Crawford leaned down the table. 'The organisation is stable enough, Gavin. And if that's the case then surely the staff . . .'

'If I may, Jim. Organisations are intrinsically unstable. People are intrinsically stable. Look at Mao Zedong's attempts at cultural revolution in China.'

There was a pause as board members tried to make the leap of intellect that Clooney appeared to think was obvious to one and all.

Diane Ellroy slipped in a question: 'Their succession planning, Jim. How do you see that?'

It was rather a clever stroke, Mark thought, since Crawford had implemented no genuine succession planning in his own company.

'Too early to say, Diane, but rest assured, we will take full recognisance of its importance.'

Colin Burroughs asked: 'Are we going to be ready to hit the ground running as far as strategy implementation is concerned?'

'We are, Colin. We'll agree where we want to go in the long term and the minute we're through the door, we'll get it in place.'

'Including downsizing?'

'Including whatever we think, whatever the new board considers will be necessary.'

'You're confident that you . . . we can effect change and make it stick, so we can achieve our strategic aims?'

'Once again, I think we have the team, right here, to do that. That's why we pay you all such a lot of money.' Crawford paused for the inevitable laugh. 'You're good. You stay with it. All the way through. The right stuff, the right strategy.'

'Jim . . .' Clooney again. 'There *is* no right strategy. As Karl Popper pointed out in his work on the scientific method: there is only the best method or strategy we have *at this moment*. There will be better. That's why there is a theory of relativity, a theory of evolution. There are many strategies – just as there are many languages. I'm sure I don't have to remind you of Wittgenstein's *Philosophical Investigations!*'

'Of course not,' Crawford jumped in, 'bedside reading for all of us.' It got a laugh but a cheap one. Mark realised that Crawford knew very well that Gavin Clooney was talking good sense and, for some reason, was intent in heading him off.

The debate continued for a while and Mark continued to minute Crawford's remarks, as he went through everyone in the room, offering each something tasty; it was a bravura perfor-mance but, to Mark's eye, neither Diane nor Peter Allbury, nor – possibly – Phil Goodman, were over impressed. Clooney was, as usual, gnomic. The rest were either anxious – wondering about their own future in the new enlarged entity – or quite plainly anticipating the prospect of action. All of them, no doubt, were already thinking about the stories they would tell once the offer was no longer under an embargo. They would enjoy all the excitement without any of the risk. Let Crawford carry that – though perhaps they should have thought about exactly whose money it was that the CEO was risking in this particular game.

Crawford finished his massaging operation with the company lawyer and a silence fell. He looked around the table, waiting for any further comments. Finally he said: 'OK, I'd like all of you to familiarise yourselves with the material and if you have any further concerns, come and see me. Otherwise, I think I can promise Ayot, and all of you, some interesting times ahead as we build on our success to create an even more successful future. I would like the board to reconvene this afternoon for the vote.'

He stood and waited . . . a canny move which ensured that everyone else had to leave the room before him and talk in groups of two or three, rather than discuss the matter as a board in the boardroom. It would remove the imprimatur of corporate governance and make any disagreement seem like backstairs plotting rather than mature, top-table consideration. You had to give it to the man, Mark thought; he really was a buccaneer.

'Well, we wondered, now we know,' Diane said, standing over him as he finished the minutes. Her presence was overpowering; her scent swirled around him like . . . like . . .

'Yes, we do and what do we think of it, now we know?' He seemed to be making sense, at least. 'What perfume are you wearing? Sorry, did I say that?' He suddenly understood how it was that someone could blush furiously. 'I meant . . .'

She leaned down, resting one hand on the table, close enough for him to see the curve of her throat and the shadow of her silver earring as it swung slightly on the lobe of her ear and the pulse – Oh Lord, he thought – the pulse of her blood in the vein just under her ear. Oh Manjit, he thought, what am I doing to you and the children?

Diane said, 'We have to talk, Mark. Not here, not even in this building. Somewhere on the outside. I mean, I don't know what he's up to, the old bastard, but I don't reckon it's for our benefit at all. He's got some private agenda and he thinks he can carry it off like . . .' She snapped her fingers.

'We'd better read the offer doc first,' he said, 'then maybe get together with . . .'

'No one yet. He'll get the vote this afternoon, no question about that. There's nothing to object to, his record . . . well, all of it; it'll go through. We keep our feelings on this between ourselves until we can be more certain.' She turned her head and looked at him, her mysterious grey eyes only inches from his, and said: 'If I'm going to be screwed, I want some kind of say in how, when and who!' And smiled and left the room, leaving Mark alone with thoughts he hardly dared admit even to himself.

Euston Road, 12:14
Hugh Mead pulled his leather jacket closed and buttoned it up. It didn't give much protection against the thin, cold drizzle that

had begun to fall but he wasn't going to stick around for much longer. His vigil outside the steel and glass of Crawford House had paid off. Ayot never held board meetings on Wednesdays. They never held them out of the regular order. And yet, this morning, the main board members had arrived at the revolving door one after the other, in a flurry of taxis and hired cars. Crawford had been in the building since eight – Hugh had been outside since seven every day this week but now he had his confirmation: something was going to break and break soon. It was time to see a man about a freelance job.

Day

sunday 31st oct. 13:15

butler's wharf, london

THE SKY ABOVE THE RIVER was a vast bowl of icy blue, the sun painfully bright, giving only the faintest of October warmth to burn off the last tendrils of mist that hung like spider silk around the piers of Tower Bridge and from the tall single mast of the Thames lugger moored by the opposite bank. On the river a chain of barges filled with garbage made their way downstream, gulls slipping and sliding in the air above the white furrows of their wake; it was a constant sight, London's rubbish being moved out to make way for more. It was said that over hundreds of years, floating islands of garbage had built up and now moved restlessly in the currents of the Thames Estuary, their flickering methane glow visible at night – no doubt luring unwary captains (of ships or industry?) to a smelly fate.

Jim Crawford finished the last of his coffee. He was sitting on his balcony, wrapped in a fleecy dressing-gown with the remains of a late breakfast on the table beside him. Andrea was taking a shower. He was . . . he was – he thought about it for a moment. He was waiting; everything so far had been preparation but now there was nothing more to be done, everything had been set up and in a few moments he would make the call that would start the whole process moving. Obviously, nothing was certain at this stage of the proceedings, but the offering circular looked good, his main board was behind him and he knew this was not only the right time but the perfect place from which to launch the bid. He owned two houses in Britain and one abroad but this flat, overlooking the river at its most picturesque and historic point, held a particular importance for him. It was payback for his childhood. The building was architecturally and historically linked to the river that ran between his boyhood home in Reading and London – the Thames – and the lessons it had taught him, lessons he had never forgotten.

It was a school trip – he must have been seven or eight and had raised the money for the outing himself, doing jobs for people on the estate where he lived with his mother. She had absolutely refused to pay – if there was any spare cash it went on alcohol, not on the child who was a constant burden. Her only contribution to his education was to return the free hair-lice shampoo when parents were asked to contribute something towards the school fete.

The idea behind the trip had been to see the Houses of Parliament but in the afternoon they had taken a trip from Westminster, downriver to Greenwich and back. It had been a grey day and the water choppy; their teacher had told them not to lean over the gunwales but he had been fascinated by the sights and sounds of the river and had run to the prow, where he could look down on the glassy green water sluicing past the rusty steel sides of the boat. His teacher, Miss East – he could see her now as plainly as if she were standing on the balcony in her yellow jacket; her dark, curly hair blowing around a heart-shaped face; her eyes, some-how, kind and interested – had joined him and told him that the very same water he was looking at here in London had been in Reading, passing under the bridges there, only a few days before. And it was as if he had been struck by lightning: the revelation that *everything changes*. Nothing is forever. The water flows under the bridge and down to the sea. It was the first real thought he'd ever had and in the days and months and years following, when he was beginning to draw in the faint outlines of his future, whenever he felt lost or defeated, he would go to one of the bridges and throw in a stick or crisp packet and watch it move downstream, away, quite literally, towards tomorrow.

And here he was, in the future, beside the river that still flowed and always would. He picked up a notebook and flipped it open to a page halfway through. The page was headed: 'The Best I Gave To You'. Underneath, there were eight lines written in black ink:

> *If you could love me*
> *Half as much as I love you.*
> *If not, remember,*
> *To another I will say:*
> *Take what is left,*
> *But in the taking know*
> *Not much remains.*
>
> *The best I gave to you.*

Nobody, as far as Crawford was aware, had even the slightest inkling that he wrote poetry; most of them would have laughed at the mere suggestion; the rest would have shaken their heads and said: what's the scheme this time. Only Miss East, wherever and whoever she was now, would have believed he could do it. Oh, there had been other teachers, some of them quite good, but only she, at junior school, had believed in him – not in his future or his talent, just believed that because he was a child in her class he was worth teaching; he meant something. Miss East and the river. Perhaps without her he would, one day, have completed the circle and drowned in that river.

He took out a pen and wrote under the poem: J. Crawford. October 1999. Then he closed the book and slipped it into the briefcase that stood open on the floor beside him. It was almost time. He got to his feet and left the balcony.

Inside the main room, he slid the glass door closed behind him, shutting out the sound of traffic and tourists, and crossed to his desk. He didn't sit but rather picked up a scrapbook that was lying on the polished beech wood. He began to flip over the pages, pausing every now and then to read a story which had been cut from a newspaper or magazine. Most of them described his triumphs. Some of them did not. It was over one of the latter that he paused, a story illustrated by a grainy picture of a group of men in dinner jackets and stiff white shirts, smiling into the camera with that unfocused look that comes after an evening of good food, over-generous drink and speeches that have gone on too long. At the front of the group, in the position of honour, stood a man slightly older than the others. His head was thrown back and there was a smile on his face, as if he had just achieved some kind of personal triumph. It was on this face that Crawford focused and, unaware that he was actually articulating the words that fell like drops of poison onto the thickly carpeted silence of the penthouse, he murmured: 'I've got you now, you bastard!'

Then he set the scrapbook to one side and picked up the phone.

Perivale Golf Club, Oxon., 13:25

John Parker balanced his weight evenly on both feet – you would have thought that most human beings did that naturally but not according to the club pro, not when they were using a two wood for a 250-metre shot off the fairway with a bunker treacherously close to the green.

'Are you going to do something with that, John, or just hang on to it all afternoon?'

The slight Canadian lilt of his partner, Mike Bray, bore just a hint of humour. Bray was no better at the game than Parker but always seemed to care *less* about losing and, conversely, did not try so hard to win. It was an attitude John Parker could not understand; what was the point in playing a competitive game if you didn't try to win. His daughter Claire had learnt that lesson at nine: she competed furiously at local gymkhanas and already had a cabinet full of rosettes and shiny little cups gathering dust. Of course Paul, his son, Paul the true believer, Paul the . . .

He cut the thought off in mid-flow and lifted and swung the wood down in one smooth movement. The pro would have been ecstatic; he hit the ball sweetly, with that 'ping' that makes the heart lift, and watched it rise up and up in an elegant arc and then gently, truly fall and land perfectly on the green where it rolled no more than a short distance and came to rest within two metres of the hole.

'I'd say that was doing something, wouldn't you, old man?' he chortled.

Bray whistled: 'If you could bottle and sell that, you'd make another fortune.'

Parker slid the wood back into his bag and grabbed the handle of his trolley. He was, as he started walking towards the hole, a happy man. If he had but known it, this was going to be the last truly happy moment in his life for a long time to come. One perfect hit, one perfect moment on a fine Sunday in late autumn.

As he stepped onto the springy surface of the green, his mobile began to ring. Bray, trying to coax his ball out of the sand, called across: 'I told you to leave that damn thing at home on Sundays, John.' He had, as Parker's doctor, the right to be angry with his patient about matters of health and relaxation, but Parker never listened to what his doctor told him anyway.

'Yes, hello?'

There was a dog barking insistently somewhere. The soft 'chuck-chuck' of Bray hacking his way out of the bunker. A laugh. A smell of tobacco – a cigar being smoked out of sight, the scent surviving, one strand out of thousands in the warm autumn air.

'John Parker? Jim Crawford.'

'Hello, Jim.' He knew Crawford from a number of committees and other City functions but had never, quite, taken to the man. There was something rather too naked about his ambition and too blatant about his own pleasure in his achievements. He was not, to put it crudely, 'one of us'. And, of course, there was all

78

that other business – but that was another time and another place . . .

'I hope I haven't caught you at a bad moment?'

Parker grinned: 'Just hit the best wood of my life off the fairway and I'm about to birdie this hole. No, you haven't found me at a bad time at all, Jim. What can I do for you?'

Bray's ball appeared over the lip of the bunker and rolled across the green, coming to rest on the far side.

'Well, a matter of courtesy, really. I thought I ought to call you and let you know . . .' There was a faint sound behind Crawford – a car horn maybe? With one part of his mind Parker tried to identify it. A ship's hooter, perhaps? '. . . that you will be receiving a bid from us tomorrow.'

'I beg your pardon?'

'For Byfield, John. I'm going to take you over.'

Parker felt a shiver run up his back – he couldn't quite identify its flavour: apprehension, caution, maybe fear, but above all, in that first moment, anger. How dare this man try and take over his company?

'That's ridiculous, Crawford.' The tone was sharp and furious enough to catch Bray's hearing from 20 metres away. He paused, his head held questioningly on one side. Parker took him in for a second, then directed all his attention back to the sliver of black plastic in his hand. He looked at it as if it were something he'd never seen before; then, hearing the tinny squawk coming from the earpiece, he slammed it back against his head.

Crawford was saying: '. . . if you felt that you wanted to talk things over?'

'Talk, there's nothing to talk about.' Parker had his voice back under control by now and, with considerable effort, managed to inject an everyday tone.

'As you wish, John.' Was that a chuckle? What was the man up to? 'I only wanted to be polite and let you hear direct. But I've taken up enough of your valuable time,' and yes, the man was laughing, he was sure of it, 'I'll let you get back to your golf. Goodbye now.'

'Goodbye, Mr Crawford.' Parker broke the connection. He damn near broke the phone too. He'd always hated people who signed off: 'Goodbye now.' And as for people who used your first name without knowing you – it was so . . . so *American,* as his wife Heather would have said.

Bray strolled across the green, an expression of mild concern on his face. 'John, is there something wrong?'

'No, nooo, nothing at all.' Parker had to keep his voice under control. Bray was a good friend but for now no one outside the company could know about Crawford's bid. He tried to sort out his thoughts as he talked: 'Just Jim Crawford. Has an idea for uh, a product line we might manufacture for him.'

Not a particularly convincing story – why would a man like Crawford call to discuss that kind of proposal on a Sunday? Still, Bray wasn't a businessman and wouldn't recognise the anomaly.

'Crawford? Should I know the name?'

Parker tried to recall his most recent meeting with the company bankers; things were good, not great, but a sense of loyalty had always been an important part of his corporate strategy and, surely, he could count on the support of his bankers and shareholders. He wrenched his mind back to the present and answered Bray.

'He's a bit of a pirate. An entrepreneur, I suppose. You must have seen him on television a few years back?'

'I don't think so.'

'Stood for Parliament in Basingstoke or somewhere. There was a scandal.'

'That's right. His wife left him. There was a woman, a mistress.'

'Lives with her now. Lost the election, had to pull out; they don't like that sort of thing in Basingstoke. He went back into business, built up this company of his: Ayot. Took a couple of other firms over, did all right with them too.' He swallowed and told the lie: 'He's the kind of man I could do business with; for all his flamboyance he's got a few sound ideas.'

Bray nodded, apparently satisfied. 'Are you going to play that?' He indicated the ball lying so temptingly close to the hole.

Parker gritted his teeth and smiled, 'Of course, old man.' He sank the putt with no pleasure at all, his mind still racing around a hundred, a thousand different possibilities, none of which he could at this moment share. He wanted to bellow at the top of his voice: 'Bloody man, what the hell is he thinking of!' Instead he pretended to be overjoyed at making his birdie and resigned himself to playing the rest of the round without betraying any sign of his anxiety. It was, he reflected, sometimes a bloody lonely business, being the Chairman.

'Come on, Mike,' he laughed, 'Let's see if you can match that.'

Heathlands, Whitchurch Hill, Oxon., 15:05
Heather Parker had known something was wrong the moment John walked in the door; after all, they'd been married more than 30 years and though her husband's career had kept him away for a great deal of that time, they had always respected each other's occupations and enjoyed each other's company. It was almost, Heather reflected at times, an arranged marriage in which both sides had put down their offers and stuck by their contracts through thick and thin.

Heather had given up her job soon after the wedding, but was active in local politics and had sat on the bench as a JP. She and John were both churchgoers though she had, without quite knowing how or telling him, somehow misplaced her faith over the last few years. Perhaps it was due to Paul, their son, who had gone into the church and was currently involved in the gay Christian movement.

She knew that in herself she could put aside all the prejudices of her upbringing and say, 'Well, why shouldn't he be what he wants? It's his right, for God's sake.' There were, however, more than enough folk in the church who were convinced that homosexuality was quite obviously not for His sake; someone had pinned a notice on Paul's church door in Sherborne: 'Bugger – Off!' It was crude and cruel and, she knew, cut her husband far deeper than it did her. She would support Paul because she loved him; John needed to find a way to support him because he thought he was right – while believing he was not. As far as John was concerned, his son was guilty of letting the family down, of a breach of loyalty that struck at everything the older man believed.

Perhaps Paul had also been the reason for Claire. She had been born shortly after their son had gone to university and, as the phrase had it, come out in public. John had been devastated and had shown, for the first time since their marriage, the vulnerable side of his nature; the side she had first come to love, and had not seen for so many years. As a consequence, they had found a new closeness and Heather, at the age of 39 (she was ten years younger than her husband) had conceived and the result, if you could call Hurricane Claire something as tame as a result, had been a delight to them both.

'Dad, you're early! Can we go now?' Claire trilled, zooming down the stairs, frantically tucking her shirt into the waistband of her jodhpurs. 'I'm ready. Well, I'm almost ready and Mum said that Trisha can come back to tea, if it's OK with her mum.'

John scooped up his daughter and kissed her nose, 'I'm sorry, sweetie, but something's happened.'

'Ohhh, Dad!'

They were simple words but contained an ocean of disappointment, and one that certainly wasn't going to be mopped up by all the mops and buckets Heather could provide by saying, 'I'll take you, love, and bring you and Trisha back afterwards.'

'But you always take me,' Claire wailed, 'and he never does.'

'What's this "he"?' John rumbled as he put her down. 'Don't I get a "Dad" anymore?'

'If you take me to riding. I want you to see me. Christine says

I'm getting better and better and I should enter for the County Show.'

John squatted and looked into her huge blue eyes. 'Hey, you can show me in the paddock, on Snowdrop.' This was her pony.

'It isn't the same, Dad. You just don't understand.' And she marched off upstairs, enough of her father's daughter not to want to show the tears of disappointment.

'She'll get over it, John.'

'If you give your word, you should stick by it,' he said, 'only I didn't know someone would be making a takeover bid against the firm when I promised.'

'Oh my Lord!' Heather pressed fingers to her lips. 'When did you find out? Who is it? How . . .?'

'James Crawford. Runs an electronics group: Ayot. He's a shark, Heather, and he's swimming towards Byfield.'

'Do you want a drink, some tea or something? Will you be calling in the board?' She'd been in the business of business long enough to know that any board member worth his salt was a double act. Wives counted, as long as they were the right kind of wife: supportive but never pushy; highly competent but never know-it-all; charming but not too charming; and above all, there when needed. It was part of the contract: his and hers. When things got tough, you didn't complain, you did something about it; problems meant solutions, not anxieties.

'I could easily get something out of the freezer for a meal or sandwiches, if you think that would be better?'

'I'll phone around in a moment. Some tea would be nice, I don't want – that's a lie,' he gave her a lopsided grin, 'I could do with a Scotch, if you don't mind.'

'Of course.'

They walked into the sitting-room where the afternoon sun was beginning to flood in through the French windows. John went and looked out while Heather poured what she called a small large Scotch from a bottle of Glenmorangie.

'Water?'

'No thanks.' The garden – Heather's area of expertise – was moving into its winter mode. Parker pushed open the window, allowing the scent of burning leaves to drift into the room.

Heather handed him the chunky cut glass tumbler. 'What are you thinking?'

He sighed. 'About all this – the house, the garden, everything we've built up.'

'It's not at risk, is it?' she asked.

'Not in that way. We won't . . . even if the bid succeeded, and I'm damned determined that it won't, we'll come out of it with more money . . .' He raised the tumbler to his mouth and breathed in the complex fumes of the whisky before taking a sip. 'I'm not sure how to explain.'

'You feel threatened?' Heather asked.

'Not threatened exactly. I can fight, I can take care of myself, I don't feel worried about me so much as . . . as about the garden or about Claire. When she ran off upstairs . . .'

'Because she hates to let you see her cry.'

'Yes, and I felt this totally irrational spurt of anger against Crawford for making that happen.' He took a deeper drink and swilled the liquor round his mouth for a moment before swallowing. 'You read the financial pages, you go to CBI committees, Government reviews, you discuss all these things rationally with your advisers and your colleagues and it seems as if it's sensible, it's businessmen sitting around a table talking about issues. And then suddenly it isn't, it's about a nine-year-old girl running upstairs so you won't see her tears because you can't take her riding today.'

He finished his whisky in one gulp. 'Right, I'd better start calling a few people, if you don't mind.'

She took his glass. 'I'll take Claire. Would it be better if she went to Trisha's today, rather than the other way round?'

'Whatever, it won't disturb us.' His mind had switched to another track; the moment of contemplation forgotten. 'We'll use this room, and sandwiches would make sense. Coffee too but I can't say when, as long as you can fit them round Claire's lesson.'

Assuming her agreement, without waiting for an answer, he crossed to the phone, flipped open the leather-bound address book and began to dial. Heather went upstairs to make it all right again with their daughter.

Flat 7, Frogwell Road, West Dulwich, London, 15:30

Beth Stewart divided the last of the wine while her husband peered at the glasses, measuring the liquid in each. Beth laughed, 'Come on, Jack, they're exactly the same.'

A slim woman, standing five foot eleven with the kind of confidence that showed she'd never worried about her height, she took her glass to the white, squashy leather sofa and sank down into it. She wore a white T-shirt, jogging pants and socks with Tintin and Captain Haddock embroidered on them; not the usual dress for the financial director of an electronics company, but as a woman in her mid-thirties, Beth was not exactly your usual sort of board member.

She drained the glass.

'Brilliant.'

Jack, in an old and torn *Aliens* T-shirt and jeans, grinned: 'Now I've got some left and you haven't.' He was the head of a large West London comprehensive and sometimes, Beth thought, got a little too close to the style and spirit of his pupils.

'It's not what you've got, it's what you do with it,' she said. 'Otherwise we might as well have left the bottle unopened in the cellar.'

'We live in a flat, we don't have a cellar.' He hooked his nose over the rim of the glass and breathed in the bouquet: 'Excellent, down to the very last drop.'

The wine was a Pinot Noir by Robert Sinsky, from the Carneros Valley in California, and not available in England. They had picked it up while on holiday in New York.

'We should have had a proper American burger with it,' Beth said.

'If we could've got something half as good as the one we ate at the Union Square Café then . . .'

'We would've been in heaven. That was just so brilliant.' Beth smiled and stretched as she recalled the two-week holiday they'd spent in Manhattan. 'Still, at least we can all eat British beef again.'

'Don't!' Jack's face was a mask of agony. 'I've been trying to persuade the governors that it's safe to put it back on the school meals menu. Only now they're all terrified it's been genetically mutated.'

'Your budget doesn't run to beef, does it?'

'Burgers are beef; at least, they're supposed to be. Generally they're reclaimed gristle or yucky, slimy bits of spinal column. And there's the ground beef in spaghetti bolognese and beef pies and beef and custard and anyway, the whole school is running around like headless chickens because of this bloody inspection.' He was referring to the OFSTED inspectors who were due in his school in a few weeks and who had occasioned an Everest of extra work.

'It's your nightmare, isn't it?'

'Sure it's my nightmare but it's come to stay all day, every day, until the whole bloody process is finished. Still, I don't want to talk about it. Sundays are sacred, right?'

'Absolutely right,' she yawned. They had both agreed, as their joint careers had begun to take off, that at least one day a week *must* be put aside for themselves alone. So far, they had managed to keep to this – though the OFSTED business was pushing very hard at Jack's resolve.

'So . . .' Putting his glass aside, he joined her on the sofa. 'Did you have anything in mind for this afternoon?'

'Yeah, I did actually. I thought we should watch that Woody Allen video before it has to go back to Blockbuster.' His disappointment was obvious. 'Or was there something else?'

'I was thinking we could screw like rabbits all afternoon.'

'It's not what you've got,' she giggled, 'it's what you do with it.'

'My sentiments exactly!' He moved closer and ran his fingers lightly over the front of her T-shirt and . . .

The phone started to ring.

. . . and Jack rolled off the sofa onto the carpet, waving his arms and legs in the air like a fly after a major hit of Vapona. 'Why can't they use the bloody answerphone like civilised people?'

'It's my mobile,' Beth groaned. 'Must be work.'

Gathering up the sports section, Jack installed himself in a lonely armchair and vanished behind the broadsheet pages. Beth scrabbled for her bag, which was down the back of the sofa, and began to search through it.

'This thing is like the Tardis,' she grumbled. 'The interior volume is 50 times greater than the surface area would lead you to believe.'

A grunt came from under the *Observer*.

Beth found the phone and flipped it open. 'Yes?'

John Parker's voice was instantly recognisable; over the past few months she'd heard it in just about every mode, from cheerful, to furious, to confidential, to bland, but in all that time she'd never heard it, as she did on that Sunday afternoon, so full of sheer concern.

Heathlands, Whitchurch Hill, Oxon., 17:22

Present at what was, effectively, the first Byfield board meeting of the campaign, were the Chairman, John Parker; the Finance Director, Beth Stewart; the Chief Executive Officer, Bill Harper; and Richard 'Dick' Worthington, a non-executive director.

Absent were Angus Howerd, the Sales and Marketing Director, who was away on a weekend break with his wife; the Human Resources Director, Tim Ericson, who had gone fishing without his mobile (wise man, Beth Stewart sighed to herself); and Tom Swift, Research and Development, who was stuck somewhere on the M25.

Beth still wore her 'I love NY' T-shirt but had changed her joggers for DKNY jeans; the CEO, Bill Harper, a small, rather precise man, had either already been wearing a suit or had found time to put one on before appearing; both possibilities typical of someone who hated to be caught unprepared in any situation.

Richard Worthington, the non-executive director, an old friend of John Parker's, was wearing a leather jacket, linen shirt (the *Field*), and jeans that were, somehow, not quite appropriate. He had been, in his youth, an A and R man for an international record label and had later gone into management, guiding a number of successful seventies and eighties acts to chart success. However, unlike a lot of the more radical members of the pop scene, his interests had lain more in the direction of country pursuits and he now ran a freshwater trout farm and owned a number of highly lucrative fishing sites. He had used his money wisely and discovered a certain talent for business and was firmly cemented – in his opinions, ideas, dress sense and hair length – at about 1983, when Spandau Ballet, Phil Collins and Bonnie Tyler ruled the charts. He had been bought onto the board more as a support for John Parker, who thought he was 'trendy' and 'with it', to vote with him and underline his expertise – and to do the occasional advertising gig – rather than, as CEO Bill Harper had pointed out at the time, to add anything to the company with a fresh approach or different skills.

However. Bill Harper himself was very much Parker's man and had not protested the appointment beyond a remark or two. John Parker was not a chairman who liked disharmony among his board members. Nor was he, Beth had thought on more than one occasion, overly keen on innovation. Harper should have been encouraged by his chairman to take a non-executive directorship to broaden his experience rather than follow the 'steady as she goes' line that seemed to sum up the company culture.

Casting a wistful glance through the French windows at the garden, where she could see a column of smoke rising into the twilight, Beth turned back to the table, and to the Chairman at its head.

'Thank you for coming, everyone. I appreciate it very much.' John Parker could no more be impolite than he could have leaped up and danced on the marble mantelpiece. 'As you know I received a phone call earlier today from James Crawford.'

'What a pain,' Worthington growled, winding the chain of his crystal round his beringed fingers.

'I think we all feel that way, Dick,' Parker said. 'I know I do, but we also have to look at what this actually means to us at Byfield because, from everything I know about Crawford, he isn't going to back off.'

Beth asked, 'Do we know if he's being straight with us, or does he have any other end in view?'

'I think we need to take his word on what he intends to do.'

Bill Harper cleared his throat and waited until he caught Parker's eye. 'John, do you think Crawford might have a point?'

Worthington jumped in: 'He's greedy, that's all; needs to expand. He should chill out.'

Beth cringed. Sharing a board meeting with Dick Worthington was like going to a club and finding Cliff Richard was playing. She had an abiding fear that he would, one day, call her 'Babe', and that she would, in response, kill him.

Parker overrode the old trendy and said: 'Go on, Bill, what are you thinking?'

'Well, were we vulnerable?' Harper did not enjoy criticising anyone, let alone his chairman, and it was clearly an effort as he took a breath and continued, 'Did we as a board leave the company vulnerable? I wouldn't bring it up, except that if we are going to fight this bid off, then we have to look at our own fitness; our own, if you like, defects.'

'If?' Beth cut in. 'Isn't that the first thing we need to decide?'

'If we fight?' Worthington's chain was becoming knotted round his fingers. 'Of course we're going to fight. Right, John?'

Silence, broken only by the sound of a jet far overhead. Beth wondered where it was going and, for a moment, wished as she often did that she was on it, heading out to somewhere new and exciting. And then it occurred to her that she was: the weeks ahead were going to be uncharted country and if she were able to cross that landscape and end up at the right destination, she would come out of this with invaluable experience. What was slightly sick-making was the fact that she did not, at this moment, know what the right destination was going to be.

None of the others appeared to notice the plane. Worthington and Harper had their eyes fixed on Parker. Both were concerned that he might decide not to fight: for where would that leave them?

'Oh yes, we fight, Beth. No doubt about it. Crawford is not . . .' He bit the remark off before it concluded. 'Better not let personalities intrude.'

'Outstanding, John.' Worthington twiddled his fingers; the chain appeared to be locked immovably.

'In which case,' Harper said, 'what can we do right now?'

'I called Nik,' Parker was referring to Nik Speller, the company's banker, 'and his instant reaction was like yours, Bill. We were vulnerable, we haven't shown much movement, and if our research and development has been forward-looking, there was still that rather unwise profit forecast you issued to the City.'

Harper went grey. 'The board . . . the board . . .' he stuttered, 'they were, you, everyone was . . .' he tailed off.

'Relax, Bill,' Parker soothed, 'no one is looking for scapegoats. We all know that balance sheets can tell us nothing at all – what's important is cash flow, and we have no problems there. Our customers are happy, and a satisfied customer is a damned good indication of the health of any business. We are loyal to our customers, our bankers, our suppliers and our employees. I don't think that will ever fall out of fashion. Loyalty is our keyword.'

This was Dick Worthington's cue – the kind of cue he'd been picking up since he'd joined the board and which allowed him to exhibit his so-called popular touch. 'I mean, I don't want to push anything here, but I think everyone feels – and I can say this from the heart, John, I mean all of us here on the board and . . . yeah, right through the whole . . . the whole company, all the companies, I mean they really appreciate what you have here, John. What we all have here. It's something real – genuine, human – and we're going to fight for it because we think, uh . . . it's worth fighting for. If that's cool with everyone.' He grimaced as he tried one last time to free his trapped fingers. The chain broke and the crystal fell to the floor where it broke into – if not a thousand – at least two pieces. Worthington shook his head, 'Man, I hope that's not a bad omen.'

Beth muttered, dryly, 'Outstanding, Dick.'

Worthington blushed and said, 'Well, the whole company, top to bottom, will be right behind you, John.'

'Thank you, Dick. I appreciate your confidence.'

Bill Harper was still looking distinctly uncomfortable. Beth knew that in everyone's mind, not least Harper's, was the spectre of a CEO who had given an over-optimistic profit fore-cast and found himself out of a job when his company profits did not manage, quite, to breast the line he'd predicted. That was not, she knew, the Byfield way; it might well be, she feared, Byfield's weakness. From her perspective as Finance Director she'd been asking a number of pertinent questions of the company as a whole: Did they have a clear aim? Did they have the strategy to achieve this aim; the management skills to make it work; the management style to want it to work; and the manage-ment motivation to make certain it did work? The exercise was uncompleted as yet but she had a very good idea of what the conclusions were going to be and nothing she'd heard so far today had disabused her of that notion. The simple fact that she was the only newcomer to the Byfield board in half a dozen years spoke volumes about the sheer lack of innovatory thinking at the top level of the group.

'Nik's main piece of advice, however,' Parker continued, 'was to keep our mouths shut, individually and as a board. Once the bid hits the table tomorrow, if we get any questions, we refer them to Nik's PR people. They'll look at what's on offer, liaise with us and prepare a preliminary statement, which they will issue.'

'Should we,' Harper's complexion no longer matched his suit, 'perhaps look at appointing a non-exec. director to the board who has some real experience of takeover bids?'

'That sounds like good sense,' Beth said. 'I can't pretend I've got any practical experience of this. I did it at university but as we all know, that isn't like life.'

Parker nodded and scribbled a few words on his note-pad. 'Good idea, Bill. I'll talk to Nik about that but we'll need to move pretty sharpish.'

'There is one thing,' Harper swallowed nervously. 'Wouldn't it, with all respect, John, have made more sense to have got Nik here this afternoon? I mean, this is going to be as much about our merchant bank and its strategies as it is about us.'

The question hung, unanswered, in the smoky late-afternoon air. Silently, Beth agreed; without the presence of the company bankers, they had done nothing and decided nothing which could not have been worked out over the phone; so why had they interrupted their Sunday to come all the way out here to John Parker's house? Was it simply prudence or was it more like the panic-stricken scattering of a herd of zebra as the lions attack?

Part Two

Downstream

Day ZERO

Offer

by

Waymouth, Paternoster

on behalf of

Ayot plc

for

Byfield plc

Ayot's Offer

Value
- Three new Ayot shares and 29p in cash for every two Byfield shares, worth 117p per share
- Cash alternative, worth 105p per share
- Byfield shareholders will also be entitled to retain their interim dividend
- The offer values Byfield at £181m

Premium
- The offer represents a premium to the pre-bid price of 30 per cent
- The cash alternative represents a premium to the pre-bid price of 25 per cent

The offer provides the opportunity for Byfield shareholders to:

- participate in the future success of the enlarged Ayot

or
- realise their investment in Byfield for cash both at a substantial premium.

Ayot

To Byfield shareholders and, for information only, to participants in the Byfield share schemes.

1 November 1999

Dear Shareholder,

The Board of Ayot believes that the acquisition of Byfield will create an electronics group which will utilise common technologies to serve a wide range of markets and which will provide a firmer platform from which an enlarged business will be able to grow.

The Ayot Group of companies is listed on the London Stock Exchange with a market capitalisation as at 29 October 1999 of £500 million. Ayot operates a number of businesses in Great Britain using a range of technologies and value-added processes. The Group has a broad European customer base, selling 30 per cent of its turnover throughout the Common Market.

Ayot's strategy is to focus on businesses related to its key areas of expertise.

Under Jim Crawford, the Group Chief Executive, Ayot has demonstrated its ability to deliver growth in shareholder value. Total operating profit has grown from £40m in the year to 31 March 1996 to £53m in the year to 31 March 1998. This year's interim results have shown continued improvement with half-year operating profits up by 17 per cent.

In contrast to Ayot, Byfield appears to have given up the pursuit of positive growth. Over the past five years it has consistently failed in its efforts to pursue new growth opportunities successfully.

Ayot believes that the acquisition of Byfield will create significant scope for further benefits from manufacturing synergies, purchasing synergies and head office cost savings. I am confident that the many common technologies and complementary markets of the two groups will facilitate a rapid and low risk integration of Byfield into the enlarged group.

Byfield has failed to deliver value for its shareholders, has acknowledged that it faces an uncertain future and has given up the pursuit of positive growth opportunities. I believe that our offer fully values your company and that the combination of Ayot and Byfield makes excellent strategic sense. I urge you to accept the offer.

Yours faithfully,

Peter J. Allbury
Chairman, Ayot

Day +1

byfield plc, goldhawk mews, london

BETH STEWART CRUMPLED UP THE CLINGFILM that had wrapped her cottage cheese and chives sandwich and flipped it into the waste bin. It wasn't exactly the meal she would have thought appropriate for the financial director of a company before she had become the Financial Director at Byfield and discovered just how often she was working through lunch.

She had discussed working patterns with Jack on a number of occasions. His take, as a school head, was that every waking hour and quite a lot of his sleeping ones were spent on the job. School problems didn't stop at six in the evening, any more than school activities did; after-hours homework clubs, PTA meetings, staff meetings and, as the horror of the looming visit from the OFSTED inspectors approached, an ever-increasing volume of paperwork to back up every school activity. He had been working on his laptop the night before, when Beth had gone to bed and he'd been working in the morning, at seven, when she got up. He'd sworn that, yes, he had got a couple of hours' sleep – on the sofa – so as not to disturb her, but she wasn't convinced. She'd tried to suggest that it was quality of work time rather than quantity that mattered – his response had been to shrug and turn back to the keyboard. So Beth had made him coffee and toast and left.

In the Tube, crushed into a corner by a man who seemed not to have washed for a month, Beth had reflected that for all her 'quality not time' philosophy, she was, almost certainly, putting in too many hours – not that she objected, and that was the problem. She loved the job, loved learning more about internal and external finance, about the City, an area in which she knew she was weak (a weakness shared by far too many directors in this country) and about the day-to-day working of a middle-sized corporation.

She knew that, to an extent, as a woman in the upper echelons of business, she was living in a false world. If she chose, if she and Jack chose to have children, then a lot of things would change. Her colleagues would expect her to put in the same number of hours and yet she would have to find time to be with her children; the fact that bringing up a child might well give her invaluable experience, that indeed being a woman gave her a different viewpoint and different skills, would still, most likely, be overlooked in relation to hours worked. Things had changed – more and more women were to be found in top positions but there was a cost – perhaps this was their problem alone or perhaps, if industry really were to move successfully into the new century, it was a problem for everyone.

For now, though, things were good; she was enjoying every moment. And there lay the danger: she was becoming absorbed by her career, just as Jack had become absorbed by his. They were both aware of the risk, which was why they'd agreed to keep their Sundays for themselves if at all possible. With Jack's inspection coming, the Sunday just passed was going to be the last for a long time on which they were both free. And she had spoiled it. Not that Jack had blamed her; he realised it wasn't anything so obvious as her 'fault' that Jim Crawford was going to try and take over Byfield. He had even agreed, when at last she'd got home, that in the long run Beth would almost certainly be better off. It was just that . . . it had happened and whatever they did, they couldn't unring that particular bell.

She sighed and picked up the pad on which she had made notes during the morning's board meeting. All the directors who had been absent on Sunday were back, though non-exec. Worthington had been 'in the studio' with some new boy band – no great loss there, except to musical taste, Beth reckoned – and the atmosphere had been bullish as the Ayot offering circular had been passed around to general contempt and derision. Contempt and derision which, Beth felt, was entirely undeserved; it was a good presentation and, if they hoped to defend themselves convincingly against it, they were going to have to come up with something rather better than they had so far. Though, on reflection, Beth wondered if the posturing at the meeting had been a man thing; the bucks of the tribe hyping themselves up with dancing and chest-beating before rushing off to club the invader to the ground. Not that anyone on Byfield's board would look particularly convincing waving a club or beating his chest. Charm, smoothness, experience, maybe even a little wisdom mixed in with the grey hairs; but no eagerness for battle. The average age of company boards was getting younger by the year, and, apart from herself and Tom Swift, their R and D man, Byfield was bucking the trend with almost brontosaurian disregard.

The office door opened a crack and Selena, her PA, put her head round. 'Tim Ericson, Beth. He wanted a word.'

It was an indication of Beth's attitude that the PA felt relaxed enough to approach her in this way – the rest of the Byfield board preserved a rather more formal attitude with their staff.

'Sure, Sel. Ask him to come in.' She slipped the banana, her second course, into the drawer of her desk as Ericson came through from the outer office.

In his middle-to-late forties, of middle height, with a middling sort of face, pleasant and never abrasive but not unassertive either, the Byfield Human Resources Director was the closest thing Beth had to a friend on the board; she liked his slightly self-deprecating sense of humour and the ability he had, quite without offending anyone, of puncturing any speech that started to get over-pompous: something the Byfield board was

somewhat prone to producing. He was also good with people –
not always a trait that is considered particularly useful in the job
– and one that, Beth feared, might make him vulnerable to any
number of pressures.

'Tim, hi. I was just finishing my sarnie.'

Ericson peered exaggeratedly round the office, as though he
was in a spy farce, then shut the door with elaborate care. He
grinned and quoted the Chairman's warning about keeping
silent: 'Walls have ears – and so do PAs . . . and waste bins.'
He grabbed Beth's bin and peered into it. 'Ah! Clingfilm. Micro
dots.'

'Micro cottage cheese, actually.'

'Not slimming again, Beth?' Ericson took a chair and moved it
close to the other side of the desk. 'You don't need to.'

'Need and want are two different things, Tim. And, in fact, I
wasn't. Slimming, that is. I happen to like cottage cheese *or* it
was all we had in the fridge this morning *or* my doctor told me it
would be good for my complexion. Choose any one.'

'Or choose them all, since this is Byfield and no one seems
able to make up their minds what to do about . . .' he spread his
arms, hands palm upwards, 'this whole bloody mess.' Despite
the humour, Beth felt there was something deeper bothering
Ericson, something related to the battle before them.

'Is it a mess?' she asked, feeling rather guilty at her own
feelings of excitement. 'The general consensus this morning
was . . .'

'Not worth the hot air it generated. Have you ever really
thought about the way we hold our board meetings?'

'I'm not quite sure what you're getting at here, Tim?'

'You know I fish.'

'You fish – yes. Never understood why anyone would, it
seems so boring.'

'That's a bit like telling a monk that meditation is boring.
Fishing *is* meditation – with a meal afterwards! What I'm trying
to say is that my fishing style reflects who I am. Right?'

Beth opened her desk drawer. 'You don't mind if I eat a banana, do you, Tim? My eating style reflects who *I* am. And, yes, I see what you mean: the way we hold board meetings reflects the culture of the company.' She took out the banana and peeled it. 'The thing about bananas, Tim, is that they only reach true ripeness for about ten minutes in their whole existence. Before, they're too crisp; after, too soggy.' She began to eat. 'Anyway, go on.'

'Everything we do reflects the style of the company, from the logo to the flowers and how many plastic cups we leave lying around after a board meeting. And at the meetings themselves: people waffle. We start with the routine stuff which goes on far too long. Accounts and housekeeping! Yeah, they're important but by the time we've got through all that – and I'm not criticising you, Beth . . .'

'Except that I present the accounts. But I take your point . . .'

'We're beginning to get tired of figures and projections. We've lost our edge before we begin to talk seriously.'

'I agree with that. The figures are yesterday. If they're not good enough, we can only do something about it tomorrow. Planning.' She took another bite. 'You know, this is a damned fine banana.'

'I'm very happy for you. Anyway, we do the figures and then we do the presentations and the same thing happens again: we spend far too long with people droning on, reading out their plans and, at the end, we don't have time to do anything other than give a quick response. There's no dialogue so there are no ideas that weren't brought into the meeting or formulated while listening. In other words, no cross-fertilisation. Nothing coming out of left field, off the wall, out of an argument. There's no life, there's no dynamic, it's all too controlled, but not by one person. If we had a Jim Crawford as CEO, then at least whatever he said or did would always have the virtue of being his idea and would be interesting because of who he is. In our case – well, who does run the board? And why are you breaking off the last half inch of that banana?'

Beth threw the skin and the residual fruit into the bin. 'If there's anything in the banana, a worm or whatever, that's where it'll be. In the base.'

'How on earth do you know that?'

'My granddad. In the desert during the war. The Arabs told him.'

'The Arabs told him? OK, fine. I guess they had some experience.'

'And . . . I suppose John Parker runs the meetings.'

'No, he lets them happen. For example, when was the last time he made sure that everyone had some input in a subject? Open, honest input. Months, a year – probably before your time anyway. It isn't that he blocks discussion, there's nothing so obvious as that: it's that certain things don't happen because we all feel it would be uncomfortable or embarrassing if they did. The company culture: you can't ever put your finger on what it is and yet it colours everything we do on the board. And what we do on the board filters down through the company. If there's a lack of clarity among the directors, then it's going to be positively muddy further down. And when you get to the nitty-gritty – the point where we interact with our customers – what are they seeing?'

'Sales are OK. Not brilliant but . . .' Beth paused and considered the last set of figures she'd looked at.

'But?' Ericson prompted.

'But maybe we should look a little more closely at what our customers might be telling us.'

'And will we?'

'Not now, not with all this going on.'

'But you do see something that's not quite right?'

'I think I do. I can't be sure.'

'And if John Parker were a different kind of chairman you could go along to his office right now – or you could have done last week – and share your feelings and he'd immediately respond. Only that never happened, did it?'

'It never happened.'

'And not for any reason you can name but just because . . .'

'Just because.' She took a sudden breath as she recalled a conversation she'd had with Parker only a month or so after she'd joined the board. 'I asked him, you know, I suggested an internal audit. Not financial, but covering everything, so we could check out our internal controls, see how we reacted in the past to various problems and how we might do so in the future.'

'And his response?'

'He didn't say no, and he didn't say yes. He did say that this kind of audit can hold up practical decisions that need to be made and that it costs a lot and then he sort of drifted . . . and Bill Harper was there, and he sort of drifted . . . like it was . . . somehow not quite serious . . . like a girlie thing, even though they'd just appointed me to the board.'

'I think they might have real cause to regret that decision,' Ericson said. 'Maybe most of us will. Because it's our fault – we . . . me, I could see how it should be and I didn't do one damn thing about it.' Momentarily, his face changed. It was almost, Beth thought, as if he'd aged 20 years in a second: the flesh sagging, going grey and coarse, the eyes dulling; the motor running down and about to stop. Then, as quickly, he returned to his old self and went on: 'Anyway, most boards don't take action until it's too late, and then they sack the CEO. What we need is a CEO who can turn around and tell us that we have a problem and ask our help.'

'Isn't that what happened today?'

'Yes,' Ericson said. 'That's more or less what happened today.' His voice was flat, offering no comment upon the frankly lacklustre performance of CEO Bill Harper that morning.

'And you think it's too late?'

'I don't know, Beth. It may be, it may not. For Byfield.'

'Look, Tim, maybe you should say what's really bothering you.' She shook her head, stopping the words of reassurance that were coming to his lips. She knew the type. Ericson was not

105

a man who could ever openly admit to being worried; you had to spot the signs and force him into a position where he had no alternative but to answer honestly. Beth had found all this out one evening when she'd been a guest at Ericson's home. He and Jack had been doing boys' things with the drinks while she had shared a sherry with Sandra Ericson in the kitchen and enjoyed a surprisingly frank conversation about Sandra's feelings as a business wife. It had taught Beth that no man, or indeed woman, is an island and that if you want to know one partner in a marriage better, spend some time with the other.

'Just stay with me a second, Tim. OK. You're worried. Fine. I'm worried about how I'll perform over the next few weeks, if I'll come out of this looking good or looking like a dog. I'm worried that I'm not spending enough time with my husband Jack and he's not spending enough time with me. I'm worried about whether I should have a baby or not and I'm worried about being worried. Now, I've shown you mine, you show me yours.'

Ericson couldn't hide the grin that crept across his lips. 'Beth, one thing I can predict: you are going to be fine, whatever happens.'

'Famous last words. Go on . . .'

'Yes, I'm worried. But my worry is better than your worry because it's a real worry. I, uh, I left school when I was sixteen. I joined a local company, it wasn't anything much: small developers who were, oddly, bought up by John Parker. Only I'd left by then. Sorry, I don't want this to turn into *This is My Life*.'

'It's fine, Tim, go on.'

'After a couple of years in a new company – it was a builder's – I moved off the site and into the office. I'd always been good at figures.'

'So why didn't you do A levels?'

'It was the family background. My dad was a builder. He was virtually illiterate, and you'd be surprised how many people in this country were – and still are. And he'd done well. Nice house, good car, holidays, all of it. He'd got it all with his own hands. Education didn't mean anything to him. When I was a kid, I looked at our schoolteachers – they had these little cars, they dressed in what I thought were dull clothes. My dad had a flashy car, my mum dressed like – like a rich builder's wife. That was success, that was what I valued far above learning all the things that teachers knew.

'So I worked my way up through this company. Local manager, district manager, then there was an opening in the central office and we moved and . . . it went on from there. I could do the job and produce the results. While other people were going to university and taking their MBAs, I was out there undergoing a real apprenticeship. I was doing the job.'

'I'm beginning to see where you're heading, Tim.'

'It's obvious, really, isn't it? I rejoined Byfield, it was still called Sheetrock then, and after a couple of years, I went on the board. Oddly, once I'd made it, it didn't turn out quite as exciting as I'd expected. Now, I won't pretend it wasn't tough at the beginning. I had to push myself harder than I'd ever done before, and, believe me, I have worked hard in my time.'

Beth had no doubt of it; in his way, Tim Ericson was the straightest man she'd ever met: no lateral thinking for him. If there was a pile of earth to move he'd pick up a shovel and start digging and he wouldn't stop until the pile was gone. Beth would have hired a digger or turned a high-pressure hose on the earth and washed it away.

'It was clear to me that I simply didn't have the kind of background, the sort of education that the majority of other board members had; it was like I was at a table where I didn't know which knife and fork to pick up. And, OK, that didn't matter too much here and now. I know John Parker, he knows me. But . . . it's obvious that if we join the big world out there – if we get taken over by Crawford – then there isn't going to be a place for any of this seat-of-the-pants style management.'

107

'Isn't that exactly Crawford's background? Started from nothing, never went to university or business school . . .'

'And probably never felt bad about it in his whole life,' Ericson said. 'But me . . . ever since I've sat on this board, there's always been that little thought, nagging away inside: you're not as good as them and one day you'll be found out. And that day is getting closer, Beth. And that makes me very scared because I'm 49 years old and if I lose this job, I won't get anything else. I'll be finished.'

'Come on, that's not true, Tim. There are hundreds of firms who'll . . .'

'Ask me onto their main boards? Like hell they will. What could I bring, what kind of experience? Everything I know about line management is 15 years out of date. I've only ever sat on one board – I've not even been a non-executive director for any other company. I can't go into teaching business studies, because I don't have an academic background.'

'What about doing something else? Fishing, start a fishing company.' Beth had to admit to herself: it sounded pretty lame.

'You're a young woman, Beth. Your point of view has a limitless horizon. Mine doesn't.'

'Oh, come on, Tim, 49 isn't old.'

'It's old enough. I can't get up at five in the morning and work a 90-hour week, not any more. I can't start again. Life, experience, hardship, success, they're all going to change you in a hundred different ways. But I am what my life has been. And like a lot of men, my life has been my work. It's what I've spent most of my time doing. And I know things are supposed to be changing but I don't think they are. Forms of work are changing, people are moving from job to job, but those jobs, the things that we do are still the most important part of our lives. We are what we do and when what we do is taken away, then maybe we no longer *are*.'

He turned his head away from her but he couldn't hide the anguish in his voice nor the way his fingers kept repeating a series of pointless movements. Beth got up, went round the desk, put both her hands on his shoulders and said: 'Then we'd better make bloody sure that Mr Crawford doesn't get hold of us.'

Heathlands, Whitchurch Hill, Oxon., 15:00
Heather Parker always felt the garden in winter had a charm of its own. The bare branches, the drifts of fallen leaves, the change in colours and textures, the berries and, still, a few sloes left in the blackthorn bush that bordered the lane. She never felt it was a dead time, only that it was still and waiting, and that under the leaves, under the bark of the trees, in the branches and hedges, insects and birds and animals were all going about their lives, following those vast cyclic patterns that have persisted in the English countryside for century after century.

It wasn't an original thought, but then, she wasn't an original woman. She was only herself, she reflected, as she took off the canvas gardening gloves and pushed them into the pocket of her apron. It would soon be time to get the car out to fetch Claire from school and another cycle would begin: Claire's stories about the day and her friends and the pony and homework and how much television she would be allowed to watch tonight. Heather wished she would read more, but children didn't seem to do that any more, not as she had as a child, when the world of books was better in every way than the life around her.

She had about ten minutes before she should leave and, as she stood in the hall easing her wellingtons off, she looked at the phone and hesitated. Ever since John had come back from the golf club with the news – she couldn't give it any other name, it was *the news* – she had wanted to call Paul. John had vetoed the idea. 'No need to worry him,' he'd lied, 'he must be busy enough with his parishioners. Let it be, I'll drop him a line sometime.'

The real reason, Heather knew, was that John could not bear the thought of being an object of sympathy to his son. And it was so horrible, that he should feel that way. Sometimes she wanted to scream at him with frustration: stop being so stupid. It wouldn't do any good, of course. Heather shook her head; men were so terribly silly.

She checked the hall clock. Seven minutes. She picked up the phone and punched in Paul's number. Even as the phone rang she wondered again if she'd made a mistake but then, with a little ping, the receiver was lifted down there in Dorset.

'Hello, the Vicarage?'

'Paul?'

'Mum, hello there! How's you?'

The pleasure in his voice was reflected on her own face. In the mirror across the hall, she could see herself smile at the sound of the familiar childhood greeting.

'Fine, Paul. I've just been working in the garden . . .'

' . . . and any minute now, you're off to collect Claire!'

'You know my routines, love,' she said.

'Of course I do. How is the hurricane these days? I had a card from her with an alligator on last week,' Claire was an inveterate sender of funny cards to all and sundry, 'and I haven't been able to find anything suitable to send back yet. Tell her I will, though, just as soon as I locate an aardvark.'

'She's fine. The riding is going well, though I worry every time she gets up on Snowdrop.'

'Of course you do, but she'll be all right. School – is she in the nativity play this year?'

'They don't do them any more, at least not at her school. I think it's something about homeless people on the streets at Christmas.'

'That sounds pretty good to me,' he chuckled and she was, as so often, amazed by how grown up he sounded. 'And, uh . . . Dad?' And she couldn't fail to notice the slight hesitation, 'still bossing the whole world around?'

'He's all right . . .' her face, in the mirror, gave the lie to her words. 'Considering . . .'

A pause – then: 'Considering what, Mum?'

'He didn't want you to know but . . . someone wants to take over the company.'

'Take over? What, sack him? Can they do that?'

'No, no, I mean another business.'

'Oh, right, now I'm with you. The kind of things they have in the bit of the paper I never read. Financial news.'

'Yes. Someone called Crawford. His company wants to take over Dad's. They've made an offer.'

'I'm not really up on all this stuff,' Paul said. 'What does it mean to Dad, exactly?'

'He could lose the company. But I'm not sure if that's what is really bothering him. Of course, it would hurt to lose it but there's something else. Something between him and this Crawford man. I don't know what. Maybe it's nothing. Just business rivalry.'

'You won't be thrown out?'

'Oh no, nothing like that. We'll be all right for money. He'll be able to go on playing bad golf for that Not the Ryder Cup Society of his. That isn't really the point.'

Paul's laugh had a slight but detectable bitterness about it. After the problems over his sexuality, money was very much the point. He had never approved of his father's wealth; even though he was not against business he could not, somehow, feel comfortable living with it. He and John had argued about the value of industry but neither had been able to see the other's point; though whether it was the 'point' or the 'other' which was the problem was undecided in Heather's mind. She suspected the latter but it had all become academic once the two men had found something they could really get their teeth into. As to who was at fault – Heather had always felt that Paul would be ready to return, to forget and forgive at the slightest hint of rapprochement from his father. So far it had never come. She just prayed – or would have if she still believed – that they would make things up before it was too late.

111

'Mum?' When she heard Paul's voice, she realised that she'd been staring into the mirror, lost, for some seconds.

'Sorry, love. I was thinking about you and Dad.'

'Oh, us. I see. Is there anything I can do? I'd suggest I came down but that would hardly be a help, I suppose?'

'I'd love to see you and I know Claire would.'

'So why don't I come? I can rearrange things, certainly enough to spend an evening with you.'

As soon as the offer was made, she felt the hesitation creeping into her voice and hated herself for what she was about to say – 'Why not come down one afternoon . . .' because she knew exactly what response it would get from her son.

'Look, you're my mother, Claire's my little sister, Heathlands is my childhood home. I won't make some sort of compromise visit, I won't creep in so Dad doesn't have to see the family disgrace. I shouldn't have to say it, Mum, but I'm not ashamed of my sexuality. I will not creep anywhere; particularly in my father's house.'

She sighed and saw, in the mirror, all the happiness drain away. 'I know, Paul. And the reason I say it is because I love both of you and I want us all to be together and . . . and . . .' She couldn't finish because he would never understand, just as John would never understand. The both of them, like children. Sometimes she thought that mothers were the only truly grown-up human beings on the planet. And then, because she had to, she picked herself up and said: 'I'll see what I can do. Maybe this time, Dad'll feel that he wouldn't mind a bit of support.'

'Good, because it only needs a nod and I'll be there.'

'Anyhow, time is getting on. I ought to go or I'll be late for Claire and she hates hanging around.'

'Right, OK. And . . . I wish it was all easier, Mum, but I do think about you and I do pray for you. Both of you. All of you.'

'Thank you, love. Bye.'

'Bye, and God bless.'

She put the phone down. The silence was everywhere around her; she could almost feel the earth spinning through space. Then she heard the cry of a vixen. It must be in the lane. They were getting closer every week, the animals. Maybe they'd move in one night and the house and everything it contained would go back to nature.

Heather shook her head, got her car-coat off the hook and the Range Rover keys from the phone table and went out to collect her daughter.

Lightoller, Bachman and Gale, RG House, Bishopsgate, London, 15:45

Bishopsgate in the City of London boasts some of the most stunning new architecture in the whole country but John Parker didn't even see it as he and Beth Stewart made their way, by hired car, to the offices of the company's merchant bank. They were to meet Nik Speller, the bank's man, and Bobbi King, from the PR agency. Beth had met Speller a couple of times socially and once when discussing a possible new issue of shares, and thought that his somewhat urbane, Oxford classics degree background was both out of date and somehow peculiarly suited to being Byfield's banker. Not that he wasn't sharp; he knew which way the wind blew as well as the boys in the US investment banks and his contacts were as good as any; and, Beth reflected, they would probably need to be!

She glanced across the wide back seat at John Parker, who was locked in a series of calculations, possible scenarios and nightmares, no doubt. He had been distant at the morning's board meeting and said virtually nothing when they had met in the foyer, where they had to wait for the car. He was diminished: older, worn, less his charming self; he seemed, as the cliché has it, exactly as if the stuffing had been knocked out of him. Well, Beth could understand that; in many ways Parker had far more of himself tied up in Byfield and its future than had Tim Ericson. He had built up a family firm, expanded, acquired, taken the company into public ownership, seen it grow and succeed and then somehow let it escape from under his hands, just as his black leather case was doing now, sliding from his knees. She reached across and grabbed it and handed it back.

'Oh, thank you, Beth. I was miles away. Are we there yet?'

Beth leaned down so she could peer out of the tinted window at the soaring exoskeleton of RG House. She felt a real surge of excitement at the feeling that she was here, now, at this moment, right in the thick of things. The car slid to a halt at the foot of a flight of steps imposing enough to have been a stage set for the Roman Empire, but since they were a real setting for a new global empire perhaps that was appropriate. The uniformed driver whipped out and opened Parker's door, leaving Beth to get out on her own and that said something about the new empire as well!

'I always find myself lost in this place,' Parker said, as they climbed the imperial steps. 'I know they've painted yellow lines on all the pavements so you can find your way to the Barbican concert hall – they ought to do the same here.'

The day was overcast and the glass cliff in front of them, hanging inside its gunmetal coloured supports, was reflecting a uniform grey. The whole place had something military about it – as though the people here took no prisoners, exchanged no hostages.

With a subtle touch on the elbow, she guided John Parker to the correct door and they went through into a vast atrium – and she had to admit, the sheer amount of unused but *expensive* space was impressive. It said: whoever has a floor in this building is very serious indeed. She liked the feel of that.

'Hi, Mr Parker, Ms Stewart. Bobbi King.' A small woman in black, with a skirt too short, too tight and way too young for her height and age, approached and handed them ID cards.

'I thought I'd wait down here – saves a lot of time and trouble. How was your journey? OK, I hope. I guess you came by hired car, makes so much more sense than taking a cab, I always find. Now don't worry, we've got coffee waiting for you upstairs, only of course it isn't the stairs, we wouldn't want to make you walk all the way up. I mean this place, incredible, isn't it just a sight to see?' They were at the lift before the diminutive Ms Bobbi King stopped talking. She ushered them in and pressed a button. 'I'm a stranger here myself,' she started as the lift began to climb silently and rapidly enough for Beth to feel a slight gravitational pull. 'I used to work with my Ex, Perry King at King Associates, but he always grabbed the really smart clients. Then he grabbed a really smart babe, only he wasn't smart enough and – whoops, divorce! Here we are. Now that's fast. Faster than Perry.'

She stepped out the lift, teetering on heels that were too high, leaving Parker and Beth to exchange looks: thank God the ride was short, or who knows what they might have found out next about Bobbi's private life!

Once again they were in a hallway where space was the design feature. There was a new-moon slim crescent of brushed steel desk at one end, behind which sat two receptionists, smart but not glamorous women in their thirties, there to give an impression of capable management. The mothers booked them in and Bobbi ushered them through into the heartland of Light-oller, Bachman and Gale: corridors, wide enough to play tennis in, lit from below with gentle light, carpets you could have slept on, pictures that looked suspiciously genuine – and if they were, astronomically expensive.

'Nik's waiting for us,' Bobbi King bubbled, leading them to a door that opened into another serious space, where Nik Speller rose from his desk and advanced, hand out ready for the shake: 'John, good to see you.'

'I'd rather I weren't here,' Parker said, as they shook. Beth tried to see if they were masons – she suspected that Parker was, but there didn't seem to be any thumb-pressing, or maybe they'd changed all that since being outed.

'Ms Stewart, how are you?' Speller shook her hand with both

of his. He had an open, uncomplicated way about him – on the street, if you wanted to know the time, he'd be the kind of guy you'd stop and ask. Trustworthy.

'I'm fine, and it's Beth, please.'

Not one to be excluded, Bobbi King asked: 'You guys want coffee?'

'I think we could both use a cup,' Beth said, falling unconsciously into Bobbi's mid-Atlantic accent. 'Black for you, John?' He nodded. 'And white for me. No sugar in either.' Sometimes it seemed that nothing could be accomplished above a certain level in merchant banking without the ubiquitous silver tray, fine porcelain coffee cups, freshly ground coffee (a blue mountain *blend* at this level – the real stuff for the big boys), a choice of milk or cream and biscuits, plain, chocolate, and butter shortbread.

Bobbi went to the table and poured the coffee. Speller picked up a document from his desk. It was the offering circular – the same that had dominated this morning's board meeting – an unassuming piece of work, no design features, nothing flashy or showy, black on white, a very professional assassin.

'You've read it?' Parker asked.

'I have, John.' Speller flicked the pages lazily. 'Owen Powys at Waymouth, Paternoster. Bit of a thug but this is a decent enough piece of work.' He let the document drop onto the desk and waited while Bobbi handed them coffee and then took a chair, sitting to one side.

'And what,' Parker asked, 'do you think?'

'Think? I think you should sell, John.'

There are moments when the atmosphere in a room changes from comfortable to chilly in a second; Nik Speller's office had gone way beyond that, it was positively arctic.

Speller leaned across the desk: 'Wait. Listen before you blow your top.' He flicked a look at Bobbi King and Beth thought: There's more to this than selling out, otherwise why call in the PR people.

Speller said, 'Look at it calmly, John. As if this wasn't your company. Think of yourself as a shareholder.'

'I am a shareholder, Nik.'

'Fine. So you read this document and see that Byfield is a reasonably well-run company doing reasonably well with reasonable returns on its shares. What are they today, incidentally?'

'90p,' Beth said, 'Up from 82 last week.'

'They'll probably slip back to 85 and stabilise for a while,' Speller said. 'So, it's all reasonable. And along comes Jim Crawford and says, "Reasonable, phooey. I can do better! Look at my company, look at my results. Look at my offer." And they do and it looks good. And, John, it *is* good. Right here and now, from the shareholder's point of view. What I'm saying, and I'm not being defeatist, is that if you want to fight this . . . and I assume you do?'

'I do, Nik.'

'Then you must be aware of Byfield's problems and you must realise that it is going to be a tough fight, and one that – even with everything we can do – you might not win. There's also the point that this is going to create a certain amount of publicity. It's not Vodafone and Mannesmann or Bank of Scotland and NatWest, but it'll be there on the business pages . . .'

'It already is,' Bobbi said, holding up that day's *Guardian* with an article by Hugh Mead prominently displayed.

'Which is going to mean you'll be in the eye of the Stock Exchange. The market in small business shares is pretty healthy at the moment, people are looking around, setting up pitches . . .'

Beth cut in: 'You're saying that if we fight off Ayot someone else might pick us up sooner or later?'

'That's exactly what I'm saying. The days when any publicly quoted company could expect to stay inviolate for years are long gone. The market doesn't work like that any more. Look back 20 years, at the top 30 companies. How many of them are still corporate entities in their own right? Two, three. Growth and change, John, it's healthy for business . . .'

Parker held up a coffee cup. 'I'm not going to disagree, Nik. I read the *Financial Times*, I have a head on my shoulders. I know what might happen later. I simply do not want a company I have helped build and run for as long as I've been with Byfield to end up in the hands of James Crawford. I'll go further than that – I would do anything I could to ensure that did not happen. Do I make myself clear?'

'You do.'

Parker drank his coffee. 'So, Nik, what do we do now?'

Speller tapped the offering circular. 'We issue a press release today – a holding operation – then we put together a defence document within the next 10 to 12 days and get it out to your shareholders. We try – subtly, of course – to alter public and City perceptions of Crawford – that's partly down to you, Bobbi . . .'

Bobbi pulled her chair a little closer to the table. 'I'll get in touch with print and broadcast journalists I know and see if we can't get something out that might plant a seed of doubt in the minds of shareholders. It doesn't need to be much – your private shareholders will be fairly conservative . . .'

'I'm more worried about the fund managers,' Beth said. Her concern had been sparked the day before, when she was doing some work on the Byfield pension scheme and comparing its performance with other funds and, in the light of the takeover, actually considering how much raw power a fund manager operating with 20 billion pounds, which was the amount the top pensions had now reached, would have in the financial markets.

'They certainly have the clout,' Speller said, 'but they're pretty responsible on the whole and they're certainly not going to take any risks. They simply don't need to, and it's quite possible that we'll be able to use that natural caution on our own behalf. Now, before I get my number-crunchers in to start on the financial aspects to the defence document, I think we should just look at our overall strategy and see what tactics we might be able to employ to upset this bid.'

'That's what we're here for,' Parker snapped. His mood seemed to be improving now the fight back was beginning. Beth flipped open her note-pad and waited, pen poised.

'So, basically, what we have is a hostile acquisition situation in which Ayot is trying to gain control of Byfield by buying between 45 and 90 per cent of its voting shares. Right now, they are offering three Ayot shares plus a cash top-up, for every two Byfield shares.'

'Not enough, that's rubbish,' Parker said. 'What are Ayot trading at today?'

'Down seven pence from Friday,' Beth said.

'That's good, it means that there's a certain amount of natural suspicion of Crawford already in the air,' Speller said, 'and that is something we can build on.'

'It surely is,' Bobbi added, her pen flying over the pages of her note-pad. 'There's nowhere I know, apart from the hairdressers, where rumours are as powerful as they are in the City. It's always struck me as crazy that financial services aren't seen as an art – a really good banker plays on the markets like . . . like a virtuoso.'

'Spare my blushes,' Speller laughed. 'Right now we're in historical drama, with Crawford cast as the black knight, who's coming to attack your castle, John. So let's look at our defences within the walls, first, shall we? The boiling oil and the men-at-arms. What have we got that might make him raise the siege?'

Speller looked quite pleased with his analogy. Beth wrote: 'State of siege, internal defences', on her pad and drew a Norman castle with little Normans tipping a vat of boiling oil on attackers.

'First, golden parachutes, and silver or tin as well, if you like.'

'Silver, tin?' Beth asked, and drew someone jumping off the wall with a parachute.

'The golden parachute is an agreement to pay top staff a high severance bonus in case of dismissal before their contracts are up. If it's high enough, any predator is bound to ask himself, can I afford this much money to go out of a firm I've just acquired? Silver and tin are the same deal for managers and even shop-floor staff, anyone who might find themselves out of a job after an acquisition. Now, since most directors' contracts run for a year, John?'

'Two in our case. But we don't have any parachutes. Never felt we'd need them.'

'You never know. It might be possible to create something but, and this is a big but . . .' he smiled at Bobbi in a way Beth couldn't quite interpret, 'shareholders don't like to see directors paying themselves over-the-odds bonuses for what is, in effect, a failure to run the company well enough to keep them safe from being taken over. If this were a merger, then the case would be different.'

'If this were a merger, we wouldn't be here,' Parker said.

'Quite. And since we need the shareholders on our side, we'd best forget the parachutes and try taking the poison pill, which is something Crawford won't want to swallow if he gets hold of Byfield.'

'For example?' Beth asked, sketching in a pill-like sun over the castle with a skull and crossbones on it.

'Byfield could merge or acquire a smaller firm before Crawford's bid comes to a vote, with the idea of making the new Byfield a less enticing prospect. Say, for instance, you were to sell your aggregate and building companies and merge with a paper-making and printing company. That would balance your electronic division with a larger paper and printing division, which is of no interest to Crawford. One of the points he puts forward is the potential cash cow the Byfield and Ayot house-building, plant and aggregate companies would become, quite apart from anything expected from the electronics side. If that weren't possible, then his bid would lose a lot of its attractiveness.'

'That makes good sense,' Beth said, 'except that the building and aggregates side contributes a large part of our overall profits and it's going to get better. That's certainly the opinion of Angus Howerd, our Sales and Marketing Director.'

'And the building firm was my first purchase,' Parker said. 'I have a sentimental attachment to it. I still know some of the men who work for us, from way back.'

'Your first purchase may be your last sale, John. Just keep that thought in your head. Beth, there are other poison-pill possibilities as far as shareholders are concerned. Certain preferred shares might have, if given conditions arise, more voting power than usual, even though, in fact, they don't usually have any voting power at AGMs. Then there are poison pills you can attach to debt securities, so that if an attack succeeds, they must be paid back immediately. However, equity holders tend not to like poison pills – it seems to them one more attempt to keep a sinking ship afloat or maybe I should say, to fill a breach in the castle walls. You might get round it by turning it into a porcupine, which is basically attaching unpalatable conditions to relations with suppliers or customers. Same thing – makes it untasty to take over.'

On the hill near the castle a large porcupine appeared.

'We've never had anything like that,' Parker said. 'It smacks of underhandedness. Not my way of doing business at all.'

'Shark repellents?' Speller asked. 'Changing the company's articles of association to alter the amount of shareholders votes needed to tip the balance?'

Beth said, 'No sharks in our moat, I'm afraid,' and drew a cruising shark in the moat, eating someone who'd just fallen off a ladder.

'A dawn raid? A surprise counter-attack, thundering out across the moat to ride the besiegers down without mercy.'

Beth decided not to attempt horses but did lower the drawbridge.

'This is all starting to get a bit fanciful, isn't it, Nik?' Parker was becoming restless. Beth had noticed before that his attention span was not particularly extended and that after a while, in any meeting, his mind began to wander. It didn't help their company board meetings to follow a disciplined course towards a defined aim; she hoped it wouldn't get in the way now.

'A little bit of fancy never harmed anyone,' Speller said, evoking a smouldering look from under Bobbi King's long eyelashes.

Well, well, Beth thought, so that's how it goes. Bobbi shifted in her chair and scribbled something on her pad. Beth caught her eye, with a questioning glance.

'Men like Crawford are often vulnerable to attack,' Bobbi said. 'Skeletons in the closet. I remember my Ex telling me that Crawford had a whole graveyard concealed somewhere; maybe we should start looking?'

Switching her glance to Parker, Beth saw that her chairman had gone pale.

'Crawford is devious, not to be trusted,' he growled, 'but remember that he is good at this kind of thing . . .'

'Sorry, John, what kind of thing?' Bobbi asked.

'He . . . he enjoys . . .' Parker was obviously struggling with some idea that he couldn't quite – or didn't yet want to – put into words. 'Just be careful when you deal with him outside of business, that's all.'

'I will.'

Speller took up the conversation: 'Maybe a Pac-man defence, which is basically turning on the predator and making a counterbid. Cheeky but it can be effective.'

Beth was finishing off a gravestone and added a computer Pac-man on it as she said: 'I think we should look at that, John,' before Parker could reject it, as he seemed to be rejecting everything else. 'If we could raise the debt, after all, he's not that much bigger than we are.'

'*I* never appeared in any of those idiotic adverts,' Parker said. 'I don't have his public . . . profile, is that what you call it?'

'This wouldn't be about profiles,' Beth said, 'it would be about money.'

Speller backed her up: 'Absolutely. And I agree, we should look at the possibility.'

Parker nodded.

'Fine, that's the inside stuff. Oh, unless this whole thing,' Speller waved the offering circular over the desk, 'is a bit of greenmail, with the idea of forcing your board to buy back from Crawford the shares he gets hold of at an inflated price. It isn't that common now, but it was very fashionable back in the eighties, especially in the US.'

'It would be,' Parker growled. 'And it would be just like Crawford to try something underhand of that nature but . . . no, I don't think it is. He wants Byfield.'

Bobbi King asked: 'How can you be so sure?'

'It was in his voice when he rang me up. Besides, I know the man.'

'How well do you know him?' Speller asked.

'Well enough to know that he won't back off without a fight and he won't surrender unless we defeat him. No treaties, no truces, this one is to the finish.'

That was the first moment during the whole campaign that Beth Stewart realised there was more to this bid than had met her eye so far. Speller didn't appear to have noticed, though Bobbi King raised her eyebrows. Perhaps it was just that the banker was more urbane and professionally disinclined to allowing *anything* to surprise him. He said, 'External allies, then. This comes down to an either-or scenario. A concert party or a white knight. To take the former first: is it possible that we might gather a group of investors and get them to buy up shares separately, and then pool them? Do you have that many friends with that kind of capital, John?'

Beth ripped the page from her pad, screwed it up and flipped it into the bin. Bobbi King grinned.

Parker said: 'It could be done – but it would take months . . .'

'Which we don't have. So finally, a white knight riding in to save you. Which, given that you seem to have no objection to being acquired by anyone other than Crawford, is probably our best bet.'

Beth said, 'Wouldn't it be a better bet for the shareholders if we'd beaten off Crawford's bid before that happened? We'd be seen as a healthier, more successful company and our share prices would reflect that.'

'Yes, but it's a big *if*, Beth. It might be possible to set something up and give Crawford a smell of it, so he backed off rather than find himself in a three-way battle and that's a chance we might have to take if we go this way. John, what's your feeling?'

'I don't want to go, but if I have to, then, yes, let it be to a white knight.'

'Fine. So we have a couple of things here, Pac-man and white knight. Now we should look at the MI6 option. Can we get into Crawford's camp and destabilise his bid?'

'How would we do that?' Beth asked. 'He's hardly going to open up the ledgers for us.'

'He doesn't have to,' Speller said. Once again he fluttered the offer doc in front of Beth and Parker. 'This should give us a start. I'll get some of our people to give it a very close reading, see what we might come up with. For instance, have Crawford's people worked out if this acquisition is better value than internal development — is getting a take-out meal cheaper than cooking it at home and is it as satisfying? What about the expertise he's supposedly buying in by getting Byfield? If you're a good cook of Chinese food, is there any point in getting that takeaway? Do you like the takeaway, can you set up a meaningful long-term relationship with the Chang Mei Restaurant and will it last beyond next year? These are all things we can ask about this document. There are others as well. What sort of combination does Crawford envisage for Ayot and Byfield: vertical, horizontal, concentric, some kind of conglomeration? And what about supply and customer demand? It's all in here, the questions appear to be answered, the figures seem to be there on the page but I have a feeling that there's been a bit of pushing and shoving to fit Ayot into the template. My instinct is that Crawford's bankers are not 100 per cent behind this offer.'

On a fresh sheet Beth drew a tinfoil box containing an unseen takeaway meal.

'You say it's a feeling, Nik. Can you firm that up at all?' Parker's attention had obviously sharpened again.

'It's difficult at this point but once we start asking the same questions he's asking about us, about him, if you follow me, I think some of the answers might prove interesting.'

'Interesting enough to head off the attack?' Beth asked.

'Oh, I doubt that. As John said, Crawford doesn't give up easily; our job, in the defence document, is to sow the seed of doubt in shareholders' minds, just as he's done here, about Byfield. At the same time, we should try and reassure the City, or that part of it that might be interested, about the health of Byfield.'

'Would having a non-executive director who knew the City be a help there?' Parker asked. 'I know Beth has a lot of talent but she's not that close to City institutions.'

'To be honest, John, it's something you should have done months ago, maybe even years ago. It's almost too late but there's probably no harm in at least talking to someone who has the necessary expertise. A fire-fighter rather than anyone more measured. Why don't I have a word and give you a call if I find anyone suitable? Then the two of you can meet up and talk things over.'

'Sounds good to me, Nik. And you'll start work on the defence document?'

'If you want us to, yes. Bobbi can put out a few feelers in the press and see what Crawford's hacks are producing.'

'It won't be headline stuff,' Bobbi said, 'but it will give us some indications and something to push against.'

'Beth, we should keep in close touch for the figures we'll be needing. My analysts will give you a call, OK?'

'Any time, Nik. I'll leave my mobile number.'

'Good. We'll need to have some kind of overall company strategy from your directors, John. One of the points that Crawford's bankers make is that your shares have not been going up – that even your modest forecasts have not been met.'

'Oh, he can say that,' Parker protested, 'but we don't falsify our forecasts. The shares reflect the kind of company we are. Besides, look at the electronics results in 1997 and the construction side last year – they're good results.'

Speller wet his finger and leafed through to the back of the offer doc. 'Yes, they're down here, but the point is made: this is good news in isolation and not part of a general trend in growth. Anyway, we can look again once we have more figures and some long-term strategy. Also, I want you to look closely at management reorganisation at board level. Could you be doing better with younger, tougher, more innovative people? Present company excluded, of course, Beth. Basically, Byfield needs more people like you on the board. I think there should be a plan.'

'I don't want a night of the long knives at Byfield,' Parker said.

'Of course not, but you do need to offer *something* in the defence document. Say that restructuring is on the agenda as a mid-term strategy. It shows you're aware of the problems. Right, I think that's it.'

The meeting was over. Bobbi King bounced out of her chair and corralled the coffee cups while Speller came round the desk to see them out.

'Now, I know it's easy to say, John, but don't worry. Byfield is a good company and it isn't about to go to the wall for the sake of Jim Crawford.'

'That's really what I care about,' Parker said, taking hold of Speller's arm. 'I don't want that man to get my company. Just try, Nik, just try as hard as you can to make sure that doesn't happen.'

Beth felt a light touch on her own arm. Bobbi King sparkled up at her and said: 'I expect you need the little girls' room?' and without waiting for an answer, went to the door and set off down the corridor. Beth followed, as she was obviously meant to and in moments found herself in a softly lit, deeply carpeted washroom.

'The boys need a moment on their own, I think,' Bobbi said, standing on tiptoe so she could check her make-up in the mirror that ran like a widescreen cinema along the top of the basins. Beth didn't really need the loo so she perched a buttock on the chrome-trimmed, brushed steel retro waste bin and waited for Bobbi, who was now replenishing her eyeshadow, to finish or to ask whatever it was she wanted to know.

'So, Beth, you don't mind if I call you Beth?'

'No, of course not.'

'John Parker, what's he like. What can we use if we have to?'

'That's a hell of a question, Bobbi. I mean, what're you going to want to use him for?'

'The *Today* programme, for instance. How would he stand up there, if we got him on opposite Jim Crawford in a debate?'

'I don't know that I'd ever thought about it.'

Bobbi put the eyeshadow brush back into her compact and snapped the lid shut. 'Well, think about it now. Crawford will use whatever it takes to raise his profile with the shareholders. This stuff matters, Beth. Is there anyone else on the board who might do some media stuff?'

'Dick Worthington. The music guy,' Beth offered.

'Is he still around?'

'He's around.' Beth's tone said it all. 'I mean . . .'

'You mean you don't like him?'

'He's a lech.'

'Aren't they all, honey. He might be useful. What about you, Beth? Could you do *The Business Show* or *Show Me the Money* on TV?'

'Oh, come on, you're kidding!'

One look at Bobbi's face told Beth that she wasn't. And though the mere idea of appearing in the media invited a whole cloud of butterflies to settle in her tummy, she did also feel that, yes . . . maybe . . .

'I suppose I could try it,' she said.

'Skirt a little shorter and tighter, a bit more cleavage.'

'I don't really see myself that way, Bobbi.' She flicked a look at herself in the mirror to see just how she did *see* herself at this moment. 'I mean, it isn't really about looks any more.' Not that she was looking bad today.

'Are you telling me you've never used your looks to get what you've wanted in business?' Bobbi asked.

Beth wondered – had she? 'I've been tripped up *because of* being a woman, Bobbi. It happened once early on and I made damn sure it never happened again. So no, I haven't used my looks, not knowingly.'

'Fine.' Bobbi didn't seem at all put out by the implied rebuke. 'You're a natural. You could make a positive impression on TV and on the financial pages with a good photo. For certain you'd be a better spokesperson than Parker or that dick, Worthington. Think about it. No, don't think about it, decide you will. I'll call you. OK, let's rejoin the boys, shall we?'

Day +2

wednesday 3rd nov. 06:50

flat 7, frogwell road,
west dulwich, london

THE NEXT MORNING, OVER BREAKFAST – coffee and grapefruit for
her, tea and toast for Jack, who was working at his laptop as he
ate – Beth mentioned Bobbi King's idea. Jack looked up from the
screen.

'What, TV? You?'

'Yes, me. Is that so odd?'

'Hey, no, no, I think it's a great idea. Uh . . . why exactly?'

'To talk about the takeover, why else?'

Jack scooped up a load of low-fat spread and slathered it on
his toast. 'Trouble with this stuff, it doesn't do what butter does.'

'Give you a heart attack?' Beth asked, detaching a strand of
grapefruit fibre from the little triangle of fruit on her spoon.
'Come on, Jack, it's a small thing, like skimmed milk, but it
makes a difference. I don't want to lose you one of these days.'

The remark was made with a smile but Jack's expression was
anything but humorous when he replied: 'Then maybe you
ought to take a bit more notice of us when we're together.'
He dug the end of his knife into the marmalade jar and came up
with a vast, shimmering globule which he dumped onto his
toast. 'OK, I know you're busy. I'm busy too. And I think I try to
give you support in your job when you need it but, right
now . . .' He indicated the laptop screen. 'I could use a little
support myself.'

'Hold on, hold on, hold on,' Beth was trying to think back to

129

the last time she'd needed support and how much, exactly, Jack had provided. 'I give you support all the time. You come home and you talk about school, about the kids, about the staff, their problems, your problems. I know as much about that place as most of your governors. Think about it, Jack. That's how it is, most evenings when we're both here . . .'

'And how often is that, nowadays?'

'You've got the OFSTED inspection coming up, of course you're busy. I've been trying to get hold of the reins at Byfield and make some kind of impact. I'm busy too.' The grapefruit was empty. She'd eaten the last four segments without noticing. What she did notice was the tension in the air. Jack was picking at his left thumb with his forefinger, something he only did when things weren't right between them. And it was true, they hadn't discussed the upcoming inspection; on the other hand, they hadn't discussed the takeover attempt either. Without quite meaning to, she voiced her next thought: 'Is there a sort of tacit feeling here, Jack, that somehow your job is more important than mine?'

He flamed into anger: 'Oh come on, that is bollocks, Beth! We've never, neither of us . . . right from the start, we've never thought like that. It's been strictly fifty-fifty all the way.'

'But it hasn't, Jack.' And she was right, she knew it with total certainty. 'Just like you think you've been supportive, you think you don't make any kind of judgement about our relative values.'

'Do you mind if we don't talk about it now, Beth? I've got a lot on. It's really pushing us all to the limit, this time and . . .' his voice took on a slightly wild edge, as if he would rather have shouted the words at her, 'I really don't think I could take any more on board without sinking. Right now. OK. I mean if you really are worried about this, then by all means let's talk when we have some time and space. OK?'

Later, much later, looking back and remembering the scene with dreamlike clarity, she was able to say: yes, *then*. That one moment I stood at the crossroads and I could have gone either way and I said: OK. Tonight. And that was it, really.

'OK. Tonight,' she said.

'Fine. We'll go round to the Rajput, have a curry or something and we'll talk it all through.' He looked at her, composing his face into the tolerant-but-don't-push-it expression he used with naughty but bright kids at school. She didn't say a word and, taking that for acquiescence, he turned back to the laptop, flipped off the screensaver and started typing, while eating the last of his slice of toast.

Byfield plc, Goldhawk Mews, London, 11:45

There were some things you simply did not think about, John Parker reflected, as he doodled a series of cartoon men around the edge of his note-pad. You did not think that one day you would wake up and look in the mirror and see your father's face peering at you; you did not think that one day your son would stand up, in your own house, and tell you that he . . . he was gay – that ridiculous word; you did not think that one day someone would come and try and take away everything you had built up in your life.

He was not a thinker, never had been; his happiest times had always been when he was working hard, building things, like in the early days. Yes, you could see the value of your effort when you built. There it was: concrete, bricks and mortar, wood, slate, glass. The actual process of making a house had always given him immense pleasure: the growth of a dwelling that would be lived in for a hundred years, perhaps even longer. It was that sense of continuity. Of the past being a foundation for the future.

On the pad it seemed as if his cartoon men had turned on each other and that some kind of massacre was in progress. The little stick figures were wielding swords and axes and there were fatalities, he was sure there were. Little dead stick figures. He ripped the sheet from the pad as the phone rang. He picked it up and Mrs Harrison, his secretary, said, 'Mr Speller for you, Mr Parker.'

'Thank you, Mrs Harrison, put him through, please.' Yes, that was the sort of man he was: Peggy Harrison had been with the company for 35 years and he'd never called her anything except Mrs Harrison and she had never expected that he would. These things, these civilities, were still of importance and when they were lost, then everything . . .

'John, how are you?' Speller sounded ebullient.

'Coping, Nik. Coping.'

'I hope you're doing a lot more than that. I've been giving Ayot's records a good going over and I think I'm beginning to see one or two possibilities.'

'That would be good news, indeed, Nik. I have to say it's getting on my nerves sitting here waiting, not doing anything.'

'Well, I have something for you. You were asking about a non-executive director who knows the City and has some experience of fighting off takeover bids?'

'You've found someone?'

'I might have done. Bryan House, do you know him?'

Parker thought for a moment but the name meant nothing. But then, why should it, he was out of touch with the City. A thought came to him: *fatally*, he was fatally out of touch. 'No, I don't know the name, Nik.'

'Obviously, he only knows what he's read in the papers, but he said he might be interested. I don't think he's an admirer of Crawford's, which is good news for a start.'

'I like the sound of him already, Nik. When can we meet and where?'

'Sooner rather than later. I took the liberty of suggesting the bar at the Landmark Hotel on Baker Street. You're unlikely to attract any attention there and it'll give you a chance for a decent, uninterrupted chat. I said eight, tonight, would probably be convenient for you. I can always ring him back if . . .'

'No, eight will be fine, Nik. How will I know this fellow?'

'He knows you, John. He was at the Innovations Awards last month and someone pointed you out to him.'

'That was the last time I saw Crawford face to face. Maybe it's an omen.'

'I can't promise anything but I can say that House knows his stuff and he's a decent enough man. He'll cost, of course, but then you'll be expecting that. Otherwise, there's not much to report, though Bobbi King would like to set up an interview for your Financial Director.'

'Beth Stewart?'

'Bobbi seems to think she could be a useful part of the defence. She's shrewd, modern and attractive; all things the rest of your board – if you'll forgive me for saying so – are not. In spades.'

'I could say, with no disrespect to Beth, that you don't judge a book by its cover.'

'No, but the cover will make you take it off the shelf and look inside. Times are changing, John, and we must change with them or . . . so I can let Bryan House know, you'll be there tonight?'

'I'll be there. Bye, Nik.'

Speller had put the phone down almost before the words were out of Parker's mouth. No bankers could afford to waste time, though it was a style to which Parker had never quite taken; and, in truth, he'd never quite taken to Nik Speller. His original banker, in the early years of Sheetrock, as it had been then, was a wonderful chap who, in Parker's eyes, had encapsulated all the traditional virtues of British banking. Loyalty, sophistication without show, a sense of history but also a grasp of the future. He still exchanged Christmas cards with Sir Giles, though the old boy was a bit squiffy in the head nowadays and someone else tended to do the actual signing. It was sad – that such a distinguished journey should end in such a way.

John Parker shook his head. What was happening to him, sitting here giving way to these idiotic and frankly rather second-rate philosophical speculations? This wasn't the way to get houses built or to run an electronics company – or, indeed, to save Byfield. He looked down at the pad. More doodles, this time of a little stick girl riding a little stick pony over a fence. He tore this sheet out carefully and folded it and put it in his wallet. Then he buzzed Mrs Harrison.

'Yes, Mr Parker?'

'Mrs Harrison, would you be kind enough to ask Ms Stewart to give me a few moments.'

Blue Mountain Coffee Bar, Euston Road, London, 13:40

Mark Chima, balancing two cappuccino cups, a raisin Danish and a lemon Danish, manoeuvred through the crowded coffee bar to the window counter where Diane Ellroy was perched fetchingly on a high stool.

'There we are. I think it's right.' Thankfully, Mark deposited cups and plates on the narrow plastic-topped counter. 'You were the raisin? I was the lemon. No, you were the lemon? Weren't you?'

Diane laughed. 'It doesn't matter. I have catholic tastes in these matters. If it's sweet pastry, I'll eat it. It's the coffee I need.'

'Tough morning?'

'No more than the usual,' she said. 'This business with Byfield generates extra work for us all, but I'm more concerned with the long-term effects.'

Mark's concern was sitting next to Diane, on this bright November Wednesday, sharing lunch. The first time he had actually been with her out of the building. It felt good, natural – after all they were colleagues and he did have something to discuss, so what could be wrong with that? So why was he going over and over it in his mind?

'There was something I needed to check with you, Diane, on the Register of Directors. You've moved and I need your new address.'

'So you can pop in one evening?'

He went red. He wished, how he wished he could control the blush response – 'Just for the records.'

'Sure.' She bit into the lemon Danish – though Mark was sure she'd actually asked for the raisin.

'And I noticed that the CEO gives his address as company property.'

'You noticed?'

'It was before my time.'

'Sure, the company pays for his place at Butler's Wharf, just like it pays for his cars and drivers and, I think, one of the country places too. It's part of his contract.'

'He's happy to use the company chequebook, then.'

'You don't approve?' She wiped a crumb from her top lip. 'As far as I know there's nothing wrong with it.'

'I think it's one more indication of how he runs the company. At the board meeting last week, OK, he got the vote and he primed the right directors beforehand . . .' Mark shook his head. 'Maybe it's none of my business. What am I, I'm the company secretary.' He took a bite of the raisin Danish. He didn't really like it – so that made it certain, he would never have ordered a Danish he didn't like. It wasn't logical. He felt a tiny spasm of annoyance at Diane for her behaviour, followed by a huge stab of contempt for himself. She was beautiful – she had the right to take his lemon Danish. If she wanted, she could have a hundred lemon Danishes, if that was the plural of Danish. It didn't sound quite right. Maybe he should look it up after lunch. Maybe he should stop thinking like an adding machine. 'Sorry, Diane, what were you saying?'

'Obviously nothing that was terribly interesting, since you were miles away.'

'No, really, please. Go on.'

'I was saying that it is your business, it's the board's anyway. Jim Crawford is charismatic and brilliant, fine, I'll go with that, but I don't feel he's good for us in the long run. I know he's a bee in his hat . . .'

'Bonnet, Diane. It's a bee in his bonnet.'

'Why?'

'There's a variant, bees in his head. It first arose in the seventeenth century, in a play by Haywood. Basically it refers to a swarm of bees that are flying round in your head like a swarm of ideas, from which nothing sensible can emerge.'

Her eyes were round: 'Are you kidding me?'

'Really, no. I looked it up once in the dictionary of slang. I was curious, it sounded odd. All those sorts of phrases, I find them . . .' bees in his own head. He stopped abruptly, as though he'd got a bee in his mouth.

Diane went on, 'Crawford's caught up with the idea of globalisation, which makes good sense. What doesn't make such good sense is him running the whole deal.'

'So let me ask you: Why?'

'Haven't we said before in a hundred different ways: The key to good management lies in the relationship between the chairman and the CEO. And as far as the relationship between Jim and Peter Allbury – well, there is no relationship to speak of. Or not to speak of. There's nothing there and from nothing, you get nothing.'

Mark didn't really want to finish the raisin Danish but if he left it on his plate, maybe Diane would notice and think it was a criticism of her for stealing his lemon Danish; and that would be terrible. Because although he did feel . . . Oh stop it! he told himself. Eat the bloody thing and be done with it.

'I suppose I agree,' he said. 'And looking from the bottom of the boardroom table, it seems to me that the CEO doesn't utilise the board to anywhere near its potential.' He took a bite of the Danish and found a sticky stretchy bit between his teeth, which he couldn't sever. He eased a bit more of the nasty thing into his mouth, but the intractable pastry was still there. He bit down as hard as he could. Nothing. It was half-in and half hanging down his chin; he must look utterly disgusting. What a position to be caught in – in front of an elegant sophisticate like Diane too! He had to do something. He stuffed the whole thing into his mouth. His cheeks bulged as he forced his lips shut and began to chew. For some reason a whole layer of the pastry now seemed to be totally intractable. Diane was looking at him with a quizzical expression. He tried to smile round the stodgy mess; this was a problem and he was going to have to chew his way out of it. 'Go on . . .' he said to Diane. Actually, he said: 'Ehhh uhhhh,' but she seemed to understand.

'The way I see it, Peter is a washout as chairman unless someone can force him to act. Now, that isn't going to be me or Goodman or any other of the executive directors, so it comes down to one of the non-execs. And we can forget Pierre, he's Crawford's man. So's Norman Brown. What do you know about Gavin Clooney?'

Mark was winning but the cost was high. His eyes were watering, his jaw ached, his throat stretched to the limit as . . . he swallowed the last of the wretched thing.

'Clooney? Not a lot.' Oh, it was blissful to be able to talk again. He took a sip of cappuccino to wash away the taste of raisins. He'd always hated raisins. 'He's only been with us six months or so – there's his academic background, his other experience.'

'Knows what he's talking about,' Diane said.

'He seems pretty independent. Doesn't say a lot unless there's something to say. Has a good grasp of overall strategy. Do you remember the August meeting, when he talked about the importance of long-term thinking, about the way business has changed, with no more vertical management and freelance-style directors coming together in . . . what did he call them?'

'Corporate clusters. I was impressed. I wanted to have a word afterwards but he had to go. Those kind of guys always have to go somewhere but I have a feeling Clooney understands that a good non-exec should be available to others on the board, not just the CEO's stooge.'

'What are you thinking, Diane?'

'I'm thinking that we should . . . I should talk to him, sound him out. Nothing formal, maybe invite him for a drink, something like that.'

Mark called up a mental picture of a rather raffish Gavin Clooney in white tie and tails dancing the night away with Diane Ellroy, clad in a silver sheath which moved like moonlit water . . . Sometimes he wondered if he was going totally bonkers. On the other hand, Clooney was attractive in an academic sort of way and Diane was a woman alone. Oh, he had to stop this nonsense.

'Yes, why don't we both see him?'

'What? Are you going to take some time out from the domestic front? What's Clooney got that I haven't?'

Ahhhhhh, wrong again. How could any human being be so totally inept at anything other than being a company secretary? It was enough to make you weep.

'No, no. Yes, I mean no.'

Diane waited and finished the last of her coffee and wiped a little foam moustache from her top lip in a gesture so touching it made him want to cry.

'I just think it would be good if we both saw him. That way, he'd know it wasn't just you.'

'That's right, he'd see it was you as well.' Her eyelashes flickered down as she looked at her watch. 'I guess we'd better get back. If you're sure you're not still hungry?'

Now why did she say that? Mark looked at her plate, at the circle of paper on which the lemon Danish had rested; he looked at his plate: no paper. He looked at Diane; she shrugged.

Oxo Tower balcony, London, 18:30

London's Oxo Restaurant has one of the finest views in the city. Overlooking the Thames from the top of a tower – built originally by the Oxo corporation, who avoided the prohibition on riverside advertising by incorporating their brand name into the architecture – it allows the diners in the glass-walled restaurant an unrivalled view up river, to the City of London and St Paul's

Downstream

Cathedral, and down past the millennium London Eye big wheel, the Houses of Parliament, Big Ben and Westminster Abbey. Of course, you don't have to dine to get the view; you can always visit the bar and, if you wish, take your cocktails out onto the balcony where Hugh and Celia leaned on the railing looking out over the river.

Celia had just asked what Hugh was looking so pleased about.

'I got an interview with Crawford. This afternoon. I talked it over with my producer Angela Daniels and we figured that, if anything, a really good piece of work on Crawford would get us over on to TV, so she rang up Perry King and we were in.'

'How did you find him?'

Hugh sipped at his drink. 'He's certainly a charmer. I think he's also a bullshitter.'

'Aren't the two inexorably mixed – like a good martini?'

Hugh sipped again. 'And this is very like a good martini and Crawford is . . . I saw him at Crawford House, which is a pretty egotistical statement in itself, until you find out that it commemorates an entirely different Crawford, who was something in Victorian engineering. There's a plaque in the reception area.'

'It's one of his favourite jokes. Only like a lot of his stuff, it isn't quite a joke,' Celia said. 'He did commission the place – in fact the company commissioned it but in effect it was him.'

'I get the impression that just about everything *is* him, one way or the other. He told me a lot about his childhood and early struggles. Quite a little achiever, wasn't he?'

'Oh yes, but then like a lot of these people, he pulls his own legend along behind him and as times change, so the legend changes. It's as if everything – life, history, people – are just part of the Jim Crawford story and when it's time for a rewrite, whole characters and sequences can be dropped and it doesn't really matter.'

'Now that,' Hugh said, offering his jacket to Celia, who was wearing a slight black dress and was beginning to shiver, 'is an interesting thought.'

'Really – are you sure, won't you be cold?'

'It's a thick sweater.'

'Then thanks. Very noble of you, Hugh.' She gave him a quick kiss as he draped the fleece round her shoulders. 'What's interesting in particular about it?'

'What he didn't say. I had all the stuff about the noble self-sacrifice of his mother. Is she still around, by the way?'

'I never heard anything about her. But then why would I?'

'Hm. She seemed a bit too good to be true, but maybe that was nostalgia, if Crawford is capable of feeling anything like that. Oh, there was some moving stuff about the hero father who died as a result of his war wounds. Then the mother got work in a factory and brought up young James all on her own – while making sure that she had time to read his school books and help with the homework. And then he started his first business delivering groceries, which went on to some pet-food scheme and he got in with the local butcher . . . And started Meat-To-Please-You. You need all of this?'

'It's all in the official biog,' Celia said. 'The salesman's bible: remove anything the customer can object to and he'll buy.'

'Yeah. Then he went on about his corporate theories: managers come together, work on some project for a while, then separate. Corporate clusters. He was happy enough to chat on about that but he clammed right up as soon as I tried to ask about standing for Parliament.'

'That was the first Thatcher election, right?'

'Yeah. Not a thing. Bang, down came the blinds. It got quite tense there for a moment. I thought he was going to call the whole thing off and demand the tapes. The most he'd say was that he had a narrow escape.'

'It's a fact that an awful lot of top executives are bad interviewees – they're also pretty awful interviewers – but this sounds different.'

'Crawford knows exactly what he's doing. But then so do I – and you know, you get that feeling when something comes alive.

You're wading through all the pre-prepared porridge these people come out with and then, quite suddenly, there's a gleam – pure gold – and you head for that, you don't let it go. Listen to Humphrys or Paxmen at their best. It's attack dog stuff and it's what the game is all about: the real stuff.'

'And that was the only moment . . .' She paused while a loud party of young men went past below performing an impromptu karaoke. Looking at her profile against the lighted curve of the dome of St Paul's, Hugh wondered just how close she was to Crawford, how many of his secrets she knew. In a lot of ways, Celia was a closed book to him, as he was, he supposed, to her. Their relationship was based on mutual liking, complementary tastes in certain arcane areas of sexuality, the shared basement flat and convenience. He wondered what would happen if either of them strayed across the border into the land of emotional commitment and came upon that fabulous beast called love? The karaoke singers drifted away and Celia finished: 'That was the only moment you felt you got close to him?'

'Yeah, the rest was all by rote. Perry King, his PR guy, would have briefed him. He's been on to all of us hacks as well. Do you know King, by the way?'

'Perry? Of course. Very competent. You know, his wife is working for the other side.'

'Surely that's a conflict of interests?'

'They're divorced. Couple of years now. I always felt that Bobbi was the brighter half of that partnership, though she started out as his PA. But Perry's OK.'

'What about the other advisers – the investment banker?'

'Owen Powys? A total bastard, thinks he's funny, makes a lot of money for the bank and for himself. This deal is pretty small stuff for him.'

'So why is he – why are you and the bank involved?'

'I'm involved because, to a degree, I work to Jim Crawford. Owen, because he sees something for himself; he's desperate to get on the list of the top 20 deal-makers of the year. I was checking out some figures and though Ayot-Byfield is pretty small stuff, the value could bring his total up to just enough to let him squeeze in. Then again, maybe he needs the bonus to buy another sports car. There's also this stuff from the Chancellor's speech about supporting entrepreneurs; maybe the bank wants to look like good boys for once.'

Finishing his martini, Hugh took both their glasses and went back inside, pushing his way through the press of fashionable bodies to the bar, where he ordered two more. Across the room he caught sight of George Packenham, a rising TV political correspondent he'd met on a couple of Beeb seminars. He waved and called over. The sunburnt Packenham – where had he picked that up? – excused himself from his group and joined Hugh at the bar.

'George, hi! How's it going? Loved the report from Washington. New England in the fall, you lucky sod.'

Packenham grinned. 'Didn't get a chance to see it, mate. Still, can't complain. How about you?'

Hugh could have banged on about the utilities programme but, compared to Packenham's triumphs, that was nothing, so he opted for: 'I'm following the takeover – Jim Crawford and this electronics company. I think it might make a good feature now that entrepreneurs are supposed to be sexy again.'

Packenham paused, his head on one side. 'Yeah, I heard something about that . . . Where was it? In the House. I can't remember where or what – junior secretary at the FO. One of Robin Cook's boys or girls. Just a word. There's some very deep briefing and somewhere . . . there was just a little mention of Jimmy and this company he wants to buy. If anything comes up, give me a call.' He flipped a card out of his top pocket and Hugh realised, at once, that Packenham hadn't come over for the sake of their acquaintance. Like a good hack, he had seen the way the water was running and was putting out lures in the hope that one day they might get a bite. Didn't matter if nothing took – sooner or later, if you put out enough, something would. 'Good to see you, Hugh,' he said, with a grin of relief at remembering Hugh's name before the end of the conversation, and drifted back across the room to his party.

Hugh looked at the card. It was very plain; it didn't need to sell itself. He decided to get his cards redone in the same style. He paid for the martinis and took them back out to the balcony.

'Thought you'd got lost.'

'I bumped into George Packenham.'

'You know him?'

'Well, I know him more than he knows me. But who knows how that might change. Cheers.'

They drank. The mixture was perfect: Tanquarey gin, icy cold; a splash of vermouth, just enough to put an oily sheen on the freezer-cold glass; a twist of lemon.

'He'd heard something about Crawford along the river there.' Hugh nodded towards the illuminated fake gothic of the Houses of Parliament. 'I'm beginning to wonder if there's more to this story than I thought.'

'They would be interested. He is a national figure, after all.'

'So was Bernard Matthews, Celia.'

'Turkeys are not electronics. They're just turkeys. They don't matter.'

'Except to other turkeys.'

'On a global scale, Hugh. They do not strut upon the stage of history.'

'Point taken. Who's good on the other side?'

'Parker's team, you mean?'

'Yeah. Someone worth interviewing, who might not be totally committed – you know the kind of thing.'

'Someone who'd talk to a hack like you?'

He toasted her with his frozen glass. 'That's exactly it.'

'The only person I know is Beth Stewart. She's the Financial Director. Very bright – very ambitious. I can't see her staying with Byfield even if they do fight off Crawford.'

'Do you have a number?'

'In my bag.'

'Great. Can you give me some background – what kind of person is she?'

'I'm not sure,' Celia said. 'I always found her slightly difficult to read. Scottish. Married to a teacher. No kids. I always felt she was something of a cold fish; never quite felt comfortable with the girlie stuff. Maybe it's just natural reserve.' She looked at her watch and finished her drink. 'We'd better be moving. You can call her from the cab.' They were due at the launch of a book by one of Celia's more exalted colleagues. Yet another sure-fire success plan for budding businesspersons; still, Hugh thought, as they made their way to the lift and descended to the ground floor, at least the drinks and snacks would be of better quality than at a literary launch.

As they walked along past the National Theatre, he punched in Beth Stewart's mobile number. After a couple of rings she answered.

'Hello, Beth Stewart.' There was a slight, rather attractive Scottish lilt.

'Hi, Beth, this is Hugh Mead from the BBC.' A slight pause to allow her the time to digest this august news. Celia raised her eyebrows and smirked. 'Sorry to disturb you at this time.'

'No, that's all right, uh, Mr Mead. How can I help you?'

'I work with *Business Today* and we're doing a programme on the general business culture at . . . at the end of the century. Millennium now, that sort of thing.'

Celia shook her head and mouthed: 'You slimy toad. Tell the truth!'

'And I was given your name by the analyst Celia Hart, whom I believe you know?'

'Yes, I know Celia. What exactly . . .'

'You're involved in this takeover battle at the moment . . .'

'Hugh Mead? That's right, you wrote an article on Monday.'

'Right. And I'd be really interested to hear your side of the story, both from the point of view of the acquisition and as a woman in business who'll be influencing corporate life over the next few years.'

'Well, I don't know if I'm that important, Mr Mead.' There was a pleasant self-deprecating laugh in her voice. Hugh decided he liked her unseen.

'Who knows – but I really would like to interview you, both for the show and maybe for the newspaper as well?'

'I don't know. Everyone seems to want me to . . .'

'Strictly voluntary,' Hugh broke in. 'Let me buy you a drink after work one evening this week. Say Thursday?'

'Well, I'm terribly sorry but . . .'

'Monday or Tuesday next week. Please, it'd be a real favour and . . .' He waited.

Celia mouthed: 'The old technique, make 'em feel guilty then reel 'em in. You slimeball, Mead.'

'I suppose I could, on Monday.'

'Great, Beth, that's fabulous. My producer will love me. Shall I pick you up at . . . Goldhawk Mews, isn't it?'

'I could always meet you.'

'No, taxi's on me. What time: Six, six-thirty?'

'Better make it half past. We're a bit busy here.'

'Great. Thanks. Bye.' He snapped the phone shut.

Celia said: 'You didn't leave your number in case she wants to cancel.'

'Oh, how careless of me,' Hugh said, and they walked on towards the Festival Hall and the big wheel, hanging over the river.

Byfield plc, Goldhawk Mews, London, 18:40

Reception at Byfield was a good deal less modern than Ayot's steel and glass cage. The best adjective would have been comfortable. John Parker nodded to the receptionist – at this hour a uniformed security guard had taken over from Mrs Glass, who presided during the day.

He could hear the whine of an industrial vacuum cleaner and

looking down the corridor he saw Adele Macdonald, who held the cleaning franchise for the office. A black woman in her fifties, she had started out as an office cleaner employed by Byfield but, during the course of a number of conversations with Parker, not only had an unlikely friendship sprung up but she had also listened to his advice and started her own company, which now employed over three dozen people and cleaned blocks all over London. Good and trustworthy cleaners were a real bonus to any firm and Parker had no doubt that Cleanaround would go from strength to strength. Perhaps out of loyalty, or to keep her hand in, Adele still oversaw the cleaning at Byfield herself. When he stuck his head round the door, she waved and called, 'Evening, Mr Parker.' She flicked the cleaner off and came along the corridor. 'I'm sorry for your problems, indeed I am.'

'You've been hearing about them, Adele?'

'In the papers. I always turn to the financial section first.'

'To check on your shares,' he joked. 'Well, don't worry, however this comes out, the share price will rise.'

'That don't matter – not that much, anyhow. I can buy and sell as easy as the next person. I was thinking more of you, Mr Parker, and what I'm thinking is that this is no easy time.'

'It has been better. Still I can't complain.'

'No, maybe not, but I've a feeling you don't like it.'

'You're right, I don't like it.'

'You think they'll win?'

'I don't really know what to think. Between the two of us, Adele, it could go either way. I'm sure they'll renew your contract if it comes to it.'

'Mr Parker, I've got a queue this long,' she stretched her arms wide, 'waiting to secure the service of Cleanaround. If they take over I might not care to *have* my contract renewed.' She laughed hugely and patted his arm. 'You take care now, and remember, if you ever need a job, you just call me.' And with another laugh, she was gone. Parker smiled. They had always got on well together. Somehow there was no side between them and he was able to be more himself with Adele than with almost anyone else in the company.

The lift pinged and Beth Stewart emerged. She carried a coat over her arm and an attaché case with the documents they would need for the meeting with the non-executive director. He held open the door and they went out to the hired car.

Landmark Hotel Bar, Baker Street, London, 19:00

'John Parker? Bryan House.' He was in his forties, impeccably dressed, utterly in charge as he stood up and held out a hand, as if he owned the soaring atrium of the Landmark Hotel and was welcoming them to his place.

'Good to meet you,' House said, pumping Parker's hand, then turning to Beth, Parker introduced her, and another bout of warm, personable handshaking took place.

'Please, sit down. A drink, what can I order you?'

'White wine for me, please,' Beth said. 'Dry, I think.'

'John . . .?'

Parker wasn't quite sure that he liked being addressed as John this early in the encounter – but then he didn't like the idea of Crawford stealing his company either, and this was certainly the lesser of two evils.

'Whisky, please . . .' he steeled himself, 'Bryan.'

'Soda – water – ice?' Having ascertained that it was water, House turned to the waiter who had materialised at their table and ordered the drinks. His own fizzy water with ice was barely touched.

Parker wasn't really sure how to start off; it had been many years since he'd been involved in what he called street-level negotiations. Usually, he was talking from the position of advantage, as Chairman of Byfield, but he was beginning to fear that this may well have produced a number of bad habits.

Bryan House obviously had no such problem. He launched straight in: 'I know we're all busy people, John, Beth, so I won't hang around asking how your journey was or anything like that. Nik Speller called this morning. He said you have a problem.'

'We're the subject of a hostile takeover attempt by Jim Crawford and Ayot. Though we have no objection to merging or becoming part of a joint venture with anyone else in the sector, we do not want to be part of Ayot.'

'Thank you, John. Admirably concise. You don't like Crawford. Does that go for the rest of your board?'

It was a question that had not, until now, been asked. Parker felt a certain discomfort because, as he was well aware, the board of Byfield had been more or less railroaded – wasn't that how the Americans put it – into following Parker's policy of rejection. House was a shrewd customer. He had turned to Beth Stewart and asked the same question.

'How do you feel about it?'

What would she reply, Parker wondered. Of all the members of his board, she was the only one who could be sure of going on if Crawford succeeded. He'd probably even keep her on the board and if not, she'd find a better job within days. If nothing else, it would be interesting to see how she balanced common sense and ambition against loyalty in the presence of her chairman.

The drinks arrived and Beth took a sip of her wine. 'Well, Bryan, I think we all feel that John has put his finger on the main point. It isn't that Byfield is some kind of virgin, that no one can touch her. She's a big girl, she's quite happy to go out on dates but, like any parent, John is concerned about her choice of partners. Ayot is undoubtedly successful but not as successful as it could be, as it should be with the kind of management team they have in place. Over the last couple of days I've been looking at their board. They're good. On the whole, I have to say, and I know John values honesty . . .'

Parker nodded, 'Three people you should never lie to: your doctor, your directors and your banker.'

Beth went on: 'As a team, Ayot's people are getting better

results than our board and I think we can learn from that and improve our performance. I say learn, rather than combine, exactly because I see Crawford's influence as a brake on their potential. As long as he's around, Ayot will not be performing at optimum. If he takes control of Byfield – and let's not kid ourselves, it will be Jim Crawford and not Ayot that holds the reins, the same thing will apply. There will be a slight improvement in overall results but no more. I think our shareholders should expect better than that. I think they will see better than that, if they stay loyal.'

Parker was impressed. Beth, of course, had no idea why he would never sell to Crawford but she had managed to come up with an admirable argument, all the same.

'OK, thank you, Beth. That sounds . . . quite convincing. I like the emphasis on the shareholders since, in the end, they're what it's all about.'

Parker poured a little water into his Glenmorangie and drank. He wanted to say: What about the employees, aren't they what it's really about? But it wasn't, not any more, so he didn't. And anyway, wasn't it all down to him, in the end? His failure. He drank again, deeper, and resolutely pushed the thought aside. 'What do you think overall?' he asked.

House shook the ice in his fizzy water. It tinkled against the edge of the glass in a most annoying way. 'I think that I, or someone like me, should have been on your board last year.'

'Nik Speller said the same thing,' Beth put in.

'It's obvious really, after the event,' House said. 'A good lesson for you, in future, Beth.'

Parker did not miss the inference that Beth had a future while he did not. He finished his drink and raised his arm to summon the waiter. Neither House nor Beth wanted another; Parker ordered a double.

'Given that someone like me wasn't on the board,' House continued, 'then the next best thing is to get me or someone like me on now, as soon as possible. I know the City, I know how it works and who makes it work and they know me. So that'll increase overall confidence in Byfield. We'll be able to talk the right language to the right people. Whether they'll listen is another matter. Whether your shareholders will listen, is another matter. I have – and there's no point in being modest here . . .' Obviously not, Parker thought, '. . . done well recently for investors so I should be able to reassure people and buy us some time while we pull the defence document together. I imagine you've issued an interim statement advising your shareholders not to accept the offer?'

'Yes,' Beth said. 'That went out first thing.'

'From what Nik has told me, and from what you've said tonight, I think we have a chance, and I won't put it any higher than that, of turning the Ayot offer aside. I think I can offer something useful in that process. If you want me on board.'

'I think we need you on board, Bryan,' Parker said. 'Beth?'

'Absolutely, John. We don't have anyone with Bryan's skills. Yes, let's go if . . . well, what terms are we talking about here?'

House thought a moment. 'Normally we'd be talking about 18 to 20 thousand for 15 or so days a year. That would be for the normal kind of input you'd expect from a non-exec; but this is a wholly different situation. To a degree I'm putting my reputation on the line so I'd be looking for something in the region of 50 to 60. Cash and equities, half and half.'

It was a lot. It was a hell of a lot. Parker said: 'We do have an employee share ownership pool which is administered by a family trust. We can sell or donate these shares to our people so, yes, there's no problem with the equity or the cash – if you can keep us safe from Crawford . . . .' The waiter placed the double on the table before Parker and, without bothering to add water, he raised it and sank it in one. 'Then cheers to you, Mr House. Welcome aboard.'

Beth raised her glass: 'Welcome aboard.'

House nodded but left his glass on the table. 'Thank you.'

Downstream

Flat 7, Frogwell Road, West Dulwich, London, 21:50

Jack wasn't home when Beth got in shortly before ten. She and Parker had stayed for a while at the Landmark after House had left, sharing their impressions of the man. Arrogant he certainly was but that was a price worth paying, they agreed, for his skills. The conversation had been a matter of keeping a delicate balance as far as Beth was concerned. She thought back over it as she put on the kettle for a coffee and shoved a frozen meal into the microwave. There had been, all through the evening, a subtext, unspoken but definitely present in her mind: one of Bryan House's most important tasks would be to take care of the succession issue. She wondered, as she set the kettle to one side and opened a bottle of wine instead, to what extent John Parker had accepted the idea that his job was more vulnerable than any other position on the board. Byfield was his company, very much as Ayot was Crawford's, even though the latter was CEO and not chairman. It was quite possible that a successful defence might include the appointment of a new chairman as well as new members of the board. This was one of those watershed moments, after which nothing would be quite the same.

House had made it plain that for her, this could be a terrific learning experience – she was in no way tainted with the company culture, her future was probably going to be made by this. For the others, most of them, win or lose, the end was in sight.

She sniffed the wine: it was white Graves from their local Oddbins. *Château l'Hôpital.* For all the big flavours of the New World wines, she often preferred the subtlety of France. And she laughed out loud, both at her own pretension and at the huge distance she'd travelled in her life, from the farm on the west coast of Scotland to here and now, drinking wine her parents would not have allowed into their teetotal household (she and Jack still hid the booze when they visited) and talking corporate finance with . . . . people who demanded and got £60,000 for 18 days work a year. It really was turning out to be an exhilarating ride.

151

The key turned in the door and Beth got another glass from the cupboard and started to pour.

'What a monster of a bloody day,' Jack groaned as he slumped into a chair at the kitchen table. He looked grey with fatigue.

'Wine,' she said. 'You need big glasses and food.' The microwave pinged. She flipped it open and looked at the slimmameal. 'I don't think either of us needs one of these right now. Why don't I call out for a pizza?'

He sat back, eyes closed. 'Brilliant. An everything pizza with chips on the side.'

She put the glass in front of him, then walked round and put her hands on his shoulders, massaging the muscles. She could feel the tension inside him. 'More problems?'

'Always problems,' he said. 'OFSTED just makes them screamingly urgent. I've got most of the staff with me but there's still a residue of the people I inherited who have this relentlessly negative attitude . . .'

As he talked, her hands soothed and she thought: we were supposed to be discussing other things tonight – our lives, our future . . .

'I'll have to bring them round somehow,' he was saying, 'or hide them. Maybe there could be an epidemic.'

And then she thought: Why bother, who needs the aggravation? Not him, not me. We can live with this. Later, we'll talk about it later, and she said: 'I'll call the Pizza Place, there shouldn't be too long a wait midweek.'

'Great. And some garlic bread.'

Station forecourt, Reading, Berks., 23:40

The station was virtually empty at this hour. Sweepers were running their odd fringed brushes over the shiny floor, a couple of bored transport police were standing by the exit doors, their attention more on the square outside, where a few late drinkers were standing around outside the pub or waiting for taxis.

John Parker yawned. It had been a hell of a day and maybe a

mistake to grab those extra whiskies at Paddington – but he'd arrived with 20 minutes to wait and didn't fancy spending time on the station forecourt where the temperature, after the clear day, was dropping rapidly. He was also at that level just a bit beyond the comfortable, when you're aware that you've had a drink too many (another couple of doubles while chatting with Beth, was it?) so you might as well go on until . . . you stop feeling anything much at all. And, by God, he needed some relaxation. His brain hadn't stopped running since the phone call from Crawford last Sunday – and the thought that it was only four days ago and not a lifetime deserved another drink all on its own. Unfortunately, nowhere was open, at least nowhere he knew of. He'd have to wait until his taxi had got him home; a 30-minute run at this time of night.

On the train he'd thought of calling Heather and asking her to come and collect him but that seemed unfair, and besides, the taxi ride would give him time to sober up a bit and then he could have a coffee or tea instead of another drink and maybe he would sleep the whole night through. But he doubted it.

His heel taps echoed on the marble flooring of the station and he drew his coat around him and slipped his gloves on as he stepped outside. The sky was still clear and even through the glare of streetlamps stars were visible. Not to the degree they were out in the country; there the show was often spectacular and, over the years, he had introduced both the children to the delights of stargazing. Paul had taken to it. Claire, so far, had only felt cold and fallen asleep in his arms when he'd wrapped her up in his coat. The thought of her, so vulnerable and defenceless, brought a prickle of tears to his eyes. How ridiculous, he thought, a man of my age snivelling over his daughter.

'Got any spare change, please?'

'Eh? . . . No.' It was his usual answer to the question; after all no one needed to beg in this country. He glanced at the bundle of coats and blankets from which a face peered up at him; not angry or resentful at his refusal, just resigned. He stopped and looked more closely. It was a child. A boy, he thought, though he couldn't be sure. Young, though he couldn't be sure of the age, either. Too young to be out at this time in this cold. And the eyes – looking at him without any kind of expression; as if they couldn't take in what was happening here, this inconceivable moment in time when he, John Gerard Parker, Chairman of Byfield plc was standing looking down at an unknown child and thinking of his daughter sleeping in his arms. He slipped off his gloves, pulled out his wallet and found a note. He didn't know what it was, a five, a ten or a twenty, and held it out. An arm came out from the bundle, a flash of white as a hand took the note and the boy – he was sure now it was a boy – nodded fractionally, not thanking, merely responding, and looked away at someone else emerging: 'Got any spare change?'

I'm a fool, Parker thought, as he strode towards the taxi queue. It's just some addict, some kid who doesn't give a damn about me or anyone in the world. He hunched against the wind as the short line shuffled forwards and the cabs came into the station and left, endlessly ferrying.

'Whitchurch Hill, please. I'll tell you exactly where when we get there.'

The cab-driver nodded and reached back to open the door. Thankfully, Parker clambered into the warmth and sank back onto the seat. As the cab swung round and out of the station forecourt he looked back to see if the boy was still there. He wasn't. Maybe he never had been, Parker thought . . . maybe none of this was really happening and soon he'd wake up. Maybe he would have that extra whisky when he got home after all.

Day

thursday 4th nov. 00:35

flat 15, south park parade, putney, london .

DIANE ELLROY LOOKED AT THE QUILT which lay draped over her lap. It had been her mother's, passed on from *her* mother and now it was Diane's and she was the last of the line. She had been alone in the world now for seven months and twenty-one days; the days since her mother had died at the home in Maine. Diane had paid, but Diane had not been there at the end, which had at least been quick. A fall one evening, followed by a massive seizure overnight, from which Mom had not recovered.

At the funeral people had said that: it was kindest that way, no long decline; she had watched TV and played cards with her friends the afternoon before and enjoyed her tea and then . . . it was over. Yes, it was the best way but it didn't stop it hurting.

Leaving her mother had been the hardest part of moving to Europe; and yet Mom had encouraged her to go. 'You're making something of yourself, honey, and it makes me proud to think of my girl over there in Europe. You know, your dad was there, in Germany in the fifties . . .'

Diane knew – Dad had been a pilot in the airforce and though he had missed the war, he had flown during the Berlin Airlift and had even appeared on television documentaries about the operation.

'Course, I always used to worry he'd find some little Fräulein out there and never come home – but he did and I guess he would've been proud too, he would have wanted you to go,

Diane. You know sometimes I can almost see him. Like he's just waiting round the other side of the door and if I listen carefully, why, I'll be able to hear him get out his matches and light that pipe of his . . . Oh Lord, that dreadful pipe!' Mom had laughed, her face as wrinkled as a Maine apple after winter in the barn, and she rambled on in the strange but somehow comforting free-association of the old. 'I used to say to him: Not in the car, Harry. But would he stop? You recall when we bought the new Edsel, Diane. You were so proud, I remember you running out to shout across to the Bellavistas, or was it Mamie Hurst, this is our new car. And you would polish the chrome – and there was so much chrome to polish on that car. I don't know what they were thinking of. Harry always said . . .'

Diane's cheeks were wet as she returned along the winding track of her own memory lane. Yes, they were tears of regret that she had not been there, and tears of loss, because she would never, ever see Mommy again, and yet they were comforting because they showed that the memories were still strong and sharp. If she had any fear, it was of the day when the pain would not cut as deeply and then, little by little, she and Mom would lose each other.

Such a time would come, Diane reflected, as she folded the quilt, wrapped it in tissue and put it away in its drawer. It was something she had to cope with alongside all the pressures of life. In a way, it gave her somewhere else to turn, allowed her to get away from the preoccupations of the boardroom. Not that she was at all inclined to back off; this takeover was going to prove a fantastic opportunity for her. Ever since joining the board of Ayot she'd felt that they could do better and now, could it be, that Jim Crawford had gone one step too far? She thought so, Mark Chima thought so – when the poor boy could drag his mind away from Diane's presumed charms. It was touching, in a way, his devotion and his attempt to hide it; touching and hugely flattering. She was ten years older than he was but in his company – when he wasn't eating paper – she felt quite the teenager again. Who could tell how that might pan out for both of them – and yet she mustn't forget the main event!

She needed a meeting with Gavin Clooney, the non-executive director, and that had to be the next item on her itinerary; though the thought of Mark attracted her more and more; it had been a long time since she'd had any kind of romantic interlude and maybe, just maybe . . .

Basement Flat, 77 Keeble Street, Victoria, London, 01:10
'How odd that Crawford and Andrea Creevy should have turned up at the book launch,' Hugh said, looking down at Celia and brushing a strand of hair from her face. 'Wouldn't have thought it was his sort of thing at all.'

'Who cares?' Celia's voice was miffed. She was lying on the bed pleasantly tired and very relaxed; work was no more than a hazy memory.

'No, I think it's very interesting. He's pushing the publicity on this one. He took the trouble to talk to me at length, thanked me for the interview, hoped it would go all right . . .'

'Oh, for goodness sake, Hugh, stop babbling!' Celia pulled his face to hers and kissed him – but it was clear from his vague response that his mind was elsewhere.

'Hang on.'

'Hugh, it's supposed to be City types like me who are consumed by their work – not hacks like you!'

'True, but you'll just have to be patient and wait. I'm almost certain that most of what he gave me was cosmetic – on the other hand . . .'

'At least Jim Crawford keeps his mind on the job.'

'What I need . . .'

'I know what you need and I need it too!'

'What I need is an interview with Andrea Creevy.'

'She doesn't do interviews.'

'Off the record. I'll buy her lunch.'

'She doesn't do lunch.'

'She does with you. Invite her and I'll just happen by, in that way we hacks have. Then you can remember something back at the office and leave me to handle the situation.'

'I wish you'd handle me,' Celia pouted.

'Will you set it up, for next week sometime?'

'Honestly, Hugh, I don't know if I can.'

'Please!' He kissed that place under her chin that she found absolutely irresistible.

'All right, all right, anything.'

'Promise?'

'I promise I'll do what I can – as long as you promise you won't exploit her in any way. She's a nice person, she doesn't need to be messed around by a rat like you. That's my prerogative.'

'OK. Deal.'

'Deal. Now don't stop . . . hmmm, that's better!'

Day +7

monday 8th nov. 11:00

lightoller, bachman and gale, rg house, bishopsgate, london

BETH FOLLOWED JOHN PARKER into the meeting room. It reflected every other space in the building – conspicuously large, minimalist, expensive, with an oval oak table around which the meeting was coming together. Bill Harper, Byfield CEO, and Tim Ericson, Human Resources Director, were seated across from Beth. Harper looked grey; Tim Ericson, clutching a bulging briefcase, gave her a tired grin. Both men had probably been at it without a break throughout the weekend.

Beth had not talked with Tim since their conversation about the future or Tim's lack of it; everyone at Byfield had been working their socks off putting together plans, forecasts, sets of figures and projections which were then couriered over to Nik Speller and his team, here at RG House, where the defence document was being put together. Bryan House, the new non-executive director, had been in and out of the company HQ, asking questions here, prompting decisions there and then vanishing into the winding streets and cloud-capped towers of the City. Beth had no great liking for the man – he seemed to her no less arrogant on closer acquaintance than he had at first – but then she didn't have to like him, as long as he delivered, and so far he appeared to be doing that. The shares had held steady. Opinion, at least in so far as it was reflected in the majority of the press, seemed to be neutral on the matter of who was winning and who was losing.

House had taken the seat next to John Parker and was leaning back, relaxed, surveying the table. In a way, Beth thought, his position was enviable, particularly compared to the Chairman, who appeared increasingly haggard and distracted as the days went by. On occasion he was able to pull himself together and act in his former reasonably decisive manner but more often now, he stared distractedly into space, as if trying to catch sight of something on the horizon. House, on the other hand, was earning big money for doing what he liked to do best with no personal involvement at all.

At the beginning, Beth had thought the same thing would apply to her: this would be a learning experience without personal involvement and not a lot more, but this simply wasn't the case; she felt a whole raft of different emotions about the battle and had discovered a sense of loyalty to the company and the people she knew – excluding Dick Worthington. People like Tim Ericson, who had given a hell of a lot to Byfield and had, consequently, invested a huge part of themselves in the company and its fortunes. Even John Parker, who she'd often characterised as pompous and out-of-date, was gaining her sympathy. These new emotions lent an edge to the events she was involved in – she'd been told that Crawford was a gambler and though she'd never been caught by that bug, she felt that if she ever was, the idea of gambling without risking real money would be absurd. It was the same here; it had become personal in a way that lifted the whole game. And for the others round the table, many of them worried sick about their futures, they too were caught up in events that were as real as . . . the taste of a knife blade in your mouth.

A waft of perfume: Bobbi King. 'Morning, Beth. I've talked to the Beeb and it looks like there's a possible spot on the *Business Show* on Tuesday 23rd, which is about a week after the defence doc is due out. Right, Nik?'

'Absolutely, Bobbi. Fifteenth we hit the ground running.'

Beth said, 'I don't know if I'm really sure about this, Bobbi. I've never done anything like it before.'

'Of course you haven't. Which is why . . . John . . .' She called across, attracting Parker's attention. 'We'd like Beth to do a TV spot to keep things rolling about a week after the defence doc comes out – so we'll need to give her a short sharp course in interview techniques. We could fit her in this Friday afternoon, if you can spare her.'

'I imagine so,' Parker said. 'All right with you, Beth?'

Bobbi butted in, 'She'll be fine, you just leave her to me.'

Beth could only shrug her acquiescence. 'Oh, Bobbi, I'm seeing this man Hugh Mead tonight. He's doing something about Crawford for Radio 4 as well as the articles he writes for the papers. I'm, sorry, I just didn't think to clear it with you first.'

'Is it a sound interview or for the print media?'

'I think it's print. He's collecting me by taxi at six-thirty this evening.'

'OK. I'll call him. We'll make sure there's a photographer free and get a picture. Where's he taking you?'

'He didn't say.'

Bobbi had her electronic diary (Byfield, of course) in the palm of her hand and was pulling out a number as she talked.

'Nobu would be great. You know it?'

'No.'

'Japanese-Peruvian. The chef is a genius. Very sexy place – Hugh Grant took Julia Roberts there in *Notting Hill*. Monday night, we should . . .' her mobile was in her hand and she was punching out a number, ' . . . be able to get a table. I'll see to it. Hugh Mead? Bobbi King.' She winked and wandered away to the far corner of the room, talking quietly.

Nik Speller cleared his throat, 'So far we're still travelling hopefully, would that be right?' He looked around the table and caught Parker's eye.

The Chairman said, 'I think so, Nik. Bryan tells me that the fund managers are holding their fire for the moment.'

'I think that's due to some of the spoiling tactics we've put out,' House waved an appreciative hand towards Bobbi, who was returning to the table.

She gave Beth a thumbs up and said to House: 'Opinion, you know how it runs. You probably create a lot of it yourself, Bryan.' There was something slightly blatant (if blatancy can ever be slight) about Bobbi's response but House seemed quite happy with her attitude.

'True, I've been talking with a number of people, both at other banks, in insurance, and to various venture capitalists.'

'What do you feel about that kind of route?' Speller asked.

'Much the same as you, Nik, I should imagine. Unless we contemplate some kind of buy-out, it isn't going to be very useful. Besides, these boys are looking to make a sizeable profit over a short period – say by ten over five years – so they can cover their duds. We don't want to be part of that. What we should be looking for are trends within the company that point to a better future, increased dividends, you know the form: we don't need Crawford because we can do it our-selves. There's nothing fundamentally wrong with Byfield and all along we've been planning this long-term increase in business.'

'Sounds promising,' Parker said. 'Bill, how does it look from your angle?'

Harper yawned nervously behind his hand. 'Well, uh, John, everybody . . . we have all been looking at internal economies, improvements, uh, anywhere we can slim down and become fitter, more efficient.'

'I'm sure you've been looking,' Bryan House said rather nastily, 'but what have you found?'

'The paper and card-making companies are not, it seems to me, delivering the kind of results that, well, justify us hanging on to them. I'm sorry, John . . .' he turned and offered a shoulder-slump of apology to Parker, 'I didn't really have time to brief you on this before we left this morning. Tim and I have been looking at the figures, the turnover, and it seems to us that if we sell them, we'll get some much-needed cash and overall, we'll be more efficient.'

Parker wasn't pleased. 'Tim, do you go along with this scheme?'

Tim Ericson was not comfortable in this company, Beth could see that at once, though she doubted the others would notice. It did, however, back up what Tim had told her about his lack of confidence. He cleared his throat and riffled through the papers in his case. 'Uhm . . . John, I have to say . . . from what Bill and I worked through over the, uhm . . . weekend, it does look as if it might be advisable. You know I hate doing this kind of thing. The cards and paper are . . . have been part of Byfield for a long time . . . uh, many years but . . . uhm, well, it's a tough situation and I'm sure . . . well, the market is changing. And if you remember, I did say a couple of years ago that the customers in that area, that market . . . they were going elsewhere. Our designs, our . . . we didn't buy into any of those franchises when we had the possibility. Look at what took off: Gary Larsen cards, those joke birthday cards . . .'

'Jokes?' Parker growled. 'Most of them seemed to be smut or totally unfunny.'

'Well, yes,' Ericson said. 'And we all agreed at the time, this wasn't a field we wanted to be in. Though the people on the ground, who were running the cards and paper, they were eager to go down that route.'

'There are standards, Tim. And responsibilities.'

House cut in: 'Yes, to your shareholders, John.'

Nik Speller said, 'I think Bryan and myself should look for potential customers for the cards and paper. The more Byfield can present itself as a business which concentrates on its core expertise the better. I'd quite like to see the builders and aggregates hived off in some way. I think we should look at that. Clear the undergrowth a bit, so the electronics is there, in clear sight. Then we can begin to look at the development inside that core business, its potential . . .'

163

'It seems to me,' Parker was white, though Beth couldn't be sure if it was through shock or anger, 'that you gentlemen are taking the business apart around me – without any reference to my feelings or my opinion.'

Speller caught and held Parker's eye. 'John, listen to me. You're with friends here, we all want the same thing: to keep Byfield out of Crawford's clutches.'

'Yes, and you're all doing very well out of it, too.'

Speller was unfazed: 'Yes, we are. And we would be failing in our duty to you if we did not explore every avenue of defence that is available to us.'

'I know, I'm sorry.' Parker shook his head. 'I shouldn't be getting emotional over this but please do remember that for me this is more than a company. That may be the wrong attitude but it is the one I have to live with. Carry on, please. Beth, have you anything to put in here?'

'I still think we should be looking at his offer price,' Beth said. 'It doesn't seem good enough to me.'

'I agree,' Speller said.

The others around the table all nodded and Bobbi said, 'Always was a tight son-of-a-bitch, Jim Crawford. Except when he was spending money on himself.'

'Whose money?' House asked. 'His? The company's? How does he spend it, on what or who? Mistresses? Yachts? Do we know?'

'We're finding out,' Bobbi said. 'He's never been shy of using the company chequebook.'

'All grist to our mill,' House said. 'His reputation in the City is generally quite reasonable. He's managed to get a long way without making too many enemies but he doesn't have that many good friends either, so maybe we can do something to undermine the reputation of Ayot. Nik?'

'We could slip something into the defence document. The main thing is to ensure it publishes next Monday and that it looks good.'

Bobbi nodded to Speller and, somehow, to Beth at the same time. She said: 'We're moving, everything is beginning to happen. Beth, I'd like a few words with you before you leave, just to go over anything you might say to Hugh Mead.'

'Is that going to be a problem?' Beth asked. 'I can pull out – I'd love to get home early for once.'

'No, there's no problem. He's probably getting briefed by Crawford's people and I do know he lives with Celia Hart, who is Crawford's broker. Forewarned is forearmed.'

'If that's settled, then,' Speller said, 'I'd like to turn our attention, if we can, to the small print at the back of the defence document. All those figures which are really going to make the difference. We need to get them right.'

Nobu, Park Lane, London, 20:30
Hugh Mead had arrived, as planned, on the dot of six-thirty. Beth had spent the half hour before on the phone to Bobbi King, talking about the takeover and what she should and shouldn't say to the reporter.

In the taxi Hugh had been pleasant, passing on good wishes from Celia Hart, filling her in about the documentary he was making for radio on Crawford's life – of which, quite naturally, the takeover had become a real part.

Nobu itself, on the first floor of the Hotel Intercontinental, Park Lane, had more than lived up to its legend. The photographer who'd met them in the bar – and was there anything Bobbi King couldn't arrange – knew the place and was inconsolable that he wouldn't be staying for dinner. However, he took a set of photos of Beth: against the glass and steel bar with a barman behind her mixing a vodka martini; being lead to her table by one of the waiters in designer (Issey Mayiki) black; sitting at her table (*the* table from *the* movie) with the lights of Park Lane behind her; standing by one of the etched glass panels that dotted the restaurant, with a large and noisy group of Japanese business men – and no women – behind her; and finally, perched on a stool at the sushi bar, though they weren't eating sushi tonight. Hugh had danced attendance, buying drinks, suggesting angles and poses until, finally, the snapper took his leave and they sat down at their real table.

As they'd arranged themselves, a cry had gone up somewhere over the other side of the restaurant – a cry taken up by a dozen or so voices. Beth feared a riot, an argument over the bill – and having looked at the menu she could well believe that – or perhaps a fatality from too much fugi fish. Hugh explained it was merely a custom of the house: complete newcomers were greeted with a cry of welcome in Japanese. It was, Beth thought, rather fun, though after listening to it half a dozen times, it was beginning to get somewhat tiresome.

Hugh was familiar with the restaurant – or familiar enough to take over the ordering and suggest various dishes that combined chef Nobu Matsuhisa's trademark style of Japanese fish or meat in Peruvian chilli sauces. Each dish was exquisitely laid out, cooked and brought to table to the nanosecond and, though Beth was a little diffident at first, utterly delicious.

Manoeuvring the yellowtail tuna sashimi with slices of jalapino chilli into the soy and lime sauce and thence to her mouth took all her attention and, after a while, she gave in and swapped her chopsticks for a fork. A choice she was glad of when the cod (cooked into flakes of pure ivory under a sweet caramelised skin) arrived. She apologised to Hugh for giving all her attention to the food and not to his questions, which she had hardly answered up till then.

'No problems, Beth. This is going on expenses so we might as well enjoy.' He toasted her with a bamboo cupful of warm sake.

'Your expenses? Does the BBC run to this place?'

He laughed. 'Not for such as I, Beth. To be honest – not a mode in which I usually like to start out the evening – Bobbi King is carrying this one, so I guess, in the long run, it'll be taken out of Byfield. Try a scallop in pepper sauce.'

She did, glad that she didn't have to pick it up with

chopsticks. 'Revelatory. You know, this meal is probably going to cost as much as my father earns in a week.'

'Do you feel guilty about that?'

'I don't think so. Yes.' She laughed. 'Well, maybe, some of the time. I don't think he would mind. He'd say: good for you, Lizzie.'

'That's what they call you, Lizzie?'

'Only at home. What's that . . .?'

'Chicken with wasabi pepper sauce. Here . . .' He expertly cinched a piece of chicken with the points of his chopsticks and offered it to her across the table. She took it straight into her mouth and, as she chewed, found herself amazed at how natural she felt with this reporter. Certainly, he was setting out to charm but, for all that, she was enjoying herself.

'You called it home,' Hugh said. 'Is that because you still think of it that way – like London is something temporary?'

'Oh no, I wouldn't want to leave. I love London. I love the fact you can be on the Strand at two in the morning and there's still a traffic jam and thousands of people. What about you – are you a Londoner born and bred?'

'No way.' He caught the attention of a waiter and ordered another bamboo flask of sake. 'Grew up in a village in Dorset. Couldn't get out fast enough. To me, close-knit communities mean that everybody knows everybody else's business. Plus the fact there's no cinemas, no theatres or decent bookshops, no restaurants, only mad, ingrown yokels who have congress with animals and attack townies with chainsaws. Oh yes, and retired couples, who've finally got that little thatched cottage every Englishman is meant to yearn for and hate it and hate each other and hate the cat. And nothing . . .' he flourished a King crab claw glazed with butter ponzu sauce, '. . . like this within a hundred miles. So, Beth, have you ever met Jim Crawford, the Beast of the Euston Road?'

'No. I heard him speak at a seminar a couple of years ago. I thought he was quite impressive.'

'Quite impressive? You want to add to that?'

'He sounded convincing when he was talking but I'm not sure how much of that was presentation and personality. I take it that you do know him?'

'I've met him. I don't know him; I'm not sure anyone does. That sounds rather wanky, I know. Mystical stuff, but he keeps himself behind a barrier. I interviewed him last week and we must have talked – he certainly talked for half an hour – but it was all like one of the glass screens in this place – it lets through the light but the frosting prevents you from seeing anything in detail. Broad strokes, no touching in with details, and it's in the details that everything really lies.'

'You could say that his kind of business thinking benefits from that; broad strategy, not being caught up in minutiae.'

'Oh yes, but it's what the man *is*. Or isn't. Sorry, that's even worse. I mean, take this meal. You know I want to get information out of you. I know that you've been briefed on how to respond to my questions. Above and beyond that, we're having a very pleasant dinner together and I feel – I mean kick me if I'm wrong – that we are both having a good time.'

'Yes, it's fun.'

'I don't think you'd ever feel that about Crawford. I suspect that, at one level, he's so secretive that his right hand really doesn't let his left hand know what it's up to. Which makes writing about him bloody difficult.'

'Why do it, then, Hugh? In all conscience, except to those of us caught up in it, this takeover is pretty small stuff.'

'True, but Crawford isn't and . . . and I think I can use this story to get myself another step or two up the ladder. I want to work in TV. I want to do more for the papers . . .'

'Well that's already happening. I've read your articles. They're very good, even if they don't support us.'

'Thank you, Beth, that's very kind.' She was surprised to see a slight blush touch his cheeks, though he turned quickly away to receive the new flask of sake and pour for them both.

168

'Let's readdress the balance, shall we? What do you think of Crawford's strategy – since you were talking about that just now.'

Beth sipped the sake, then ate some more cod.

'I don't think he's got a strategy except to buy Byfield. If you take a close look at the offer doc, that's all it really comes down to. Nothing really long term at all.'

'Wouldn't he say the same about Byfield?'

'Yes, but he'd be wrong. Oddly enough, and to a certain extent this is an accident, at least it wasn't planned, if you look at . . .' she stopped herself, suddenly, hearing Bobbi's voice imperative in her head: 'Sorry, Hugh, this is embargoed until the defence document comes out.'

'OK, that's fine.'

'Byfield actually does have a better long-term strategy, as far as electronics goes, than Ayot. We are thinking about the future, about new services and not just about what works now, today. OK, we haven't been that dynamic about it and we need to firm up our strategy, but the basic company culture, of loyalty to our suppliers and customers, actually produces a better long-term approach than Ayot's short-term profits do. And this goes particularly for research and development. It seems as if we've been lagging but we have a first-class team under Tom Swift and they've had the time to lay down the kind of firm foundations on which Byfield can build for long-term and profitable growth.' She wondered if Hugh would swallow that – and if he'd pass it on. It was right enough, Byfield *did* have some brilliant young researchers in its electronics division but it was also true they had been woefully under-used. That would all change – though whether Byfield would have the time to do it or not was another question. She went on, 'Yes, so far Ayot's profits have been increasing but for how long and by how much?'

Hugh finished the last dribble of sake. 'Go on, Beth.'

'Byfield will do everything that Crawford says he'll do but better, because we know our staff and our markets.'

'Aren't you and Ayot in the same market?'

'It seems that way but if you look more closely, Crawford has always gone for the . . . can I say quick fix?'

'You can say anything you like, Beth. Pudding?'

She was surprised to find that everything had gone. 'What do you recommend?'

'It has to be the tropical sorbet, with warm pineapple soup and gyozas.'

'Go on, educate me.'

'Little spoonfuls of chocolate, nut, pineapple and apricot wrapped in dough and deep fried. Believe me, the taste is worth a dozen companies.'

'I'm in your hands!' She laughed and then wondered what it might be like actually to be in Hugh's charming, capable hands. And thought: My God, I'm turning into a slut!

He ordered. She went on: 'Crawford's market is essentially different: it's still the old DIY, frozen food, pile it high, sell it cheap approach; Byfield has always been committed to the quality market. Maybe too much so for our own good – but that can be mended. Trying to fit a Ford Fiesta, no matter how good a car, together with an Alpha Romeo is not going to work.'

'An interesting point, Beth. But what if Crawford says that he also has a high-performance car and that, in fact, they'll fit together perfectly?'

'We know that isn't true.'

'Do the shareholders know that and will they care? Markets change – maybe a mid-performance car can serve them all.'

'Just a moment, Hugh. You said that Crawford says Ayot shares our market?'

'Yes.'

'Then he's lying, isn't he?'

'Left hand, right hand. Is a lie only a lie when you intend to deceive? What if it's business strategy?'

'My parents would say a lie is a lie in any circumstances.'

Hugh grunted and said nothing. There was a silence, prolonged until the pudding arrived, and, in its turn, this demanded a longer, but highly appreciative silence. The serious talking was over for the moment but both Beth and Hugh had something to think about.

Day

friday 12th nov. 07:40

17 carrington street, ealing, london

'MUM, I CAN'T FIND MY GLOVES! Where're my gloves?'

'Where you put them last night.'

'I don't know where I put them last night. If I did, I wouldn't have lost them!'

'Think, all right. Just think.' The microwave pinged and Manjit Chima took out the cooked porridge for Rajinda's breakfast. The bowl was hot and burned her fingers so she dropped it onto the worktop, where it skittered towards the edge. Mark made a dive, caught it just before it toppled, hung on despite the heat and transferred it to the table.

'Just eat your breakfast, Rajinda, all right, we'll find your gloves in a minute.'

Rajinda's brother, 15-year-old Ravi, came zooming into the kitchen still pulling on his shirt and bellowing: 'I need the money for the school disco, Dad.'

'How much?' Mark asked, reaching for his wallet.

Rajinda chimed in: 'And you said you'd pay for the violin classes, Dad!' Why she wanted to play the violin was beyond him but then he seemed to have lost touch with his children recently.

'Wait, what disco, Ravi?'

Manjit took two slices of toast from the toaster and put them down in front of Ravi. 'You should eat more on these cold mornings, heat inside is better than layers of clothing outside,' she said with practicality that was becoming increasingly irritating to Mark.

'I don't want porridge,' Ravi snapped, 'it makes you fat.'

Rajinda wailed: 'What do you mean? I'm not fat! Am I fat, Mum?'

'You're not fat,' Manjit said.

'I am, I am fat. It's obvious,' Rajinda howled. 'Look at me. Why do you keep making me eat porridge?'

'You are not fat,' Mark said. And it was true. Rajinda was as slim as Manjit had been once, and his eye settled on the well-rounded form of his wife. She looked over her shoulder from the stove, as if to say: Well whose fault is that, and Mark was damned if he knew.

'Eat your porridge, fatty,' Ravi said.

'Shove off, dickbrain,' Rajinda hissed.

'I will not have that language in my house,' Manjit said. 'Do you want porridge, Mark?'

'No thanks.' He felt as if he'd choke on the stuff.

'See, Dad doesn't eat porridge! Why do I have to eat it? Just because you want me to be fat.'

'You are not fat!' Mark bellowed.

'She is,' Ravi sniggered.

Before he could stop himself, Mark reached across the table and grabbed Ravi's arm. He saw the shock cross the boy's face as he hissed: 'Apologise to your sister, then eat your toast and go to school.'

'But what about the disco . . .'

He got no further before Mark said, 'Do as you are told. Now.'

Sulkily, he apologised to Rajinda, who nodded, smirked and returned quite happily to her porridge. Mark pulled out a five-pound note and gave it to Ravi who pushed it away and said: 'I don't want it now. I don't want to go to the disco.'

Mark noticed tears gathering at the corners of the boy's eyes before Ravi got to his feet and rushed out of the room, leaving the money on the table.

Manjit turned from the worktop and they looked at each other. Mark knew that they needed to talk – about Ravi, who was obviously tense and worried as exam year approached; about Rajinda, who was obsessed with being slim and dressing in a way quite inappropriate; above all, about themselves. They needed to talk and yet, somehow, they never did. When Mark got home, he was usually exhausted or Manjit was going out – she taught a physics evening class to GCSE and A level standard – or the children were around, as they were now, or there was some social event at the temple or it was a local council meeting and they had promised to attend. It was all too much and somewhere in the middle of everything, they were lost, as if they were trapped in a maze.

And yet, looking around the large kitchen, walking through the house, with its three roomy storeys, or strolling in the back garden, you would have said, as their friends and parents did: Look how well they've done.

Rajinda finished her porridge and, picking up on the silence that hung in the air between her parents, said, 'I'll just go and look for my gloves. I expect they're upstairs.'

Mark said nothing. Manjit muttered, 'Yes, you do that, love.'

'OK, I'm sorry, I shouldn't have done it,' Mark said, as soon as they heard the door to Rajinda's room shutting. 'It was stupid but . . . he was being annoying.'

'He *was* being annoying,' Manjit said. 'He's often annoying but you don't usually grab him that way. What's wrong with you, Mark? Are you going to do that again sometime – to Rajinda, to me?'

'It was just the noise, the . . . the everything.'

'Are there problems at work?' she asked.

'No problems,' he said. She had never evinced the slightest interest in his career, beyond the fact that it was a career. He supposed he had never shown any interest in her work either, but you could hardly compare his job at Ayot with teaching a couple of nights a week at the local adult education college.

'Everything is fine,' he went on, and it was – work was more exciting than it had been since he'd joined Ayot.

Manjit began to wash up, plunging cups, the porridgy bowl and plates into the sink. She tipped Ravi's unfinished toast into the compost bucket. She had built a compost heap in the garden and religiously recycled organic and every other kind of rubbish. She was probably happier in the garden in her shapeless cagoul and wellington boots than anywhere else. It was not an interest Mark shared. He sometimes sat out there in the summer and had played with the children when they were young, though truth to tell he wasn't terribly good at playing, and on the whole, preferred not to be outside.

'If it's not work, what is it?' Manjit went on. 'It must be something that's upsetting you.'

He shrugged.

She said, 'Mark, I'm trying. Can't you see that? I am trying to speak to you.'

'I can hear you, Manjit. I'm not deaf.'

'Tell me, then. What is wrong?'

Well, frankly, Manjit, you're boring, you're not sexy and I've fallen in love with another woman who is ten years older than you and . . . and . . . and what could he say to her? That he was afraid to tell Diane what he felt, that even if he did, he wasn't going to leave Manjit and the kids – he'd shoot himself before he did anything like that – and that the thought of spending the rest of his life living here in Ealing, doing the same things week in and week out, was driving him utterly crazy. Oh sure, why don't you sit down and make yourself a cup of coffee, Manjit, while I destroy your world? And yet, was this any better? Looking at each other across the kitchen with nothing to say.

'Maybe I'm just overworking,' he said, to break the silence. 'We should have a holiday. Something really . . . different. Go back home for a month next summer. Find out about . . . life and where we came from.'

'The kids want to go to America,' Manjit said, in the same

175

spirit and with the same sense of defeat, of backing away from a vital moment. It was band-aid time; patching it up until . . . it happened again.

Two doors slammed upstairs, followed by the thunder of feet coming down. The kitchen door burst open. Rajinda waved her gloves: 'See you, Mum, Dad,' and was gone.

Ravi grabbed the five-pound note and said: 'See you, Mum' and, avoiding Mark's eye, rushed out after his sister. The front door opened and slammed.

'He seems to have got over it,' Mark said.

'Has he?'

'Look, I'd better be moving too. Don't want to be late.' He got up, went across to Manjit and gave her a perfunctory kiss. She smelled of . . . herself, porridge, sleep, the house, of everyday. She didn't smell one little bit like Diane Ellroy.

Liberty's Coffee Bar, Regent Street, London, 13:12

'Hey! Hi! How are you?' Hugh leaned down and kissed Celia on both cheeks. She gave him a look composed equally of scorn and admiration.

'This,' she said, 'is my flatmate Hugh Mead. Hugh, Andrea Creevy.'

In her forties, Andrea Creevy carried her age well. Not a beautiful woman, she had an open, used face with laughter lines around her eyes; a face on the edge of losing its youthful looks which was, somehow, all the more attractive for it. Hugh reached out and shook her hand. She had a good firm grip and looked him straight in the eye as she said, 'Celia mentioned that you'd like to meet and talk about Jim.'

Hugh was wrong-footed for a moment. He had assumed that Celia would deliver up an innocent Andrea Creevy, not one who was part of the plot; but a good hack is never at a loss for long and, ignoring Celia's knowing smile, he launched straight in: 'Yeah, I'm doing a documentary for Radio 4 on Jim Crawford and it seemed to me that you might be able to . . .'

'Tell you the things nobody else knows? I don't think so, but I don't mind talking, if that's any use to you? I don't want anything recorded, though.'

Hugh sat down between them. They'd been having salads and some kind of egg-based tart. He took a nibble of the crumbs on Celia's plate. 'I couldn't record here anyway, and I'd need your permission so there's no need to worry. I'd be happy to talk and if there was anything, then perhaps I might persuade you to come in to the Beeb and we could do some recording there. But only if you are totally happy. Ow!'

Celia swatted his hand away from her lunch. 'Order your own, Mead.'

'I'm not hungry. I had a sandwich earlier. I will get some coffee – shall I order for all of us.'

'I have to go,' Celia said. 'Andrea, great to see you, and we should do it again.' The two women kissed and Celia picked up four bulging carrier bags and, after giving Hugh a peck and the whispered admonition, 'Don't mess her around,' she hurried off towards the lifts.

Andrea appeared quite relaxed and said, 'I've heard a lot about you, Hugh. Celia seems to like you. Did I say that? *Seems* to like you?' She giggled. 'Sorry, let me rephrase: Celia likes you.'

'I think we like each other.'

'Does that mean that you two might, uh . . . . make a go of it?'

Hugh had an interior flash of Celia in latex, uncoiling like black light. 'I guess you never know.' After all, when a couple knew as much about each other's fantasies as did he and Celia, then perhaps marriage was the only thing left. 'But, if it's not rude, and do say if it is, you and Jim Crawford never actually tied the knot, did you?'

'No, still living in sin after all these years. Not that there's an awful lot of sin these days.'

'Gone out of fashion, hasn't it?'

'Yes, though I'm not sure how good a thing that is. Maybe we all need a little bit of righteous fear.'

'I'm sure you don't, Andrea. Hold on, I'll get the coffee.' While he queued at the counter he took a surreptitious look at her through the lunch-time crowd. She sat still, her head on one side, relaxed, not twitching or impatient. She seemed pretty straight – maybe she wouldn't want to betray any secrets.

'Here we go.' He put the two cups down and sat, moving his chair so he faced Andrea. 'You met Jim Crawford in 1978?'

She paused to taste the coffee. 'Yes. He was standing for Parliament. It was the first Thatcher election. There was a really strong feeling around that the country was ready for change. I don't suppose you remember?'

'I was still at school.'

'Jim was quite big in the local Conservative Party. He donated money, they used his house – he had a place outside Reading – fêtes and things. To a certain extent, I'd have to say he bullied his way through the various selection committees. Not that they didn't like him . . . well, most of them.'

'What was he like then?'

'He was magnificent. I know that sounds absurd but really, if you'd seen him . . . There was so much life in the man. He's still something of a natural force but then . . . just being in the same room, you felt he could make things happen. And he had – the business was growing, he employed a lot of people locally, this was just before the DIY, so he wasn't a national figure, but all the same, in Berkshire and Hampshire, he was well known.'

'And married?' Hugh offered, trying to gauge from Andrea's reactions how far he should go.

Her mouth turned down fractionally at the edges. 'Yes. Patricia. I don't know how that happened. She was – to be fair I never really knew her and the "other woman" is never the best person to give an opinion of the wife.'

'I don't know,' he grinned. 'Maybe you see each other more clearly than anyone else.'

'Believe me, Hugh, and I know, it isn't like that. She was . . . I think, if you want my opinion, he married Patricia – and no one ever called her Pat or Tricia, it was always Patricia – because of his mother.'

'Go on?'

'As you may or may not know, Jim's mum was . . .' She shook her head and screwed her eyes up. Hugh said nothing and waited until at last she continued: 'Something of an alcoholic. In a way, Jim kept her going after the . . . let's just say he kept her going.'

'After the what?'

'Something happened. I'm not really sure what, but it threw his mum right off course and she started drinking.'

'When was that – later, earlier? Did she work? What about the father?'

'Whoa, boy, whoa.' She held up both hands to make a stop. 'I don't know who his dad was. From what he's said, it was just a one-night stand but that's all I know. The mother, and I never met her, was dead; she died when Jim was 18 or 19.'

'Of drink?'

'Drink-related. I can't say more than that. She was never much good to him – except I suppose she loved him; and Patricia was everything she wasn't, except, of course, she didn't love him. She wasn't a warm woman and Jim needs that kind of uncritical, all-round insulation when he's at home.'

'Not what you'd think of first thing. He has a fearsome reputation. He's the buccaneer.'

'It's possible that even Blackbeard liked to sit down at the end of the day with Mrs Blackbeard, the cat, a cuppa and the newspaper.'

'I guess. Patricia was Mrs Crawford when you two met?'

'She had ambitions for him. Her father was a big local businessman, a mason, the whole thing, though Jim never joined. He always rather disliked that kind of clubbiness.'

'But he wanted to join the House of Commons club? It wasn't just Patricia?'

'No, if Jim hadn't wanted to, he wouldn't have stood. And if he hadn't stood, I wouldn't have been a volunteer on his election team and we'd never have met and he might have been Leader of the Opposition by now.'

'Only it didn't turn out that way.'

'No, it didn't turn out that way.' She sighed and looked down at the surface of her coffee, quite unconscious of the noise and clatter around them.

Hugh prompted: 'The campaign was under way?'

'Yes. And . . . oh, we were canvassing – that's the real tough end of politics, nothing glamorous about going from door-to-door asking people how they might vote; and I was paired with him and one thing led to another, as it does. A long hard day, a few drinks, a hotel room – he could afford that – one night together and somehow, the next day, the local paper got to know. Patricia was wild – the local party dropped him like a hot potato . . .'

'But why, Andrea? People have affairs. Even in 1979 they had affairs. Was it so bad?'

'It was bad considering there were those in the party who didn't want him. You must remember that I was on the outside. I wasn't a member of any ward party, I never went to the social events. It just happened I had time on my hands and I was asked – it wasn't even a Reading constituency, we were bussed over and bussed back. I was just a little person who happened to spend one night in a hotel room with a fascinating, exciting man who made me feel that I mattered.'

'We all need to feel that. More coffee?'

'No thanks,' she said, smiling as she remembered the old days. 'He was asked to stand down. I wasn't there, and he never talked about it. I know that Patricia was prepared to forgive him. That didn't go down terribly well, no one "forgives" Jim Crawford. And he never "forgives" anyone else. He just walked out. There were no children. It was easily settled and . . . he, we left the area.'

'He came straight to you?'

She grinned, 'Oh, please, there was no strong man in tears with young lover scene. He walked out of the local party and walked into the DIY business and sold his house, moved to London and *then* picked up the phone and asked if I'd like to come and see the new place. I was surprised – I never thought I'd see him again after that night.'

'There it is – true romance.'

'I don't know what it is, Hugh. I reckon we take the best we can get in this world. Sorry to be philosophical in Liberty's at lunch-time.'

'No, no, that's really brilliant, Andrea. It fills in a lot about the early years. His mother and . . . whatever it was that turned things bad . . .'

He waited but she volunteered no further information. 'So what about life after that – alongside Blackbeard the Entrepreneur?'

As she talked, he gave every impression of listening but his mind was elsewhere – back in the seventies, back even earlier, with the mother who was a paragon of the matronly virtues and, at the same time, an alcoholic. It looked as though there might be a seam of pure gold somewhere in the Crawford story, if only he could root it out – and if there was one thing that was absolutely certain in his mind, it was that those roots lay in Reading, back in Crawford's childhood and climb to power.

Butler's Wharf, London, 17:35

Jim Crawford was leafing through the *Financial Times* when the phone rang. He put the paper to one side and picked up the receiver. The voice was familiar, well bred, slightly arrogant. As usual, it didn't bother to identify itself.

'I was reading all about you in last Sunday's paper.'

'I'm surprised you have the time.'

'Oh, opposition, you know. One has to fill in the time some-how.'

'I see an old friend of yours will be up in court any day now.'

'Unwise of the fellow, don't you think? Messing with the Egyptian.'

'I don't have an opinion. What can I do for you?'

'Hurry up, old chap. Push this thing through. The business, you see, the business won't hang around.'

'And it's not as if you have as much influence any more, right?'

'Absolutely. And if you don't get a bloody move on, neither will you.'

'Do you have any kind of date?'

'Don't be silly, old man. They don't bandy dates around, those people at the Foreign Office. All too bloody scared of Cook and the whips. Don't want to lose their jobs, you know.'

'Who does?' Crawford muttered. 'Not you.'

'I expect I could always pick up the odd directorship.'

'Don't count on it.'

The other chuckled. 'We never count on anything, do we, Jim? We always try to make sure the odds are well stacked in our favour. Well, I'd love to chat but I really must go. I believe Michael Portillo is making a visitation somewhere in London this afternoon and I wouldn't want to miss that!'

The phone was put down without any further ceremony. Crawford listened to the dialling tone for a few seconds, then put his receiver down and walked out onto the balcony.

Heathlands, Whitchurch Hill, Oxon., 19:35

The gate off the lane was open and John Parker made a mental note to remind Heather to keep it shut at all times. One never knew who was wandering around these days, and even the country was no guarantee of safety. Then he thought: Am I overreacting to everything nowadays? He shook his head as he guided the Jag under the carport next to Heather's Range Rover.

When he climbed out, he paused a moment on the drive. It was a clear night – though it had been cloudy in London, and the moon, though bright, was far from full and didn't obscure the nearby stars. He quickly found Orion – a constellation of which he'd always been particularly fond. As the seasons changed and the great hunter began to slide slowly round into the night sky, he always felt a lift, as if to say: All's well, Orion's back in his place.

This year, somehow, the old magic was missing. Somehow? No, he knew exactly how. The gradual chipping away of everything he had built up – everything he had inherited. No, no, he told himself: Put that aside. Selling the publishing and the printing division – he must not let that spoil what was good in his life. Heather and Claire. This house in the country. Stars. Orion the hunter. Tonight he would forget it all – like Scarlett O'Hara, he'd think about it tomorrow because if he didn't get some time out soon, he was going to end up mad.

The front door opened and Claire called: 'Dad, you'll get cold.'

He turned back to the house. 'No, I won't. I've got my overcoat on.' In fact he was carrying it so he slipped it over his shoulders before he reached the porch.

'You cheated,' Claire gurgled. 'I saw you, you put it on.' She gave the sleeve a yank and the heavy Burberry slid off his shoulders. 'See. I know everything. I am the all-seeing Claire. And Mummy says I can't watch *Buffy the Vampire Slayer.* I can, can't I? Why can't I?'

'Buffy the what?' Sometimes his daughter's world and pre-occupations left him utterly confused. He picked her up and walked into the hall, pushing the door shut behind them both.

'Oh, come on, Dad. She slays vampires, well, bad ones. At school.'

'There are vampires at school?'

Claire wriggled from his grasp and zoomed away. 'Wait!'

He took his coat off. The smell of food drifted through from the kitchen: pork, roast pork and, since they'd bought the meat from a nearby organic farm, the quality would be high enough to produce real crackling. And John Parker loved crackling above almost any other food in the world. He called through: 'Hello, love.'

'In the kitchen,' Heather called, as she always did when he got back before dinner, though there was something different about her voice tonight.

'Look, here you are, look!' Claire thrust a magazine at him. Sure enough, its cover was titled *Buffy the Vampire Slayer* and there was a picture of a group of young people on the cover. American teenagers, it looked like.

'Everyone watches it, Dad.' Claire was entrenching, already suspecting that he would support her mother. 'It's all right, really. It isn't scary. Paul said it was . . .' She stopped and a silence fell. Then, gamely but knowing she'd already lost, she ploughed on: 'Paul said he thought it was all right.' She took the magazine and ran back through to the kitchen, leaving Parker alone in the hall.

'Heather?' he called.

'Hello, Dad.' Paul came through from the kitchen. He was wearing a sweater and slacks, no dog-collar. He approached his father as if to hug him and Parker stepped back.

'What are you doing here?' The words came out like cold, jagged splinters of ice; he hadn't intended them to be that hurtful, not to make Paul stumble to a halt. It was all too much, that was the problem; the takeover, Crawford, and now Paul – he really didn't need it.

'I was talking to Mum. She was worried,' Paul said, a tremor of tension in his voice. 'I thought maybe you . . . she at least might need a bit of support.'

'She told you, then?'

Parker went through to the sitting-room and straight to the sideboard where the whisky decanter stood. He poured himself a glass – a double, a treble, whatever – and drank it down in one movement. He felt Paul enter the room behind him. 'Drink?'

'I've got some wine in the kitchen. You're not to blame Mum, you know. She cares, she's worried.'

Parker poured himself another and turned round to face his son. 'Yes, yes, she's worried. We're all worried. It's a difficult time. There was no need for you to take the time to come up. I'm sure you're very busy.'

'Dad, I'm not one of your executives; you don't have to make a speech. You don't have to say anything, if you don't want.'

'I've said all I had to say.'

Paul didn't reply but Parker could see it cost him an effort as he folded his arms and leaned against the door jamb in that way of his – fey was the only word to describe it – and, as it always had since Paul started doing it at the age of 14 or 15, an unreasoning anger arose in him.

'Don't do that!' he snapped.

Paul unfolded his arms and shoved his hands in his trouser pockets. When he spoke, his voice was tight with tension. 'I came because I thought you might want your family around you; I didn't arrive in the daylight, so you won't have to explain my presence to the neighbours. I thought . . .'

'I doubt it,' Parker said. 'You always did whatever you wanted, never mind anyone else.'

'Would it have been acceptable if I'd gone into the business? Would you have preferred having a gay son on the board?'

'What makes you think I would have let you on the board?' Parker threw back the whisky. It tasted sour. Even so, he poured another. He was furious that this evening – the food, time with Claire, time away from Byfield and the takeover – had been spoiled by Paul's selfish desire to appear like some kind of good shepherd. Well, he was no one's sheep.

Paul advanced across the room; his face was pale. 'Dad, this has to stop. It isn't doing anyone any good. Please . . .' He held out his hand, expecting Parker to take it.

'Paul, I accept your right to live your life in any way you choose. I simply can't see why you have to . . . not only make trouble for yourself but . . . What kind of example is it for Claire, eh? What does she think of you and . . . and . . .'

'And the fact that I have a close and loving relationship with someone who happens to be a man? I don't think she has any trouble with that at all.'

Parker batted the proffered hand away. 'You don't know, how could you know that?'

'Because we talk about it, Dad. That's what rational people do. They talk, and explain and share their feelings.'

'You talk to my daughter about that kind of filth? Hanging round public toilets picking up who knows what!'

'Dad, I've never hung round a public toilet in my life.' An indulgent grin flickered across Paul's face, as if really, the old man had gone quite gaga this time. It shot, like a stream of vitriol, straight to Parker's heart.

'I forbid you to talk to Claire about your . . .'

Paul took his arm. 'Stop it, Dad, please, before you say something you regret.'

'The only thing I regret is you, Paul. That I ever had a son like you. I wish . . . I wish you had never been born.'

A high wail, like an animal in pain, arose from across the room and Claire's white, horrified face appeared above a chair-back. She opened her mouth but nothing beyond a sob came out.

Parker bellowed: 'Now look what you've done with your stupid self-indulgent . . . Get out of my sight! Just get out, Paul. Just go!' He started towards Claire but she backed away from him, her face twisted and wet with tears.

'It's all right, Claire, it's going to be all right.'

He reached out but his arms were brushed aside by Heather, who materialised beside the chair and swept Claire up into *her* arms. Her eyes were red too, as she stared at him, clutching their daughter.

Out of sight, Paul sighed and said, 'I'm sorry, Mum. I thought it would be better. I'll call a taxi.'

Heather said, 'I'll take you. Claire, get your coat and gloves, we're taking Paul to the station.' She put Claire down and the child ran out to the hall.

Parker heard Paul murmuring reassurances. He said, 'There's no need to take Claire, she can stay with me,' but even to him the words sounded crass and stupid and empty.

Heather didn't reply. She walked past him and out to the hall, shutting the door, shutting him in with the whisky.

Day +14

monday 15th nov.

THIS DOCUMENT IS IMPORTANT AND REQUIRES YOUR IMMEDIATE ATTENTION.

Ayot's
derisory offer
grossly undervalues
your company

IT FAILS TO RECOGNISE BYFIELD'S RECENT SIGNIFICANT
INVESTMENT TO GENERATE FUTURE GROWTH.

IT FAILS TO REFLECT BYFIELD'S LEADING MARKET POSITION.

REJECT THE BID. TAKE NO ACTION.

BYFIELD ELECTRONICS (HOLDINGS) PLC
(Registered in England No. 2100005643320)

Directors:
J.G. Parker
T.H. Ericson
W.H. Harper
B. House*
A.R. Howerd
E.J. Stewart
T.E. Swift
R.R. Worthington*

*non-executive

Downstream

189

Ayot's bid for Byfield is driven by its fears for its own future prospects over the diffused area of its existing markets. In particular, the inability to concentrate on its core business because the peripheral businesses are drawing too heavily on central finance. Forty-eight per cent of its business is in the supply sector, concentrating on domestic markets while its electronics sector is producing frankly poor results. Ayot management should concentrate on building its business up rather than mounting an opportunistic raid upon Byfield in pursuit of a quick-fix solution.

During the course of this bid, many Byfield customers have expressed their anxiety about the impact of a takeover by Ayot. I view this, myself, with great concern. Byfield's supplier and customer relationships have been built up and nurtured over many years; loyalty and service are the foundations of the group's future prosperity. Do not let Ayot reap these benefits on the cheap. None of Byfield's directors has any intention of accepting this offer and our financial advisers are fully supportive of our position on the offer.

Yours faithfully,

John Parker
Chairman

Downstream

'So what about this piece of tripe!' Crawford slid the defence document across the table. Owen Powys trapped it under a finger.

'Have you actually read it?'

Crawford laughed. 'I have people to do that for me, Owen. All this small print – never could be doing with columns of figures.'

Powys sat down and opened the document. 'Getting Bryan House on board at Byfield was a good move. I imagine it was Nik Speller who put them in touch.'

'I know the man,' Crawford said. 'Pushy bastard but good. Knows a lot of the right people. It's still too late, though, isn't it? He can't pull anything out of the fire now.'

'I wouldn't be too sure.' Powys turned to the letter from John Parker. 'They identify one or two points that might cause us problems. Down the line, maybe, but there all the same. They draw attention to the lack of balance across Ayot's corporate activities. I know this is something we've talked about before and you've always pooh-poohed the idea.'

'And I still do, Owen. That criticism has got about as much future as a fart in a hurricane.'

'Maybe, maybe not,' Powys looked at his fingernails. They were impeccably groomed – something Crawford thought damned odd, but then what else did these people have to spend their money on? You can only own so many cars, have a flat so near the City and a house so deep in the country and it was human nature after all. Who saves? Not 29-year-olds with five million in the bank and the world before them. Crawford knew of at least one young investment banker who had turned down a £400,000 pa position, because the job title wasn't grand enough. He snorted at the thought and, when Powys directed an enquiring glance, said: 'Nothing, Owen, go on.'

Powys said, 'We'll need to keep an eye on the share prices – and on the derivatives. A shift in opinion now could make a real difference down the line.'

'Never liked derivatives,' Crawford growled. 'It's not real money, it's not real anything. It's playing games.'

'Games matter if they affect your business, Jim. And this document might do that. The point about your approach to day-to-day management? Can you deny it?'

'No, but the results are consistently good.'

'But aren't Byfield implying that with a different style of management, they'd be a lot better?'

'That's hypothetical, Owen. You can't argue against what isn't there.'

'No, but you can use it to alter opinion. I know you've always been a cash man, a builder, a producer, but if I asked you: What is value, show it to me . . .'

'You're beginning to sound like Gavin Clooney, my mad professor.'

'Maybe you should listen to your mad professor some time. After all, you pay him to be on your board. Perhaps we should trot him out at a press conference.'

'Hardly likely to stand up against this!' Crawford opened his brief-case, pulled out a paper and spread it across the table. Illustrating an article by Hugh Mead was a half-page photo of Byfield's Financial Director, Beth Stewart, sitting on a stool at a sushi bar. Taken slightly from above, it emphasised her long legs, crossed, the tights lending them a glow cut off by the severe black of her skirt. One elbow rested on the bar, chopsticks were held lightly in the hand; her head, with a beautifully cut bob, was slightly turned, as if she were choosing a dish and, through chance or art, one of the overhead lights had caught the sweep of her cleavage in the black V of her jacket. All in all, she looked stunning. The article was entitled: 'Riding the Takeover Roller-coaster'.

Owen grinned. 'Yes, caused quite a sensation with some of our guys. I think Ms Stewart has just done her career a lot of good. And she's pretty shrewd in the article – though I did think that Mead was your man?'

'Check with Perry King on that. If he was overwhelmed, who can blame him? Though I imagine Celia might have a few questions about the divine Ms Stewart.'

'She backs up everything in the defence doc – it's well done, complimentary. And people will read it, if only to find out something about the girl.'

'Is there going to be a problem, Owen?'

'I don't think so, despite all this.' He folded the paper and returned it to Crawford. 'They do draw attention to the quick-fix aspect of the acquisition and link it quite cleverly to your supposed dislike of the humdrum; I think we'll have to give it a few days and see.'

'They can hardly point to a dynamic management style.'

Powys indicated a line of print in the Byfield chairman's letter. 'They've had the good sense to sell off the printing and publishing business.'

'By God, though, that will stick in Parker's throat!' Crawford seemed almost glad. 'Do they have a buyer?'

'I think House and Speller have someone lined up. Uh, from the speed at which it happened, I'd guess that Speller, at least, if not Parker, had this one up their sleeve from Day +1.'

'Speller maybe, not Parker. The publishing is one of the original businesses. It was family-owned for years. Goes back to the last century. Oh, no, he couldn't sell that without a whole world of pain.'

'Some of our Wall Street people used to have this expression for really doing a number on someone,' Powys said. 'They'd be like, Hey, we really ripped his face off, didn't we?'

'Yes, that's it,' Crawford said, 'that's it exactly.'

Byfield plc, Goldhawk Mews, London, 15:10
Beth unpinned the newspaper photograph from the notice-board. It was the third copy she'd taken down already today and she was beginning to regret ever having done the interview. Her secretary Selena was wildly enthusiastic and the boys in the

post room had taken down Gail Porter and put her up instead. It was all getting a bit ridiculous.

'Beth, hold on a moment.' Tim Ericson was leaning out of his office, a big grin on his face.

'Not a word, Tim!' Beth warned.

'Would I? I was only going to say bloody good job. I mean what you told him in the interview, it's all good stuff. Let's hope it makes some difference.'

'A lot of it was down to Bobbi King, who co-ordinated the defence doc and the interview.'

'Absolutely. She might not look it, but she's a very smart cookie.'

Beth was about to ask Tim why Bobbi didn't 'look' smart, when John Parker appeared from the lift. He was worn, that was no surprise, but today he looked even more worn than usual. Beth supposed that the sale of the printing and publishing divisions was hitting him hard. He'd been out to lunch with Bryan House at Chez Nico, showing himself in public, relaxed and unconcerned. She hoped he'd looked better than he was right now – otherwise he wouldn't have convinced a blind man.

'John, how did it go?'

'Come along to the office, Beth. And you too, Tim. And collect anyone else who might be around.'

In fact, only Beth, Tim and Angus Howerd from Sales and Marketing were on the top floor at that time so it was a small, impromptu gathering in Parker's office. Beth sat next to the desk, which was piled with copies of the defence document. The only other objects were photos of Parker's wife and daughter, and Beth wondered how they were coping.

Angus Howerd, a bearlike man who wore hairy sports jackets rather than suits whenever he could, perched by the window, opened the top a slit and lit his pipe. The rest of the building was smoke-free, in fact the whole company operated a no public smoking policy, but Parker was too polite to issue any kind of fiat as far as his own office was concerned. And Beth had to admit, Howerd's tobacco had a delicious, scented tang. After puffing away for a few moments, Howerd said: 'Good picture, Beth. We'll all look at you very differently in the future.'

'More to the point, Angus,' Parker said, arranging himself behind the desk, 'it was a good interview and made a number of points we needed to make.'

'And that,' Howerd responded, 'we could state in the document with total certitude. Absolutely, John. We couldn't have bought publicity this good.'

There was a palpable change in the atmosphere of the room – Howerd was no slouch and even if he did feel his future was at stake, he was obviously enjoying the battle; in fact, apart from Bill Harper, the fight had put something of a spring in everyone's step. Routine management just wasn't sexy – takeovers, in spite of, or even because of the risk, definitely were.

Beth said, 'Since you paid for the meal, or our fees did, then, actually, we did buy that particular piece of publicity.'

'Raw fish, wouldn't do for me,' Tim Ericson said. 'I hope your lunch was more digestible, John?'

'House . . .' the non-exec had not yet been admitted into first-name relations with the rest of the board; Beth doubted he ever would be – just a tad too abrasive for the Byfield old-timers. '. . . he appears to feel we are at least holding our own. The risk is always that these kind of measures,' Parker tapped a pile of documents, 'come too late to do any good and show up what wasn't done before. What we should have done.'

Well, Beth thought, you're finally beginning to get the message.

Parker went on: 'We did have one or two natural advantages in place, however, so we aren't total failures, at least in Mr House's eyes.'

'I shall sleep easier for knowing that,' Angus Howerd rumbled around the stem of his pipe. 'Go on, John, tell us how clever we were.'

'Having someone from research and development on the main

board, for a company this size, apparently showed we were serious about research. As we are. We may not have utilised the talent at our disposal but it is there. We have a bloody good R and D Director in Tom Swift and a lot of very bright young people coming up with the kinds of ideas which are going to pay off in the future. That allowed us to play the quick-fix defence against Crawford.'

If this was the case, Beth wondered why Tom Swift had never really been given his head; he did have a lot of ideas but only the most certain were taken up and he had never been tied into the company through stock options. He could walk out the door any day of the week – in fact, like a lot of brilliant people, he was more concerned with getting on with his research and being with his team of geeks than with corporate management, but that was no guarantee for the future. She considered bringing this up but, like so much, it was too late to do anything about it now and she contented herself by asking: 'Will it work?'

'The consensus among our advisers is that, alone, no, it won't. However, if the City begins to feel nervous about Crawford's long-term business prospects . . .'

'Is there any reason they might?' Howerd asked.

'Parts of Ayot are definitely underperforming. As Beth points out in the her interview, it could . . . maybe . . . if it combines with the quick-fix solution and the doubts we planted in the document about his board being under-utilised. All together, House and Nik Speller think it might make him back off. If Ayot shares start falling. If City opinion turns.'

'Sounds like a lot of "ifs" to me, John,' Ericson said.

'Me too, Tim,' Parker said, 'but we're doing all we can, and we can't do any more. We have to wait and see.'

Beth pulled a document off the pile and turned to the figures at the end. 'The decision . . . your decision, John, to bite the bullet and sell publishing and printing, might be the thing that swings it in our favour. It took courage to do it . . .'

'I can tell you, Beth, it took more than that. It was like pushing a needle into my heart. My great-grandfather started the stationery business and . . .' He was unable to go on, in the grip of deep emotion.

'I'm sure we all admire you for that, John,' Beth said. 'Let's see if Crawford can match it.'

Crawford House, Euston Road, London, 17:15
'Celia, I'm pretty damned pissed off at you.'

Celia Hart took the rebuke like the professional she was. 'Really, James, I thought it was all going well.'

'That's not what I mean.' Crawford shut the door to his office and strode across to the circular sofa and the round table strewn with papers and magazines. He sat down. 'You had lunch with Andrea the other day?'

'I did, though I don't quite see what business that is of yours.'

Crawford nodded, 'True, and I don't want to seem like a . . .'

'Caveman?'

'I don't like it when my people are set up.'

Celia followed him across to the sofa and sat down opposite, sinking into the soft, bouncy material. 'Is that what I'm supposed to have done?'

'That friend of yours, Mead . . .'

'I thought Hugh was on your team, James. He certainly talks to Perry King.'

'Hacks are never on anyone's team, Celia. You know that.'

She leaned forward, something dangerous glittering in her eyes. 'I hope you're not about to accuse me of unprofessional behaviour, James. We're friends and we've been friends for quite a while – but if you come out with that . . .'

He held up a finger: 'For goodness sake, Celia, stop acting like . . . a woman. Of course I'm not accusing you of anything like that – it's just that Mead spent the lunch date pumping Andrea for old stuff about me and my career.'

'He's doing a profile, James. What do you expect?'

'I expect him to talk to me, straight.'

'He did. Didn't he?'

Crawford got to his feet and walked to the window. 'The past is the past. I'd like it to stay that way. I've nothing to be ashamed of, Celia, don't think that; it's just that when Andrea and I got together . . . it was a bad time. And she felt that, in some sense, Mead had pushed her into saying more than she intended.'

'She's a big girl, James. We're all grown-ups here and we have to cope. I told her Hugh wanted to do an interview; there was no trickery involved. OK, he's a professional, she's not – but 20 years with you ought to have taught her something about manipulating the media.'

'Flattery will get you everywhere,' Crawford said.

'It won't get me out of this squashy sofa without showing my pants. Will you give me a hand?'

Crawford left the window and, taking Celia's hand, pulled her up. She stood close to him for a moment. 'Of course, you could have left me to struggle up on my own, James.'

'Yes, that might have been interesting.' He paused. They stood almost nose to nose – Celia, in her heels, a little taller than the financier who said: 'But then we are on the same team, aren't we? Try one of these.' He offered a conventional seat. 'They're slightly more respectable.'

'Thank you. Now, before we go on, are you really pissed off at me over Andrea?'

'No, I couldn't be, not for long. But I do feel protective of her.'

Of her or of what she knows? was the question Celia didn't put. Instead, she said: 'I'll have a word with Hugh and ask him to check with you before he writes anything based on Andrea's interview. Not that I can guarantee it'll make any difference. Hugh is a bit of an opportunist but he's pretty straight as far as his work is concerned.'

'Fair enough, Celia. I don't ask for more that that. Now, down to business.'

'Which is?'

'Byfield.'

'The defence document? What do you think of it?'

'Not a lot. Owen Powys and his boys and girls are giving it a good going-over; they'll get back to me with anything I need to know. Did you see that Parker had to sell his publishing and printing?'

'Looked like good sense to me.'

'To you and to me but to him . . .' Crawford shut his eyes for a moment and seemed to savour the silence. 'He's losing what he cares about. That hurts.'

'Is that quite nice of you, James?'

'Oh, I never said I was nice. Talking of which . . .' He pulled the paper out, laid Beth Stewart's photo on the desk and tapped Hugh Mead's byline. 'Your boyfriend gets around a bit, doesn't he?'

'You could say he's cornered the market in Crawfords and Parkers.'

'In pretty girls, too.'

Celia squinted down at the photo. 'He has taste, I'll give him that. What exactly does this have to do with anything? You don't want me to do a calendar pose for you, do you?'

'I wouldn't say no, Celia, but right now I'm more interested in this young lady's figures.'

'Beth's figures?'

'She gives a good interview; from what you said about her when we were first planning this acquisition, she's one of Parker's better board members.'

'Oh, certainly. Apart from Bryan House, the new non-exec, she's head and shoulders above the others. She's got a real future.'

'And does Parker know what he's got in her?'

'If he didn't, he certainly does now.'

'Good. I want her.'

'I beg your pardon, James?'

'I want her on my main board.'

'Hold on; if you're going to win this battle, you'll have her anyway when you get Byfield.'

'Let me put it another way, Celia. I want John Parker to lose her. I want her to be the one who tells him, when the time comes, that Byfield is lost.'

Celia felt a cold shiver travel up her spine. There was something almost reptilian about the way Crawford was sitting there, nothing moving except his eyes, as he talked of betrayal. She had never seen him in quite this light before and she wasn't at all sure if she liked what she was looking at.

'That would be asking a lot of Beth.'

'Betrayal, Celia, is part of growing up. I think it would do Ms Stewart good to learn that lesson and if she really is as exceptional as you say, it'll help her grow.'

'But what will it do to John Parker?'

'It'll weaken him. And he'll lose.'

'Surely by that time the takeover will be finished? He will have lost already.'

'Yes, Celia – I think we should invite Miss Stewart onto our board. Why don't you have a word with her? Nothing blatant. Trail your coat a bit. See how she responds. Then get back to me.'

'Is this punishment for setting up Andrea, James? If so, you should know that I can absorb a lot of it – and I keep coming back.'

'It's just a business approach.'

Going down in the stainless-steel lift, Celia wondered what on earth Crawford thought he was up to. Was this thing personal in some way she didn't know about? He undoubtedly *was* angry at Andrea's indiscretions and this made Celia all the more avid to hear exactly what she'd told Hugh.

thursday 18th nov. 10:00

waymouth, paternoster, city of london

THE TWO BANKERS MET IN POWYS' OFFICE. They each had a copy of the defence document and a pad for notes. Carpenter said: 'I've been looking at the shares, Owen. I can't say I like what I'm seeing.'

'No, and I wouldn't say it was totally unexpected either.' Powys opened the defence document to Byfield Chairman Parker's letter, as he had done a few days before with Crawford present. Carpenter's attention was rather more acute, however, than the entrepreneur's had been. He craned over as Powys highlighted a number of points, then flipped to the back of the document, where he drew the thick marker along a whole row of figures.

' "Time and again," ' he quoted, ' "Ayot has talked of merging their plant with Byfield's aggregates and building companies but where is the evidence that supports the so-called profits this is supposed to produce? Byfield currently hires plant in a market which it knows well – and which, in return, knows it well." '

'Crap writing,' Carpenter said, 'but not crap itself. If their figures are correct, and I see no reason why they shouldn't be, the overall effect of tying Byfield into an unbreakable plant contract with Ayot would not lead to any increase in profits.'

'Right,' Powys said. 'Crawford was selling us a future, a derivative. And a pretty dodgy one at that. It was his way of tidying away loose ends.' He pulled his note-pad closer. 'Ayot's shares dropped after we went live, as we'd expected. Once the City had time to digest the document, they climbed again but, since the Byfield fightback, they've been slipping.'

'If dealers don't get the right vibes, they're not going to support the company.'

Carpenter pulled out a pen and noted down a few figures. 'Have you got Ayot's results to hand?'

'What're you after, Chip?'

'Comparative results from the various companies. Crawford is going to need to regain the confidence of the City if this is going any further.'

'Should it?' Powys asked, as he leafed through the original Ayot offer document and found the figures Carpenter wanted.

'No point in pulling out, not from where we stand. Basically, we've started running down the hill, we've got faster and faster and, even if we wanted to, we couldn't stop without falling over. And that's not good business. We got into this . . .'

'Against your better inclinations, I have to admit,' Powys said.

'I supported you, Owen, Nobody forced me. And, let's be honest, this is far from down the drain yet. In one sense, I think we could say it might be about to get rather interesting for all concerned.'

'Old Chinese curse Chip. May you live in interesting times. So who gets to tell Jim Crawford the bad news?'

Carpenter shrugged: 'You, of course, you're his banker. Besides, it's not really bad news – just a change of direction, a slight blip in our preordained course. Yes?'

Day +18

friday 19th nov.
three phone calls

owen powys to james crawford 08:15

POWYS: Jim, not too early for you?

CRAWFORD: The concept early doesn't exist in my world, Owen. I'm here on the end of a phone whenever you need to reach me. What can I do for you?

POWYS: It's really more what I can do, what I have to tell you, say to you.

CRAWFORD: Tell, say? What's been happening there, Owen? Too much Red Bull and vodka last night? Someone take *you* over this morning?

POWYS: We, uh . . . we've been looking at your figures. Jim. And . . . we feel that, uhm, you should consider very carefully selling the, uh, plant side of your business. At least that. Maybe the food too. Jim?

CRAWFORD: Yes, I hear you, Owen. I'm thinking . . . why now?

POWYS: Have you looked at your shares recently? Sorry, obviously, uh, of course you have. And . . . and you'll see . . .

CRAWFORD: Down 12 per cent last night.

POWYS: And no better . . . another slight drop this morning.

CRAWFORD: Forgive me for mentioning it, Owen, but aren't you fellows meant to make sure this doesn't happen?

POWYS: Jim, Jim, you know us. If we go with a deal, then it's a deal half done before it even hits the table. But if a few dozen fund managers start pissing their pants over this . . .

203

CRAWFORD: Stupid kids –

POWYS: And they did a good job over at Byfield with their defence.

CRAWFORD: That's good? Their defence is good?

POWYS: Not in the long run, no, of course not. It won't make any difference, well, we hope it won't and we will ensure it won't . . . And if we want to do that then we must be as certain as we can . . .

CRAWFORD: That our offer is foolproof?

POWYS: Exactly, Jim, yes. We can't give them anything to pick on. Pick out. Whatever. No objections. And, in general terms the plant company . . . as you pointed out, building work is increasing, people need . . . will certainly need cranes and . . . and . . . diggers and . . . So it'll sell. Easily. And the City will see that you mean, uhm . . .

CRAWFORD: Business?

POWYS: Yes. And to be honest, Jim, the food supply, the frozen foods, they don't really deliver – get rid of them too. You'll have a lot of extra cash and it'll be clear, absolutely clear that you're concentrating on your core business.

CRAWFORD: Do you have customers lined up, Owen?

POWYS: There are a couple of numbers I could ring as soon as you give me the go-ahead.

CRAWFORD: Obviously the board at Ayot would have to OK it. I can't guarantee that they'll agree.

POWYS: Knowing you, I don't see any great problems.

CRAWFORD: It isn't always a question of waving a cutlass over people's heads, Owen.

POWYS: The thing is, Jim, when you start a process, you can't always stop it when it goes off in a different direction. If you tried to go ahead without this sale, I would have to say . . . my advice, and the advice of my colleagues, would be that it would probably fail. And that if you pulled out . . .

CRAWFORD: I'm not going to pull out.

POWYS: If you even considered it, I really do think that the shares would not . . . they wouldn't climb back up, Jim, because in the eyes of the City, this has, uhm . . . it's identified a flaw in . . . a fundamental flaw in Ayot.

CRAWFORD: Stick to your core business. Yes, I see that. Well, OK, let it be known that Ayot is looking to divest itself of the plant and food companies. Don't make any deals.

POWYS: That'll be fine for now. As long as we deliver. It'll reassure them, show them . . .

CRAWFORD: That Jim Crawford is still in the game.

POWYS: Exactly.

CRAWFORD: I've got some damned function next week – Entrepreneurs and the Future. Speeches and bad wine. I wasn't going to go but maybe I should.

POWYS: I think so. It'll show confidence and you could drop a few words in the right ears.

CRAWFORD: Yeah, and you'll earn yourself another Lotus or some other damn flashy piece of machinery. I'll be in touch.

End

hugh mead to sally cohen 11:15

OPERATOR: Good morning, *Reading Argus*.

MEAD: Uh, hi. Could I speak to Sally Cohen?

OPERATOR: Who's calling, please?

MEAD: Hugh Mead. She knows me.

OPERATOR: Hold on, please.

COHEN: Hugh?

MEAD: Sally, hi! How're you doing?

COHEN: Pretty good, pretty good. You know, busy and all that. How about you? Are you still with, Rachel, was it?

MEAD: No, no, that was uh . . . haaa . . .

COHEN: Whoops!

MEAD: You and Tim?

COHEN: Like an old married couple. Actually we're thinking of doing the deed next year. I'll send you an invite.

MEAD: Great. Uhm, now, uhm, well, Sally, I wonder if you can help me with something?

COHEN: Whatever, if it's in my power – and if it's any good, I get a part of it!

MEAD: I love it! I'm doing a profile on Jim Crawford.

COHEN: Sorry?

MEAD: The entrepreneur. He's mixed up in a takeover battle right now.

COHEN: I saw something. I don't know.

MEAD: He started out in Reading . . .

COHEN: Long before my time, Hugh.

MEAD: Both our times. The thing is, I wondered if – he stood for Parliament but there was some kind of problem. He was chucked out.

COHEN: Doesn't mean a thing, I'm afraid. What you could do is go through the back issues. If you came down, that'd be easy enough to arrange.

MEAD: Yeah, I'd like to do that but I was also wondering if you have anybody . . . I s'pose it's too long ago . . .

COHEN: 'Berkshire Ups and Downs'. It's a column we run. The old days, memory lane. The guy that writes it has been around for ever. He's retired now, lives out near Pangbourne. Harry Burton. King of the Hacks, he calls himself. Spent his whole life on the *Argus*. Copy boy to chief reporter. I could give him a call . . . If anybody knows anything, it's him.

MEAD: Would you? I could get down anytime if he wanted to talk.

COHEN: The problem with Harry is getting him to stop. Do you want to give me your mobile number and I'll see what he says?

HUGH: Sally, you're a star. It's 0956 89 897.

COHEN: Fine, and if you do get down, and want to see the archives, let me know. We could have a drink together.

MEAD: Old times' sake, Sally.

End

celia hart to beth stewart 14:00

HART: Beth, Celia Hart.

STEWART: Celia, how are you?

HART: I'm fine. What about you? Are they keeping you busy?

STEWART: I could say *you're* keeping me busy.

HART: I guess. Where are you, Beth, if you don't mind me asking? That doesn't sound like any office I know.

STEWART: I'm at Bobbi King's, being groomed for some TV thing I'm doing. The *Business Show*.

HART: Yeah, I saw Hugh's interview and the piccie. You looked fabulous and sounded even better. Definitely one for our side. Do you have a couple of minutes?

STEWART: I think so. Hold on. (faint) Bobbi is it . . .? Yes, that's fine, Celia.

HART: Because I was talking to Jim Crawford the other day.

STEWART: Yes?

HART: And he was very impressed with the article too. He thought you talked good sense.

STEWART: I think Hugh made it sound better than it was.

HART: Hey, I know the boy – and he's not that good. He wrote it how it was. Certainly, that's what Jim thinks.

STEWART: I . . . I suppose that's very kind of him.

HART: Realistic, Beth. Jim isn't given to kindness in business. He's impressed and . . . he'd like you on his team.

STEWART: What, sorry?

HART: He wants you on his board. He's offering you a directorship.

STEWART: You mean after the . . . if the takeover goes through, he's saying he wants me to stay at Byfield?

HART: No, Beth. He's offering you a place on the Ayot main board. Increased responsibility, increased salary, increased career prospects.

STEWART: Now?

HART: Effective from now, though you'd stay on the Byfield board. Nothing would change there. When the time comes, and only if the situation warrants it, you'll be able to, uhm . . . point out the inevitability of the acquisition. You'll also be able to offer good severance terms to the other directors.

STEWART: Celia, I'm not quite sure what you're offering me here. I mean . . . am I supposed to be some kind of spy?

HART: Beth, it's nothing like that. Crawford doesn't need secret information. He's going to win, sooner or later. He knows that, you know that. Your chairman is probably the only person in the whole business who doesn't. What we need to be looking at now is the accomplishment of a smooth integration. Proper succession.

STEWART: You'd need Tim Ericson for that . . .

HART: You see, that's what we want. Your judgement short-term on the merging, long-term in respect to the new entity. It's a good chance and, don't worry, no one expects you to stop fighting your corner right now. Go on TV, do your stuff. I know you'll be great. It's only when the situation becomes inevitable that we're all going to need someone who can point out what must be faced and what must be done. Will you think about it?

STEWART: I suppose . . . I suppose I have to, don't I?

HART: I think you do, Beth and, you know, I'm really confident about the way this is all going to turn out. In about five years you'll be CEO of something really major and I'll be working for you.

STEWART: I don't know, sometimes it all seems . . .

HART: Hey, have fun on TV. I'll look out for you.

End

Day (+22)

crawford house, euston road, london

'HOW DID HE DO THAT?' Diane Ellroy's impeccable eyebrows climbed up her forehead in disbelief.

Mark shrugged: 'The old Crawford magic.'

'I thought at least Phil Goodman would put up some kind of objection. I always figured he was hot for trucks and bulldozers.'

'Obviously he's hotter for good business sense.'

'You think it is sensible, Mark?'

They were standing by the glass wall, looking down onto the Euston Road which was, as usual, nose to tail with traffic.

'I'm not a director, Diane. I just take the minutes.' Overhead a police helicopter floated into view, its identification lights bright against the gloomy, lowering clouds. Mark pointed to it: 'Maybe they're staking him out.'

'I doubt it. Crawford is too damn slippery for the cops or anyone else.' She gave an exasperated shake of her head – and her hair moved exquisitely, a curtain of black above the column of her white neck. Mark wondered what it would be like to press his lips against that flesh and then he thought, This is getting boring: isn't it time you put up or shut up? And the thought of setting himself a deadline made his stomach churn with fear and delight.

'The board had to go with him,' he said. 'There wasn't any choice. Even Gavin Clooney seemed . . . well, not to object for once.'

'Hey, it's exciting, you can't deny that. Suddenly the old humdrum day-to-day decisions are up there on the big screen. We're in the papers – not the trades but the real thing. They talk about us on *Newsnight*. That foxy financial director over at Byfield gets to strut her stuff in the *Guardian*. We're human, we love this stuff and Crawford knows it. And knows how to use it. You know what Emerson said: in skating over thin ice, our safety is in our speed. But I would like to know what Clooney really thinks about it all.'

The ex-academic was across the room, chatting to Burroughs from human resources. Crawford had left as soon as he'd secured the board's backing for the sale of the plant and food supply companies.

'Let's go see, shall we?' Diane turned from the window and went round the solid, black rectangle of the boardroom table to join Burroughs and Clooney. After a few moments, the Human Resources Director left and Mark drifted over to join Diane, as she was saying: 'Were you really behind him today?'

There was no doubt that Diane could be direct when she chose – what if she responded positively to his advances? Another swoop of the stomach, was he really going to try it? He must be crazy . . .

'Behind him, Diane? On the whole, yes. Given the position as we face it today. I feel that in the long term it is always better to be pro- rather than reactive; which is where we stand . . .' he looked around, as if to orientate himself, 'currently.'

'Reactive – being forced into making moves we might not have considered a few weeks ago?' Diane said.

Clooney laughed. 'My word, you do jump on one.'

Jump on me, jump on me, Mark fantasised. Clooney merely continued: 'Since you put it that way, yes.'

The short answer rather caught Diane and she was silent for a few moments. This didn't bother Clooney one bit: ruminative silence was his natural habitat.

'Is it a good thing?' Diane asked, at last.

'Good – is a relative value in business. I don't want to sound like *1066 and All That* . . .' Clooney chuckled at a reference which neither Mark nor, from her expression, Diane picked up. 'Good corporate governance demands . . . should I say . . . ?'

'You should say whatever you want,' Diane laughed, 'we're sitting at your feet on this one.'

'I don't want to start lecturing, thank you very much, but the idea of a working interrelationship, as it were, between industry, banking and government, on a day-to-day basis has still a long way to go in many parts of the City. Yes, we are on the road to Damascus but too many of us have not yet met our, uh . . . so as to say, moment of . . . blinding revelation. Some of us are still Saul and not yet Paul.'

He chuckled and Diane offered a smile and said, 'What if Saul never makes it to Damascus? Maybe he buys a pair of Raybans?'

'I beg your pardon?'

'Sunglasses. No revelation, no change. No missionary journeys, no letters to young churches. That wouldn't be . . . *a good thing?*'

'No,' Clooney said thoughtfully, 'no, not at all a good thing. In the long run.'

'And as you say, Professor, strategy matters.'

Clooney considered this a while, then nodded and said: 'I must leave you. Perhaps I might buy you a sherry sometime. At my club. No, I don't think they let, uh . . .'

'Women?'

'Exactly. I'm resigning. I know, do you like sushi?'

Even Diane Ellroy was floored by that one. 'You? Sushi?'

'I taught in Japan. Spent five years there on and off. I have quite an affection and a considerable respect for their corporate culture. Give me a call.' He produced a card. 'That's my mobile or you could e-mail me.' He tipped an invisible hat and wandered off.

'Sharp as a needle,' Diane said.

'I think it's a pin,' Mark said. 'What do you think?'

'Pin, needle, who cares. Sorry, you're so serious, Mark, I can't resist it.'

His face fell.

'Hey, I didn't mean to upset you.' She reached out and brushed his cheek with her fingers. 'Cheer up. You can have *my* mobile number.' She produced a card and slipped it into his top pocket. He was aware of a beaming smile – like he was favourite in the country-bumpkin-idiot-grin competition – blooming across his face. He tried to control it but simply couldn't. Diane said: 'That's better. And yes, I think I will go and eat sushi with Dr Clooney as soon as possible.'

Mark somehow knew it was now or never. In what was the single most courageous act of his life so far, he said: 'Diane, will you come and eat something with *me* one night?'

And she said 'Yes.'

Byfield plc, Goldhawk Mews, London, 14:00
Bryan House said: 'No, John, it doesn't.'

Beth pushed the follow-up offer document Ayot had issued that morning across the boardroom table. 'I agree with Bryan, it doesn't make any difference.' She examined her words: Did *they* make any difference? Since accepting Celia's – and thus Crawford's – offer of a place on the Ayot board, she had found herself caught in a maelstrom of emotions and thoughts, which threatened to drag her down into total confusion. She was determined to be loyal to Parker and Byfield and never to offer any advice that contradicted her duty as an officer of the company – in so far as she was able. And it was in that little 'so far' that the trouble lay.

'I simply don't see what you mean, either of you.' If he had looked tired and under pressure last week, this week the screw had turned still further. For a moment, at the beginning of the meeting, Parker had seemed elated, as if the news of Ayot's sale of its subsidiaries indicated at least a half screw-turn back. Now, these hopes were being destroyed. 'For God's sake, Bryan, Beth, it shows the man can't keep a grip on the everyday running of his companies. So why let him run a larger business?'

Bryan House opened the new Ayot document. 'This makes a very persuasive case for the sale of their food and plant companies, John. It looks like prudence. Not, I admit, a quality one would normally associate with Crawford, but here it is. With the support of his advisers, and the board, sales have been arranged, there's more money in the kitty, therefore they'll be able to finance the research and development of which we boasted in our document.'

'We can finance that,' Parker said.

'But not to this extent,' Beth said.

Bill Harper, Byfield CEO, joined in: 'There's no increase on the original offer – if our shareholders didn't accept it then, I don't see that this sale is going to make any difference.'

'Good, Bill,' Tim Ericson said. 'I still think we have the loyalty of our customers and the loyalty of our suppliers . . .'

'And the loyalty of the bank,' Parker said. ' And while we have that, we can still fight.'

'I'm concerned,' Beth said, 'that no white knights have come along. This still seems to be a straight contest. Bryan, any thoughts on that?'

House considered a moment. 'Good point. My feeling is that they are waiting. There's nothing – sorry, John – terribly interesting in either company, not enough to draw others into battle at this point. Why not let both sides tire themselves and then, if it still looks tasty, step in with fresh troops and a new battle plan?'

'They're going to let us sink, aren't they?' Parker muttered. The flesh of his face was like old putty – Beth thought she had never seen a man look so tired and yet so incapable of sleep.

'We can't say at this moment.' House appeared confident but then so he should; that was his job.

Angus Howerd, who kept reaching for his pipe and jerking his hand back, asked: 'What are the shares doing?' He should have known but perhaps could not bear to look.

'His up 15 per cent, ours holding,' Beth said, 'but I wouldn't count on a stable position for long. Something has to happen soon.'

'We can't give up, I won't give up!' The shout was torn from Parker's throat. He clenched his fists: 'We must keep fighting. This offer . . . even if it were tenable, it's still too low. It's insultingly low. We can't let ourselves, we won't let ourselves . . .'

Dick Worthington, who had been no more conspicuous in his absence than his presence but who had made it in today, said: 'No one's talking about giving up, John. This is like one of those great Bruce Springsteen ballads where you struggle and you struggle and then . . .' Worthington fell silent, remembering that as a rule in Springsteen songs after the struggle came defeat or death on the highway or debts that no man could pay. Fortunately, Parker was not familiar with the Boss's oeuvre and took Worthington's remarks at face value. The pony-tailed non-exec went on: 'You should take some time, John. Go home, chill out, grab some Zs. You're very important to us here, we need you ready to get down and boogie – so how about it?'

'It's a temptation, Dick, but I have to attend this function tonight. It doesn't go on late but, uh . . . I said I'd be there and, now more than ever, I need to stand by my word.'

'OK, but get home early.' That was it for Worthington.

Beth unclenched her ears and started listening again, 'As you know, I'm doing this TV show and they want to record it at four, so I need to be on my way.'

Parker smiled: 'If you do half as well as you did with the interview, then you'll do us proud, Beth.'

She smiled while knowing that there wasn't a lot more to say about the situation. 'I'm feeling absolutely terrified. At least it's a recording, so if anything ghastly happens, Bobbi says they can do a retake. If it was live I don't think I could hack it.'

'Hey, TV, it's only . . . TV.'

'Thank you, Dick, I'll keep it in mind.'

Downstream

In transit: Park Lane / Kings Cross / Soho, London, night
The function suite of the Regent Park Hotel was filled – with crowds of suited men mainly, and a few women, also suited, for this was a business occasion. One of many that existed, as far as John Parker could comprehend, simply because they existed. The last time he'd been here, it was business innovations; this time it was entrepreneurs – so there must at least be a chance of meeting Crawford again. Not a prospect he looked upon with any pleasure at all. He ordered another whisky at the bar; it arrived as a double, which suited him just fine. He tipped it back, enjoying the rich seaweed and iodine tang of the West Coast malt. One of his favourites and he certainly needed something decent tonight.

The extempore board meeting he'd called this afternoon to celebrate Crawford's reversal had turned into a nightmare. House and Beth Stewart had both made it plain that this was not a get-out for Byfield and, as they had explained patiently, as if to a child, he had felt a huge embarrassment at the pathetic glimmer of hope he had nourished. It was not a mistake he should have made in the first place, and making it in front of House was even worse – he trusted and liked Beth Stewart – but the non-exec, for all his talent, was not a man to inspire warmth or loyalty.

He'd intended, after the meeting, to call Nik Speller to re-assure him about the continued will to fight but the effort of picking up the phone and asking for the number had been too much; or maybe it was the fear of Nik's response. Instead, he'd had a few nips from the bottle of Scotch he'd taken to keeping in his office, and had come to the conclusion that since Byfield, in all its incarnations, had always been loyal to its bankers, they, surely, would be loyal in return. On that score at least, he could feel reasonably comfortable.

'John, how's it going?' It was Chip Carpenter, one of the junior geniuses from Waymouth, Paternoster, Crawford's bank, but Chip had nothing to do with the takeover.

'Chip – not bad, considering. A drink?'

'White wine. Dry.'

'As it would be for a banker,' Parker joked and ordered the wine and another whisky. 'How's the family?'

'Oh, fine, fine. Boy's away at school now.'

'Gives you a bit more time.' Parker realised that both he and Carpenter were uncomfortable in each other's company and had nothing to say. Nevertheless, they were going to have to stand and talk politely about something until they'd finished their drinks and one of them found an excuse to get away. It was a bit like having a death in the family – and finding that your friends and acquaintances somehow can't rise above the embarrassment.

'Kate wasn't wild about him going, said six was too young but . . . once he's settled, we'll only have Corinne to worry about.'

And the conversation wound on, through the wine and whisky, and then Carpenter saw someone he had to speak to and Parker waved him off and they agreed to meet up some other time. And Parker ordered another whisky, avoiding the barman's eye – after all, what business was it of his.

There was a buffet supper, the same buffet supper as always, and Parker decided to give it a miss, staying at the bar, steadily drinking or was it drinking steadily. He felt as if he had a crack in his soul and that no matter how much he tipped down, he would never manage to fill himself up. So that was all right then. And anyway, why should he go home to Heather's frosty looks and Claire's hurt? Oh, she'd forgiven him: he'd gone up at bedtime and explained that sometimes even daddies had problems and they got angry when they didn't mean to. And she'd said: 'Then you do really like Paul, don't you, Dad?' And he'd said, Of course I do, he's my son but sometimes things happen and . . . people get angry with each other and . . . and . . .

Had he been lying to his daughter? It was so difficult to think clearly about anything. He felt as if he wanted to open the top of his head, get hold of his brain and wring it out like a sponge and then lay it on a rock in the sun and let it bake until there was nothing left in it at all.

He ordered another drink and the barman said, 'You could have bought the bottle, Sir. Would have saved you time.'

Had he drunk that much? He felt fine. Better, in fact, than he had for weeks. Since this whole bloody business had begun. Maybe Dick Worthington had been right, he should go home and see Heather. Make it up to her. Why not? She was a grand girl.

He nodded goodnight to the barman and made his way through the crowds and up to the hotel lobby. Here the guests were coming and going, porters were carrying cases, life was happening just the way it always did. Collecting his coat, he made his way to the revolving door and stepped out into the cold – and it hit him like a boxer.

His head swam and he missed his step, turning his ankle on the kerb. A hand gripped his arm and pulled him upright.

'Careful, John. Don't want to injure yourself.'

Crawford. Standing there grinning, his own coat over his arm.

'It's all right,' Parker said, conscious that he was slurring his words. 'I can manage.'

'I'm sure you can, John. Shall we get you a taxi?'

Crawford raised his arm and a taxi approached. Parker reached out and pulled the wrong way at the handle. Crawford detached his gloved fingers, and opened the door so Parker could lurch into the leathery darkness. He breathed deeply and shut his eyes as the taxi pulled away from the hotel. His head was steady, no swirling and whirling. Thank God for that.

He grunted and opened his eyes – conscious at once that he was not alone. Crawford sat beside him, relaxed, looking past the driver's head.

'What are you doing here?'

'Just making sure you get home all right. Wouldn't want to get lost, John, would you?'

'I'm quite capable of my own home, of seeing my own home

way,' Parker said, furious at himself for mixing up the words. It made him look as though he couldn't hold his drink; it made him feel as he had this afternoon in front of Bryan House. 'I can . . . get home.'

Crawford didn't answer; just sat there like something made out of granite. Parker grabbed the door strap, pulling himself upright. It was a crazy situation. He felt allright – everything inside seemed quite clear, but he wasn't able to get the words out. What the hell do you think you're doing? Driver, stop this taxi immediately. They wouldn't come and still everything was crystal clear. Even the way Crawford's lips turned up at the edges in a slight smile.

He made an immense effort and said, 'Where we going?'

Crawford turned towards him, like an idol; massive and somehow menacing, the lights of cars and shopfronts sliding crazily across the glass behind his head. Without reply, he turned back and, after a long pause, there was a grunt: 'You'll see.'

Parker tried to catch sight of a landmark and work out in which direction they were heading but either they were in a part of the city he didn't know or his memory was functioning no better than the rest of him. The streets seemed darker and there was a great wall running alongside them that fell away as the taxi did a U-turn and came to a halt. Crawford leaned forward and paid and opened the back door, letting the cold night air in. For a moment Parker felt control return to his limbs and slid across the back seat and stepped onto the pavement. Above his head a neon sign buzzed and fizzed; he craned up to read CAS NO.

'Casno, what the hell is that?'

'Casino, John. Where people throw their money away. You know?' Once more Crawford had him by the arm and was leading him up a couple of steps and into a seedy entranceway, lit with yellow strip lights behind dusty glass. 'Not quite the standard of place you're used to but good enough to take anyone's money. Come on, get your coat off. It'll be hot in there.'

Parker unbuttoned his overcoat and handed it to an elderly woman in a shabby uniform who hung it on a bent wire hanger. Crawford let go of his arm and said: 'Coming?'

He should turn and walk out now, never mind his coat, he could leave it.

'Go on, if you want to run away . . .' The words were gloating. Had Crawford actually said them or had they only echoed in Parker's head? 'Run away!' No, he'd never run away from anything. He breathed in deeply and turned to Crawford.

'So, Jim, this is your club, is it?'

Was there a second when Crawford was taken aback? Parker was sure of it, before the other laughed and said: 'Good for you, John. Yes, this is one of them. Come on, I'll buy you a drink.' He walked to a pair of swing-doors and pushed through, leaving Parker alone in the lobby. The woman in the coat-check cubbyhole began to cough thick, phlegmy hacks; someone passing outside bellowed: 'Fucking bastard,' with extraordinary violence; and Parker stepped forward and through the swing-doors.

The casino was dark, hugely dark with pools and strips and bars of dirty yellow light, etched solidly against the gloom. Within the lights were blackjack and roulette tables, a long bar with mostly empty stools and a few booths at the far edge of the room, where shadowy figures crouched over cocktail glasses. The smell was of damp carpets, cigarette smoke, and the kind of electricity that Parker always imagined rising off insane people. It didn't make sense, he knew that, as he followed Crawford to the bar, where he slumped onto a stool, resting his elbows on the wooden top; it didn't make sense but then, how many things did, anymore.

At the end of the bar a television flickered down from the wall at a crazy angle; football played in a blizzard or maybe the blizzard was coming from the TV and they were playing in the sun. Crawford beckoned the bargirl, who didn't appear to be wearing anything under her open blouse, and whispered something, passing over a bank note.

'Whisky for you, John?'

'Why not?'

'Will Grouse do? I don't think they run to the single stuff.'

Parker shrugged. 'Anything.'

The bargirl returned with a bottle of Grouse. It didn't have a cap. She smiled wanly and placed two glasses beside the bottle. Looking closely, Parker thought he could see a scar running up the centre of her chest, between her two small breasts. He blinked and when he looked again, she had gone. Maybe he'd seen nothing at all.

Crawford poured for them both, filling Parker's glass almost to the rim. 'Drink up. You can toast your young lady.'

'What?' The whisky was good, warming and smooth; it was what he needed, it made everything right again. Fuck Crawford, who the hell did he think he was anyway? 'Lady? What are you talking about?'

Crawford jerked a thumb over his shoulder at the TV where Parker recognised Beth Stewart, her mouth moving silently as she gestured and smiled to the camera. The picture was crystal clear.

'She's good,' Crawford poured more whisky into Parker's glass. 'You're lucky to have her, John. Sorry about the sound; I'm afraid they don't really like to listen here, unless it's racing. Still, I'm sure you can trust her to put your case.'

'Case? There isn't any case and you bloody well know it. This is just a game, isn't it, some stupid game you're playing. You think you'll win – well, maybe you will, Jim Crawford, but you'll still be a little . . .'

Crawford turned away and called to the bargirl, who switched back to the football and the blizzard. 'Come and watch me lose some money, John, you'll like that. And don't forget your bottle.'

Without another word, Crawford went to a wire-fronted booth, shoved a wad of banknotes under the grill and received a pile of chips which he took to a vacant place at one of the roulette tables. Pouring himself another, Parker wandered unsteadily over and stood behind Crawford, who looked up over his shoulder.

'Nothing fancy about this place. It's here to gamble in, that's all.' He pushed chips onto a red square. Others round the table followed suit, some betting on red or black rather than an individual number. The croupier, a young woman in a silvery sheath dress, said: 'No more bets, ready to play,' her accent pure estuary, and spun the wheel, dropping the ball after a pause.

Parker looked around at those who chose to patronise this place; there was, certainly, nothing glitzy about it at all and nothing classy about the clientele. Middle-aged men and wo-men, most of them smoking, most of them with coarse, indoor flesh and clothes that appeared to have been stained over years with nicotine. Or perhaps that was the lighting, which made the backs of his own hands look pale and sickly and turned his jacket sleeve to something he'd rather not be wearing.

'Red 24. Ladies and gentlemen, red 24.'

Crawford's chips were dragged away and Parker toasted that. At the next spin Crawford lost again and Parker finished his glass for it. After that, Crawford won, so Parker went and got the bottle and refilled and drank for each of the next five spins, which left Crawford with an empty space in front of him and Parker with an empty bottle.

No one at the table seemed to notice, no one seemed to care. They sat there in the green-yellow light, their clothes lost in the gloom, their faces hovering like tired balloons slowly deflating and Parker had a sickening feeling that there was nothing inside their flesh at all, no bone, no gristle, nothing and that over time they would get smaller and more wrinkled and . . .

'Five thousand down.' Crawford got to his feet with a grin. 'Do you gamble, John?'

'I don't. Stupid . . . very stupid.'

'At least it doesn't mess up your liver, like this stuff.' He took the bottle from Parker's hand and put it back on the bar – which is where they were suddenly, though Parker couldn't quite work out how they had got there. No more than he could account for being outside again, swaying in front of a busy road. His legs felt as if they had been filled with all the helium that had been sucked from those slack balloon faces inside.

'Easy, don't want to lose you yet.' Crawford guided him over a crossing. It was difficult now keeping control of his feet; they were blown up so, and had got caught in sheets of old newspaper. At the centre island he stopped and grabbed the metal railing, trying to get himself together. The steel was cool under his palms but when he pulled his hands away, one of them seemed to stick.

'Station? I . . . I should get the train.'

Crawford jerked him forward. 'Wrong station, John. Kings Cross. Interesting place, though. Lean here, that's it . . . give yourself a moment.'

Rubbing some feeling back into his numbed face, Parker peered up at the Victorian façade of the station. A huge wall of stone; how did it stay up there? He turned to ask Crawford, but he was talking to a man in a leather jacket. After a moment they parted and Crawford returned.

'Feeling better? Good, I've got something for you.' He pulled Parker forwards and once again, there was some kind of a gap and they were standing in a doorway near some stairs under a dim light bulb and the man in the jacket was there and a girl who seemed very young and pale.

'Her name's Chrissie. Say hello to John, Chrissie.'

The girl smiled, and Parker knew that if they smiled in hell, this is how it would look. 'Hello, John,' she lisped.

'G-get away.' He tried to ward her off with an arm. The leather man pushed between them and grabbed . . . actually grabbed Parker around the neck and spat words at him in a language he didn't understand. He felt himself slammed against the wall, his head hitting the plaster with a crack he could hear quite clearly. And yet he didn't seem to be hurt – only terribly, terribly scared.

His mouth was full of water and he realised that only Crawford could save him and that was why they were here.

'Please . . .'

'Here's your money.' Another wad of notes appeared in front of the pimp's face. He let go of Parker who slid down onto the staircase.

'There's more than enough, take it and go. Take her too.'

Parker looked up at Crawford. Above his head the light bulb glowed evilly through the dust.

'Come on. Let's get out of here. These people . . .'

Now Parker found himself in a taxi again. His hand hurt and he looked at it; there *was* something sticky all over his fingers. He tried to scrape if off against the seat.

'My hand?' he mumbled.

Crawford didn't appear to hear him. He said, 'So, you don't like girls, John.'

'Not that . . . horrible. Why?' A wave of depression, of self-loathing swept over him. He tried to say: You bastard, but the words eluded his slow tongue, like little lights, playing around the inside of the cab, flickering here and there.

Crawford barked something and the cab stopped. Once more, money changed hands. So much money tonight, Parker thought, as he found himself on the pavement and the little cloud of firefly words flickered past his head, swallowed up by a great tumult of noise and light and colour that burned into his brain. He shut his eyes; it was still there – the clatter, the beeping, the wails and snatches of music, a monstrous production line.

'This might interest you more, John. Do you play games?'

Parker tried to listen but the words were falling away down a long funnel and then rushing back into his face '. . . play games . . . Oh, you play . . . always . . . got away . . .'

'Wha . . .' He tried to hold on but it was glass he was leaning against and there didn't seem to be any purchase. His cheek was pressed against the window and yes, he could see through into the world inside. Where was Crawford? It didn't matter now. He was OK, he was fine, insulated; nothing could touch him. He even laughed and pushed himself upright and floated inside on his helium-filled legs. He tried to take some money out of his pocket but now his fingers had swelled into little balloons.

'You all right, then?'

A quiet voice, cutting through everything . . . cool water running over his forehead.

'I think so. A bit too much to drink. You know?'

'Yeah.' A boy, young, with blonde hair, a tiny silver bar through his eyebrow.

Parker reached out his fat, bloated fingers and as soon as they touched the bar they shrank back to normal. The boy smiled and his whole face came alive and was so beautiful, so touching that Parker had to turn away as if an angel had suddenly appeared, here in the games arcade. He found himself smiling in answer.

'I'm Kevin,' the boy said.

Parker said, 'I'm John. Pleased to meet you, Kevin.'

He held his hand out and the boy took it and said, 'Would you like to go somewhere?'

'He's with me. Clear off.' Crawford again, taking his arm, pulling him away.

'No . . . please . . . I want . . . I want . . . just to be with some-one.'

'Nearly there, now.' Another jerk on his arm and . . . they were somewhere else, dark this time. And there was the smell of rubbish.

'Why did you . . . he was . . .'

'Too young . . . old man.'

'No, not that, never that . . .' And he saw Claire, turning away from him as she had on the night he'd shouted at Paul. It was like a light turning off – and it had stayed off ever since. A light . . . then a slab of darkness came up to meet him and he felt something hard against his cheek. It was good to be still at last.

'Why . . . where?'

Turning . . . he was turning. Hands. A face. And the sky. Night sky. Clusters of light. Star clusters.

'Orion,' he said.

And Orion the hunter looked down on him and said, 'Have you no darkness inside you?'

Darkness?

And Orion said, 'Good night, John.'

Part Three
The Weir

I think one could very well say that business, as we see it presently constituted in this country, should certainly be able freely to advance its interests and achieve its corporate goals without, as it were, undue tinkering by government agencies, irresponsible litigation by the legal establishment or the existential dread contingent upon the threat of being excluded from the corporate realm wherein one exercises one's talents to, so as to say, bring home the bacon! And yet, we must never forget, we operate in a world that is by no means solipsist; and our sought-after freedom is, in itself, contingent upon accountability. As Kierkegaard might have put it, had that gloomy Dane's life taken a different route, purity of heart in business means to accept one thing: that we do not work for ourselves, but strive only for the shareholder and will, of a surety, be called upon to give an account of our actions; and we shall, on that day, be judged by the main board and if we are found wanting we shall be cast out.

Gavin Clooney, *Corporate Governance*, 1992

Day

thursday 25th nov. 06:25

basement flat, 77 keeble street, victoria, london

HUGH PUT THE PLUG IN PLACE and filled the basin with hot water. As he washed, Celia drifted into the bathroom and started the shower.

'What time did you get back?' she mumbled, slipping off her robe and stepping under the hot water.

'Two-thirty, something like that. We were finishing next week's show. A rush job.'

'No Crawford biog yet, then?'

'We're getting there, but Angela wanted to do something on Internet share buying. It's fascinating, changing the whole shape of the Stock Market. Overnight millionaires . . .'

'Yeah, and wasn't that guy who went crazy and shot a load of people in America some kind of private trader?'

Hugh worked the flannel into his ears and had a memory flash of his mother holding him at the basin doing exactly the same. He shuddered. 'People lose as well as win. I was just wondering if amateur trading might make any difference in the Crawford business?'

'Perhaps,' her voice came from clouds of steam and water behind the semi-transparent shower curtain. 'You know Beth Stewart is probably going onto the Channel 4 share show to see if she can do any good, whip up any support for Parker.'

'Will she?'

There was a pause, then the shower was turned off and a

deliciously pink Celia appeared, like Venus from the waves. 'Oh, I think Beth Stewart is in a totally different game nowadays. And no, she won't make a lot of difference, not if Crawford is determined to keep pushing ahead.' She wrapped a towel into a turban round her hair, keeping it up in the way that only women know; then she slipped another towel round herself and went through to the bedroom.

After cleaning his teeth and shaving, Hugh followed. Celia had already done her make-up and was pulling her skirt up. She'd never been one to hang around. 'What are your plans for today – are we going to meet up later?' she asked.

'I don't know, I'm going down to Reading.'

'Oh, really? This is Crawford stuff?' Her fingers paused on the hooks of her waistband, her interest piqued.

'Yeah, this guy Burton, who knew Crawford in the old days, he called back, invited me down, so I figured, why not, let's give it a go.'

'Why not indeed.' The hooks engaged, she brushed the material flat over hips and thighs and took a blouse from its hanger. 'I must say, Crawford has been rather odd the last couple of days. I think something happened.'

'Something happened? What does that mean – anything – nothing?'

'He's caught up in a way I've never seen before. It's probably nothing. Anyhow, I'd better be moving; Owen Powys is seeing the old pirate today so he'll probably want to talk it over. They're rushing out a final offer document. Give me a call if you're going to be late.'

'I might stay over. Depends how much there is down there.'

'OK. Well, have fun and be a good boy, or don't!'

She kissed him and hurried through to the hall where she grabbed her coat, then paused and came back through to the bedroom door. 'Like he felt bad about something. That's what it is – like he regretted something, and I don't think Jim Crawford ever regretted doing anything in his whole life.'

232

Hugh looked up at her and rested his right leg on his left knee, his shorts dangling from a toe. 'Maybe I'll find out,' he said.

Waymouth, Paternoster, City of London, 11:00

'Well, Owen, how's it coming?'

'We're getting it together, Jim, we've been at it all night.'

'I thought you were looking a tad less smooth.'

'Only a tad, though. And I'm still not totally convinced about the size of the new offer.'

Crawford returned to his chair regretting that Powys was obviously too busy to think of offering him coffee. He needed something to clear away a feeling of – as he characterised it to himself – moral indigestion he hadn't quite been able to get rid of since the evening he'd spent with John Parker. Not that he felt guilty – they were all playing at the big table and, as Andrea had said once, if the game *was* rigged, at least it was rigged for everyone. No, it was more a feeling that the event hadn't quite lived up to the publicity.

'You don't think we should be offering so much cash on top of the share exchange?'

'I think you might get it for less. The way their shares are moving . . . I think some of those amateur investors are being pointed towards a potential profit. It only takes a snowball to start an avalanche.'

'Did you make that up, Owen, or is it investment banker's law?'

'I made it up. But you know what I mean: Ayot can gain control with anything between 90 and, theoretically, 45 per cent of the equity. Once the shareholders see the way the ground is shifting, they're going to be shit-scared they'll be too late to sign and send off the acceptance form and that you won't need to buy their shares. The more the balance tips towards Ayot, the faster the rush to sell. A self-fulfilling prophecy.'

'I see all that,' Crawford said. 'But I'm also aware that the market is volatile right now and that you can't predict exactly how they'll jump. Years ago, when I was a salesman, my motto was: Go one step further than the next fellow to make sure of closing the sale. That's what I'm doing here. It's no loss, after all.'

'Well, it is a loss, Jim. If you pay more than you have to – it's cash you could be using for something else.'

'I don't want something else, Owen. I want Byfield and I want it fast.'

Powys said: 'Do you think you might level with me?'

'Call it instinct.' Crawford smiled. 'And let's go with the new offer. I want it out by Monday 29 November and I want the minimum time to unconditional acceptance.'

Powys checked his diary. 'Fourteen days. Which would make it 13 December.'

'Then I'll order the food and the champagne for that evening. At Butler's Wharf, eight sharp. I'll expect you there.'

'Sometimes, Jim,' Powys got to his feet and opened the door for Crawford, 'your confidence overawes even me. I just hope it isn't over-confidence.'

'Don't ever hope, Owen. Make sure. That's why I pay you. Now, can you see me out of this fortress?'

Riverside Town Housing Development,
Maidenhead, Berks., 12:30

The site was a river of mud with grimy white concrete foundations standing clear, some of them already with three or four courses of bricks in place. John Parker stood by the gate, under the large sign showing how the development would look next year when it was finished. And, he had to admit, it looked good – the houses were small, but then houses were nowadays and the river wasn't exactly alongside. It wasn't much of a river either – but it was there and once the ground was decently landscaped, Riverside would be a pleasant place to live, with two-, three- and four-bedroomed houses for young professional people moving into family life. Or so the brochure said. And he might as well take that for gospel since he almost certainly wouldn't be around when the development was formally opened.

He trudged through the gate and onto the site. There was a pervasive smell of drains – work was being carried out on the main sewer, so perhaps that was it; or perhaps there was no smell and he was in the grip of an olfactory hallucination.

Only it wasn't hallucination he had to fear, it was obsession. He had little coherent memory of that night – there were flashes, moments that kept coming back to him: the faces above the roulette table; that stairwell and the man reaching out to grab him. Later he'd checked; there was no bruising on his neck and he had to wonder, did it even happen? Did they really go to Soho and see that boy . . . Kevin . . . whose face had haunted the edges of his consciousness ever since?

And after – he'd woken to a dull pounding head, in an alley, where there were only the closed back doors of clubs and restaurants. He'd stumbled into a bin full of swill, which had soaked his trousers. And he'd walked, he could remember that, and somehow found a minicab. He knew he'd paid some huge amount to get back to the office at Goldhawk Mews, where Adele Macdonald had been about to leave after delivering the wages to her team of cleaners.

She'd looked at him and, with huge generosity, had said nothing; just taken him into the building, got him to the wash-room where she'd helped clean him up, then helped him upstairs to his office where she'd put him to sleep on the couch. When he'd woken at seven the next morning, his suit was on a hanger, cleaned and pressed. There was a new shirt, still in its packing. He didn't know how she'd done it and when he'd called, later in the day, she'd said no more than that old friends help each other out and had he called his wife to reassure her.

He *had* called Heather, first thing; her response had been cold and distant, his explanation perfunctory. Neither seemed to have the energy left to care.

'Mr Parker, how you doing?'

A man of Parker's age, wearing a donkey jacket, thick trousers and boots with the socks turned over the top, his face weathered and lined, came stomping across the water-filled tracks that had sunk deep into the mud. He stuck out a hand and Parker shook it.

'Billy, hello there. It's been a long time!'

'Must be near 15 years since you've been on a site, Sir.' Billy Griffin was of the old school of navvy – he gave respect and expected it from his bosses. He'd started out as a labourer and was now site manager. He and Parker had known each other since the building firm had been brought into the original company. Back then, Parker had often found time to visit the sites and Billy had always made him welcome. Now he too would be part of John Parker's past.

'Going up well,' he said, indicating the brickies and their hod carriers at work along the scaffolding.

'Well enough. It's a good little site, should go like a dream. In the office, they tell me we've sold three-quarters off the plan. They'll probably change hands again, most of them, before we're finished.'

Parker felt a stab of fury. It was a good firm, they did their job and delivered; it didn't deserve to be sold to someone like Crawford.

'Just thought I'd stop by, Billy. In case you've seen anything in the papers . . .'

'I've seen some stuff, that's for sure. And Tim Ericson gave me a call. Said I'd be all right; whatever happened, the building side would carry on.'

Tim was another old-timer from the building days who still enjoyed being on site and getting mud on his shoes. 'He's right, Billy. You'll be fine.'

'And what about you, Sir?'

Parker shrugged. 'Probably about time I retired, anyway.'

'We're the same age,' Billy laughed. 'I tell you what, you ever need a job, come and see me. Big chap like you, be a natural as a hod carrier . . .'

Parker looked at a young man carrying his hod full of bricks straight up a ladder and along a horrifically narrow plank without missing a step.

He shook his head. 'Somehow, Billy, I don't think so.'

Crawford House, Euston Road, London, 14:00

G123: Notice of increase in nominal capital. To the Registrar of Companies. Ayot plc gives notice in accordance with section 123 of the above Act . . .

'Come in.' Mark Chima pushed the form to one side and stood up as Diane Ellroy entered his office. She seemed slightly flushed – something Mark had never noticed before. 'Are you . . .' He stopped himself – what the hell was he going to say: why are you flushed? Please!

Diane took a chair and sat down facing him across the desk. She laid a folder next to the companies form he'd been working on.

'You wanted these, Mark?'

'No hurry, that's fine.' He put the figures to one side but Diane didn't get up and leave. She leaned further across the desk, giving him an unnerving view of her breasts (you wanted *these*, Mark?) and said, 'I'm seeing Gavin Clooney tonight. I called this morning and he suggested Mitsukoshi, so we're meeting at eight. I'd like you to be there.'

So that was it – she was flushed by the first steps in actually betraying Crawford; or was it by asking him to dinner? By rights, he should have asked her, but this would allow him two bites at the cherry. Two bites at Diane! Too much.

'That's great. Uh, what made you actually . . . well . . .'

'There's no reason why I shouldn't consult a non-exec; that's what they're there for, Mark.'

'Even when it's about planning a boardroom coup?'

'Is that what we're doing?'

Mark reached down to the bottom drawer of his desk and pulled out a copy of form 288b, resignation of director or company secretary. He gave it to Diane.

'If it goes wrong, he won't show us any mercy.'

'Come on, Mark, he's a fighter, he expects others to fight *him*. Besides, look what they're saying about this final offer.'

Mark, like everyone else, had seen the document.

'It's over the top?'

'Yeah. This seems to have become some sort of personal crusade without a Jerusalem.'

'Sorry?'

'The game isn't worth the candle, Mark. It is not serving the shareholders or the long-term development of the company and . . . and hell, he should move on, we all know that. If he stays, we'll find ourselves involved in more and more adventures and sooner or later one of them will go pear-shaped. Then *we* will be filling out these things . . .' she pushed the form back across the table, 'for real. Are you going to come along or not, Mark. In or out?'

There was no real question. 'Oh, absolutely, Diane. In.'

She breathed a sigh of relief. 'Great. I always felt we had a lot in common, Mark, but I didn't want to take anything for granted. I know you've got a family.'

Manjit, the kids . . . yes, he had a family but set against Diane . . . and what did that mean, 'set against Diane'?

'I'm just the Company Secretary, I take the minutes,' he joked. She said: 'That won't make any difference if Crawford gets a glimmer of what we're doing. He likes a fighter – but he also believes in first-strike response.'

'We're not talking about stopping the takeover, are we?'

'Unless Byfield have got something pretty spectacular to pull out of their pockets – I don't think so. Besides, for all the overbidding, we might as well get hold of them now. It'll be useful in the long run and strengthen our core business. No, it's not today I'm worried about – it's tomorrow. I'll meet you at the restaurant at ten to eight. You know where it is?'

'I can find it.'

The Old Forge, Pangbourne, Berks., 14:45

As he had told Beth Stewart, Hugh Mead wasn't a lover of the countryside at the best of times – and a bleak, rainy day in November was far from that; even in the car, with the heater turned up and Vivaldi blasting out of the speakers, he felt himself shivering at the sight of the soggy countryside, the bare trees and the grasses beaten down along the hedgerows by the wind. Not that they didn't have winds in the city, or rain or grey skies but somehow there was always somewhere you could escape to for a drink or a movie.

Still, he wasn't here for fun but for work; and he'd spent the morning going through the microfiche archives of the *Reading Argus* for the years Crawford had been prominent in the town. It had been pernickety, exasperating work and he'd never been that good with machines but in the end, his patience had been rewarded.

He noticed the signpost, half hidden by the overhanging hedge, and pulled off the Pangbourne–Oxford road onto a winding lane, which took him away from the town, down toward the Thames, which wound through the water meadows at the bottom of the valley. Here, yet another sign, more dilapidated, covered with lichen, directed him along a rutted track towards the Old Forge; which proved to be a stone cottage with outbuildings on the bank of the river.

An elderly man in moleskin trousers – from the first time they were fashionable, Hugh thought – a baggy grey sweater over a shirt and a flat cap perched incongruously on his head, came out to meet him. He waved a stick at the corner of the yard which seemed marginally less boggy than the rest and Hugh pulled over.

'You won't sink in there,' the old guy said. 'At least, not much.'

Hugh looked down at the spongy turf under his feet. 'What do you do when it floods?'

'Swim! Harry Burton.' He stuck out his hand.

'Hugh Mead, Harry. Glad to meet you.'

'I've heard some of your stuff, Hugh, and read a couple of your pieces. Being interested in Jim Crawford. Not bad.' He winked. 'Not bad – that tasty little director girl you interviewed. Wouldn't have refused that job. Come on through.'

Hugh followed Burton into the cottage, where a log fire was blazing. The place was furnished with large comfortable arm-chairs and wooden bookshelves, floor to ceiling, stuffed almost beyond capacity with a bewildering array of titles. Hugh would have been hard put to say what Burton wasn't interested in, from the few he caught sight of; and what spaces there were, in the hall, up the stairs as far as he could see or in the sitting-room or kitchen were covered with framed front pages from the *Argus*.

'Hardly anyone ever comes,' Burton said, noticing Hugh's interest. 'It's vanity but harmless vanity. See there.' He pointed at a yellowed sheet with the headline: 'Home from Spain: Berkshire Volunteers return from Spanish War'. 'The week I joined the paper as a copy boy. Fifteen years old.'

'And you were there . . .'

'Apart from the war, I went right through. Could have shifted, I had offers. The *Express* wanted me but somehow I couldn't leave the old place. No ambition, I suppose. Today they'd throw you out for that.' He filled a pipe. 'In my day it was different.'

'You were still reporters, wherever you worked. That doesn't change.'

'You don't think so?' Burton lowered himself into a chair beside the fire. 'I feel the cold – sit back if it's too hot for you.'

'No, it's fine, Harry. I feel the cold too. You mind if I record this?' He produced a BBC digital recorder. Burton held out a hand and looked at it.

'Nifty piece of stuff, Hugh. Saves using shorthand – though I don't suppose you youngsters . . .'

'I know it, don't use it much but I can if I have to.' Hugh knew his man – this immediately won Harry Burton over; he could recognise Hugh Mead as a fellow hack. Fortunately he wasn't able to recognise him as an opportunistic liar. Hugh breathed a sigh of relief and flipped on the recorder. There was hardly any need to remind Harry of the rules. 'Jim Crawford, Harry. Tell me about him.'

And Harry did. It was pretty much the standard biography. Poor boy made good, good boy made better. Gifts to the town, even after he'd left; the occasional visit still, opening the gym at his old school. Otherwise a non-stop ascent. And not worth driving down the M4 to hear.

Burton had finished a couple of pipefuls before he finished the story and the mantle clock – Presented to Harry Burton, King of the Hacks by the Boys in the Composing Room – had ticked its way to four forty-five.

'Well, that's it, Hugh. You know as much as I do.'

Hugh decided to take a chance. After all, what did he have to lose? 'Bullshit, Harry. I don't think I know any of the *interesting* things you know. You've given me the official biography, that's all.'

Burton shrugged.

'Come on – I spent the morning at the *Argus*. I read a lot of your stuff. You were better than this. Crawford's more interesting than this. What about his mother – or his father?'

'In my day, Hugh, we didn't always print it all – not in a town like this. People had a right to their privacy, to their tragedies, if you like. It wasn't the fashion then to spread it all over the front page.'

'That was then and this is now, Harry. Look at the clock – King of the Hacks. That's a hell of a title to be proud of – not King of the PR Men.'

'Maybe some things are best left buried, Hugh.'

'Only in novels by Stephen King – and if you ever read him, Harry, you'll find that those things best left buried don't generally stay that way. They claw themselves out of the ground and come looking for you!'

Harry Burton laughed. And thought about it for a moment. And finally said: 'Let's get a drink. My local's just along the old river path. If you don't mind getting those smart shoes a bit muddy, we could wander along for a pint or two.'

If this was the price of the story, Hugh was happy to sacrifice his shoes – a true hack, he thought. 'Fine by me, Harry. Let's go.'

'Just along the old river path' was a claim about as accurate as Hugh's shorthand skills. The path was stony and uneven and damned slippery; the river was high and rushing; the plants on the verge were wet and clingy; and after about 20 minutes following along behind Harry Burton – who seemed in his element, stepping out with the energy of a man less than half his age; in fact, with considerably more energy than Hugh was able to summon up – the bottoms of Hugh's trousers were sopping, he bore a handful of nettle stings and a vicious piece of blackthorn had swiped him painfully round the ear.

For the first stretch, Hugh had tried to keep some kind of conversation going but as his breath got shorter, so the roar of the river got louder and when at last the white pebbledash of the pub came into sight, Hugh was able to make out a ragged line of white foam stretching away across the flat darkness of the water. There was a mossy, coppery smell and the sound of the screech-owl – something Hugh hadn't heard since he was a child. The ground beneath his feet became paved and Hugh saw they were walking alongside a lock. The roaring was coming from the weir, on the other side of the small island which housed the lock-keeper's cottage. Burton stopped and leaned on the lock railings.

'They don't let anyone through after dark at this time of the year.'

'Oh.' Hugh could hardly hear him above the rushing of the water and besides, could think of nothing else to say; he just wanted to get inside.

Harry Burton had other things on his mind. He pointed over

the island, to the weir itself, which dog-legged across to the far bank. Above the falling water there was a fragile wooden bridge raised up on stilts.

'That's where it happened,' he shouted.

'What?'

'Jim Crawford's brother. That's where he drowned.'

The pub was full: estate agents, shop-keepers, the kind of people who lived in the country; Hugh wasn't interested. After buying a couple of pints, he grabbed Burton, sat him down and said: 'His younger brother?'

'They used to come from the town and play here,' the old reporter said. 'It was easier then. Fewer fences, you know. It wasn't all keep-out signs and anyway kids, you know kids. Timothy, Tim Crawford. It wasn't much of a story. I wrote it up. I was covering the district then.'

'I didn't see anything on the microfiche.'

'Were you looking that far back? This is the fifties.'

'No, no, I wasn't. What happened?'

'The same thing that always happens, Hugh. Children playing, one falls in, the other can't swim – stands there watching. I didn't make much of it. It was a picnic, see. The mother had brought them. And she was . . . I talked to people on the estate. She was a drinker. Single mother. That wasn't common back then. It was tough for them. It was going to be even tougher. I didn't see any reason to make a big story of it. Maybe that was being a bad reporter – if so, I can live with it.'

'Did you speak to the boy or the mother?'

'The boy was in shock. They didn't call it shock then and they didn't have counsellors to help you get over it. It happened . . .' He took a good draught of his beer, wiped foam from his lip and sat for a few moments, staring down at the tabletop, obviously seeing it all again.

'You see, I thought of the boy, the one who didn't die, going back to live with a mother who was an alcoholic, who would be crippled by guilt that she had let her youngest child die.

I couldn't help thinking of them, shut up together in that flat with the ghost and the guilt and the anger and . . . God knows what happened or how Jim Crawford survived the next few years. His mother didn't. I kept an eye on the family. She was in and out of the local asylum; there were rumours at the boy's school of . . . things that had been done to him. Burns . . . other things. It was the fifties, Hugh. Things were different then.'

He took another drink, finishing the pint.

'Years later, I did a story about this young fellow who had started his own business: Meat-To-Please-You, and I found it was the same boy and he seemed OK, then. Another one?'

Hugh was driving; he knew he shouldn't but he couldn't stop Burton now. 'Yes, thanks.' He would have bought them himself but he knew the old man's pride needed to buy in return.

'I got to know him,' Burton said when he'd put the two full glasses down, 'over the next few years we met up at functions and I interviewed him on two or three occasions. And, you see, the thing is, he lied. All the time. He lied about things that I knew were not the case. And I never said anything, not to him, not in the paper. Oh, they weren't big lies, not about things that mattered; always small. I don't know why he did it and it never seemed to matter beside the rest. That need to succeed . . . whatever the cost. That utter determination that no one, no one would ever get the better of him.'

'Did you ever . . . about the drowning, did you . . .'

'No. What good would that have done, Hugh? Can you tell me that?'

'I can't, Harry. Will you excuse me . . . I need the lav.'

In the toilet he called Celia's mobile and left the message that he wouldn't be home until tomorrow. With what he'd learned this afternoon at the *Argus* archives, he had the feeling it was going to be a long and boozy night.

The Weir

Mitsukoshi, Regent Street, London, 20:20

Gavin Clooney's expertise with chopsticks was, Mark thought, like something out of *The Matrix*. No one could move that fast, that dextrously and yet talk at so measured a pace.

'Years of practice, I might say,' he said, 'and greed. Since freshness is all . . .' he gathered a piece of toro and leek and popped it in. 'Delicious. And good for you too. Diane, try the yellowtail.'

'Thank you.' Diane was good but not as good as Clooney. She was, however, a good deal more desirable, in a metallic black top which swooped down over her chest and, Mark would have sworn, outlined her nipples – he would have sworn but dared not look again. Which meant, of course, that every other view in the restaurant was giving him acute neck ache. How could she do it to him – unless it was Gavin Clooney; but if her interest had been directed at the non-exec, her smiles had been all for Mark. He had a feeling, both intensely wonderful and frightening, that something would happen tonight and that after it, nothing would be the same; though whether it would be his future or the future of Ayot that was changed, he didn't know.

'What you should be aware of, Diane, Mark . . .' Clooney was saying, 'is that my position as a non-executive director, indeed the ideal position of someone like myself, is, in a sense, exactly that: ideal. It does not exist in the real world, so the best we can do is an approximation. In a sense one might be seen as an officer of the company, not necessarily *de facto* but *ab* . . .'

'Gavin, I didn't do Greek . . .' Diane said.

'Latin.'

'Whatever.'

'I can't both be a decision-maker and a monitor of those decisions, if you take my point.'

Mark and Diane both nodded.

'I have always seen myself as an adviser, a neutral voice, as much as possible providing an overview *for* the whole board – *of* the whole board and its decisions. It goes without saying that we, all of us on the board, should monitor our actions . . .'

'Gavin, what do you think about the way Jim Crawford is running things?'

'It isn't that simple, Diane.'

'I was afraid it might not be,' she said. Mark concentrated on picking up a turbot sashimi without disgracing himself. He was, for all the difficulty with the chopsticks, finding the food quite interesting – some of the time.

'What I mean,' Clooney went on, 'is that it is more a matter of asking: How does the CEO's method of running the company allow us as executive and non-executive directors to see and judge him. Carlyle once wrote, I believe in *Frederick the Great*, that in every object – or indeed subject – there is inexhaustible meaning; the eye sees in it, what the eye brings means of seeing. Thus, the significance lies in the eye of the beholder. When you have a powerful CEO with complacent shareholders, it tends to become difficult to be, in any way, effective as a creative critic. *Salus populi suprema est lex.* Sorry, Diane. Cicero. The good of the people, the shareholding people, we might say, is the highest law and not the ambition of tyrants. That latter sentiment is not, of course, Cicero.'

No,' said Diane.

'Absolutely,' Mark agreed, not quite sure what was the most extraordinary thing about this evening: the sushi, the discourse or Diane. He supposed that even asking the question must say something about something. He took a deep breath. 'Dr Clooney, do you think it is in the best interest of those shareholders that Mr Crawford should remain as CEO of Ayot?'

Diane swivelled towards him and mouthed: Well done!

Clooney sucked his teeth, put his hands behind his head and stretched.

'Behind anything which *is* anything – then there *is*, surely nothing. To put it another way . . .'

'Yes, please do,' from Diane.

'Behind any speech which is good for anything, there lies a silence that is better. Silence is as deep as eternity; speech as shallow as time. And yet, having thought in silence, we must deliver up . . .'

Diane said, 'Shit or get off the pot, right, Professor?'

Clooney grinned. 'Absolutely, my dear. In which case: Yes.'

It took Diane and Mark a few moments to disentangle the meaning from Clooney's verbosity.

'You think he should go?' Diane asked.

'My advice is that the board should decide. But also that they should be properly briefed in the matter.'

'Allbury won't do it,' Mark said.

'Allbury may have no choice,' Clooney said. 'If there is one single aspect of the problem that we might pull out and say: There, there it lies, then it would be the relationship – the dynamic – between the CEO and the Chairman. Now, normally, if a chairman were ineffective and, for whatever reason, could not be removed, I would advise that one of the non-executive directors was given, as it were, a senior position. I don't feel that would be appropriate here. As you put it so charmingly, Diane: Mr Allbury is going to have to shit or get off the pot. I think he will choose the former . . .'

'He'll vote against Crawford and stay on the board?'

'For the time being, Mark. To lose a CEO may be seen as necessary, to lose a CEO *and* a Chairman would certainly be careless. *Festina lente*, eh?'

'Hasten slowly,' Mark said.

'But hasten?' Diane said.

'Oh, yes.' Clooney said. 'And now, let us give our attention to the food and we can start to untangle other things later.'

The rest of the meal slipped by like a sliver of sashimi swallowed with hot sake and by half past ten Mark and Diane were standing on Park Lane watching Clooney's taxi slip into the stream of traffic.

'Well,' Diane said. 'That was interesting.'

'Yes,' Mark said. 'Shall I call you a taxi?' Hating himself for chickening out but he just couldn't . . . could he? Things like that only happened in dreams and he was not, never had been, a dreamer.

'Why don't you do that, Mark.' Her voice was neutral; he stuck his hand up and, dammit, a taxi arrived almost at once. He opened the back, she climbed in, turned towards him; he said: 'It's been a great night;' she said: 'Do you want to come back with me?' and he, knowing exactly what would happen if he did, said: 'Yes.'

Day +25

friday 26th nov.
four phone calls

celia hart to beth stewart 11:10

STEWART: Hello?

HART: Beth, how's tricks?

STEWART: Well . . . you know. Busy . . . and, uh . . . busy.

HART: That's the way we like it, right?

STEWART: Yes. I, uh . . . what can, can I do something for you, Celia?

HART: Not really for me, Beth. I was with Jim Crawford yesterday. One of his lunches. Gavroche. That's one thing I have to say about the man; there's nothing cheap about him at all. I think you'll find that quite liberating once you're on board.

STEWART: To be honest, I'm finding it a bit . . . I don't need to burden you with this stuff.

HART: No, that's fine. We'll have a lot of time to get to know . . . to think about the future and . . . Once this is over.

STEWART: So . . . we're approaching that kind of time. I mean . . . you'll be responding to our . . . to the . . .

HART: Monday, Beth. The final offer. It'll be on the table then. And I have to tell you, it's a good offer. It's a very good offer and . . . your shareholders . . . your fund managers, it's a lay-up, they'll want to take it and so will your private shareholders. There's going to be . . .

STEWART: So you're saying, that's it, from Monday?

HART: They'll have to vote but there isn't going to be a lot of time. Monday 13 December, that'll be the final . . . the last day for fulfilment of the offer conditions and you . . . well, if you don't know, I can tell you it'll go like . . . faster and faster as everyone wants to get on board.

STEWART: You're sure of that . . . obviously you are. I can see, once you were going to come back with a final offer then, yeah, it was . . . all over.

HART: Jim wants you to make that very clear, Beth. To John Parker.

STEWART: Bryan House is . . . is . . . he'll be there and . . .

HART: He wants you to do it, Beth. He wants you to be in charge of the acquisition from your end and you'll be working with whoever you designate from Byfield – short-term, since most of them . . . you know most of them will have to go.

STEWART: I think that was going to happen anyway. Once this started, win or lose, we were going to have to change.

HART: And succession . . . Is your non-exec on top of that?

STEWART: I don't know what's in his mind, not for sure but . . .

HART: I think you'll find that you'll have an important place in whatever he's thinking. What about John Parker?

STEWART: I don't know, Celia. Sometimes he seems like he's going with it, other times he wants to fight to the last man . . . the last shareholder.

HART: It isn't going to work, though, is it?

STEWART: No, no, it isn't.

HART: That's your first job, Beth. You have to tell him so, make him see it. Then we can go forward . . . Byfield and Ayot . . . and do some really exciting stuff. Yeah?

End

owen powys to nik speller 12:20

SPELLER: Owen, old man. Nice to hear from you. Been keeping you up nights, has all this?

POWYS: We eat work over here, Nik. But yes, we've been busy. How about you?

250

The Weir

SPELLER: We try to keep our hands in.

POWYS: Good defence, I thought.

SPELLER: Thank you.

POWYS: Though it was piss-weak in the end.

SPELLER: You know, I am surprised that your man – and I assume that you're calling because there will be a final offer?

POWYS: It'll be with you on Monday.

SPELLER: I would have thought that he might . . . well, have put this one down?

POWYS: No chance. And when you see the offer . . . it is a very good offer.

SPELLER: Obviously I can't comment without . . .

POWYS: I just wanted a word . . . your man House will be looking at the succession on the board?

SPELLER: You might assume that to be the case, Owen.

POWYS: We like your Miss Stewart.

SPELLER: Everybody likes Miss Stewart. Bobbi King thinks she walks on water.

POWYS: Good. That's good. Tim Ericson is a good hands-on manager for the switch over but . . .

SPELLER: You'll obviously be looking at Tom Swift at R and D. Possibly Howerd but otherwise . . . the CEO?

POWYS: He's history! Bryan House – we like him as a non-exec.

SPELLER: Aren't you quite well set up with, uh . . . those fellows?

POWYS: Jim Crawford is thinking about a change.

SPELLER: Aren't we all?

POWYS: Yeah.

End

gavin clooney to peter allbury 14:15

CLOONEY: Peter . . . Peter . . . I, uh, thought I'd give you . . . if you've a moment? Not that I want to disturb the Chairman in his . . . time off.

ALLBURY: I was feeding the pig, Gavin.

CLOONEY: Of course, charming little . . . now don't tell me . . . kune kune . . . New Zealand, if I'm not mistaken? Fascinating place. So many climate changes – good wine too. Better than the Aussies, I think.

ALLBURY: Was there something, Gavin?

CLOONEY: There generally is, don't you find? I was wondering, Peter, if we might . . . if you would care to join me for dinner one night soon. Soonish.

ALLBURY: It's very nice of you, Gavin but I am rather . . . with Christmas coming up and . . .

CLOONEY: Because there are one or two things I should like to chat over . . .

ALLBURY: . . . it is busy and perhaps after the new year?

CLOONEY: I think, perhaps, if you'll forgive me for so saying, *not* after the new year. Rather sooner. Yes?

ALLBURY: Does anyone . . . Will anyone else be there?

CLOONEY: Thought I might sound you out, Peter. Just between friends, eh? The two of us, a little wine . . . half-decent game pie? Rules, perhaps. They do a nice line in game, don't they?

ALLBURY: Gavin, is this . . . should I be thinking about . . .

CLOONEY: No, no, no, no, my dear old thing. Your advice is what I want, so as to say – and perhaps we might go on from there? *Experto credite*, eh?

End

hugh mead to george packenham 17:00

PACKENHAM: Yeah, hello?

MEAD: George, Hugh Mead.

PACKENHAM: Oh, yeah. Hi!

MEAD: When we met at the Oxo Tower the other day – you were saying something about Westminster?

PACKENHAM: Was I?

MEAD: Yeah, George, you were.

PACKENHAM: Yes . . . I guess I was. If I remember . . . the FO.

MEAD: Do you remember . . . before the election . . .

PACKENHAM: Does anybody in this brave new world?

MEAD: One of the appropriations committees? Crossly, Patrick Crossly, he was chairman – then after the election . . .

PACKENHAM: I remember it. Something to do with Indonesia. Systems, some kind of systems.

MEAD: Would it be possible to find out if the deal is still going through?

PACKENHAM: What's on your mind, Hugh?

MEAD: Maybe something, maybe nothing, George. Perhaps you could check that out for me and I'll call you back whenever?

PACKENHAM: I'll see what I can do. Call me tomorrow evening.

End

Day (+28)

monday 29th nov.

Increased and Final * Offer

by

Weymouth, Paternoster

on behalf of

Ayot plc

for

Byfield plc

Acceptances should be dispatched as soon as possible, and in any event so as to be received no later than Monday 13 December. The procedure for acceptance is detailed on pages 29–32.

*Weymouth, Paternoster reserve the rights to increase or otherwise amend the increased offer should a competitive situation arise or should the panel so agree.

Ayot

To Byfield shareholders

Dear Shareholder,

In our original Offer Document we showed the success of Ayot under its management team, demonstrated the poor performance of Byfield and laid out the benefits that will arise from the combination of Ayot and Byfield.

We can now show that the so-called change in management outlook claimed by Byfield in response is totally false, as are the extravagant claims concerning their research and development department. In addition, the thoroughly mediocre Stock Market performance and the extravagant remuneration paid to Chairman John Parker cannot be overemphasised.

Byfield have tried to deflect attention from their poor corporate governance and their equally poor record of generating value for all their shareholders by alleging our bid lacks industrial logic. Later in this document we deal with this argument and demonstrate its implausibility.

I believe you have a clear choice:
- accept Ayot's increased Offer at a premium of 45 per cent to Byfield's pre-bid share price and participate in the future success of the combined group or realise your investment in Byfield for cash at a 40 per cent premium.
- or hope that Byfield will manage somehow to live up to the extravagant promises they have made since the bid.

I urge you to accept the increased offer.

Yours faithfully,

Peter J. Allbury,
Chairman.

Byfield plc, Goldhawk Mews, London, 13:00
Present at what was, effectively, the last Byfield board meeting of
the campaign was the whole board. John Parker sat at the head of
the table – he appeared to be vague, preoccupied with something
else, only occasionally shaking his head and returning his attention to the matters in hand. Bill Harper was pale-faced and tired –
they all were – but Harper seemed tired beyond tiredness, as if the
worst that can happen has happened so there is no point in
talking about it any more. Tim Ericson was tense, picking at the
skin on the edges of his thumbs until he drew blood. Howerd and
Swift were more relaxed, they could both contemplate a future
either in or out of the company. Dick Worthington was . . . Dick
Worthington. Bryan House was turning the pages of the Ayot
final offer and grunting to himself approvingly. Beth Stewart was
wondering if there was any way she could get out of saying what
had to be said. She caught House's eye and he shrugged expres-
sively down at the document.

'It's a very good deal for our shareholders, and that's a fact,' he
said. 'Almost too good a deal. Can't really understand what
Crawford is up to.'

'Paying over the odds?' Harper croaked. 'It's . . . I thought we
might have headed him off with the sales, I really did.'

House's raised eyebrows said: Then you're a fool. What
actually came out was: 'If there's anything I've learned in
business, it's that no one really knows.'

Tom Swift had been making notes. 'Well, it won't make much
difference to most of us, since our share participation is actually
pretty feeble.'

Parker winced in his chair, but he could not deny it. 'It's a bit
late for all that now,' he said. 'Bryan, what about our fund
managers? How do you feel they'll go on this?'

Beth couldn't believe her ears. The question was pointless; it
was obvious how they'd vote, they had no reasonable choice.

'What can I say, John? Most of the fund people take the view
that management is not their business.'

'But surely,' Bill Harper said, 'they'll want to play a part.'

'Some do, some don't. In fact, looking back, I would say that the Byfield attitude has been to discourage, as much as it can, the kind of fund management which likes to take a part and get to know the managers who actually run the company. It may be by choice or by chance, but our big investors take the view –'

'You're sure of this?' Tim Ericson put in.

'I'm sure – it's my job to be sure, Mr Ericson. They take the view that their responsibility is to their clients and that does not include solving management cock-ups.'

Beth realised he was using the term on purpose, to drive home to everyone the finality of their position.

'They would rather sell than meddle, I think.'

'But there aren't any great problems,' Harper said, 'nothing that can't be solved given a little good will and the backing of our customers. Can't they see that?'

House's answer was quiet and deadly. 'No.'

Dick Worthington chose the ensuing silence to make his final contribution. 'John, Mr Chairman, I think right now we're all looking to you for leadership here. When the herd is stampeding and the river is rising and the cowboys are in a panic, then I guess it's time for the man in the white hat to get up on his . . .'

And Beth did something she'd wanted to do for months. She said: 'Dick, please be quiet.'

He shut his mouth with an audible slap.

'What about the banks?' Parker asked. 'I know Nik will stay with us – we have a long relationship with Lightoller's – old Sir Giles and I . . .' he tailed off for a moment, then gathered himself. 'Together with the bank and venture capitalists we could still put up a decent fight.'

A silence, and Beth cleared her throat. 'I'm sorry, John, but that won't happen. I talked with Nik this morning.'

Bryan House nodded but said nothing to help her.

'There isn't going to be any fight-back. Not from him, not from the venture capitalists. This game is over.'

Bill Harper shot her a suspicious look: 'You seem to know a lot about it, Beth.'

Now House stepped in. 'Of course she does. It's her job to be in touch, on top of the situation.' The rebuke to Harper was implied but none the less sharp for all that.

Parker said, 'Beth, you're young, you're bright; can't you find any way . . . anyone we could go to? Is there nothing we can do?'

'No, John, there isn't.'

'Beth . . .' It was Tim Ericson. He obviously knew which way the wind was blowing. 'I . . . I mean who . . . you know what I mean, don't you?'

'Yes, I do, Tim. They'll want you to stay on for at least the changeover period.'

Harper looked at her even more suspiciously. 'You do know, don't you?'

'It's been clear, Bill, for quite a while, that this battle has been lost. Ayot have managed to identify a number of weaknesses in our corporate governance.' The calm tone in no way reflected the turmoil she felt inside at what she was doing. 'One of the major shortfalls has been the lack of succession planning. Being on the Byfield board is not a job for life. Some people seem to think it is.'

Angus Howerd whistled through his teeth. 'That's telling us and no mistake, Beth. I think I'll light up, and don't bother to tell me not to; I have a feeling my job prospects are not, in the long-, the mid- or even short-term, terribly good.' He pulled out his pipe and began to scrape out the bowl onto the final offer document.

Beth had no answer so she fell silent. Tom Swift shot her a look along the table and she nodded. He was all right, he was very much part of the deal, she suspected. Her problem might be inducing him to stay on. 'Tom, perhaps we could have a word later,' she murmured.

'Please, Ms Stewart . . .' The words were torn from Parker, 'at least have the decency to wait until I'm out of the room before issuing your orders.'

'John,' she said, 'it's not like that.'

'Isn't it?' he snapped, then subsided again.

Bill Harper said, 'I imagine the usual process will be followed as far as . . .'

House said, 'It hasn't happened yet. It will happen. It's a process, that's all. Organic growth. Things change, things grow.'

Harper didn't look convinced. Neither did Angus Howerd or Dick Worthington and, Beth could see quite clearly, even Tim Ericson's relief was only skin-deep. He knew that once the merging was done – he was done.

Beth said, 'Yes, the normal conditions will apply. Don't worry on that score.'

'I wasn't,' Tim said. 'On that score.' He sighed and Beth remembered the conversation they'd had in her office and the way it had ended, with her saying: Let's make sure Crawford doesn't get his hands on us.

'I imagine you'll want my resignation?' Parker addressed the question directly to Beth. She felt like Judas.

'That's not really my responsibility, John but, yes, they will want your resignation. When it goes through.'

Howerd had got his pipe alight and from behind the aromatic smoke said, 'How long's that going to be?'

'The closing date for acceptance of Ayot's offer is Monday 13 December.'

'Somehow appropriate, I think,' Howerd said.

'It'll be a done deal before then,' House said. 'And there's a great deal of work to get through, so I suggest we get down to it.'

John Parker looked bleakly along the table, as if his gaze was focused on Antarctica and he knew he had nothing whatever left to do – except to find an angel.

Day (+32)

waymouth, paternoster, city of london

'IF IT WASN'T SO EARLY, I'D DRINK A TOAST,' Chip Carpenter said, raising an invisible glass of champagne to Owen Powys across the table.

Powys returned the salute. 'Thank you, Chip. We seem to have come through all right. Not that there was ever any doubt about it.'

Apart from the latest voting returns the table between them was bare – though it might well have been piled with money since, as both men knew, the bank would be taking a tidy little profit out of this one.

'Doubt, no,' Carpenter said. 'We did have our moments, though. When Jim was reluctant to sell his plant and food companies.'

'No choice in the end, and it tightens up the whole operation. My concern is still the final offer price.'

'Too high,' said Carpenter.

'Too high,' said Powys, 'and that has been reflected in the share price. It isn't moving as freely as it should and that is reflected . . .'

Carpenter took up the litany, 'in the opinion of the City.'

'Yeah. It was an offer too far.'

'Yes . . .' Carpenter's eyes had narrowed, as they always did when he was, as his colleagues said, up to something. 'I bumped into a couple of old friends the other night. At Rules.'

260

'Nice place. Good jugged hare. Not really my scene. Who?'

'Gavin Clooney and Peter Allbury. Very matey they were. It struck me that Allbury had a little more fizz about him than usual. As if the sinew had been stiffened a bit.'

'Did you hear what they were talking about?'

'It was just a few words across the room. When you brought up the City opinion – the behaviour of Ayot's shares . . . putting two and two together and coming up with . . .' He let the words trail away.

Powys tapped his teeth with his Mont Blanc. 'Basically, day to day, Crawford is not good news. Let him go out and start up something or buy something – yeah, fine, but once he gets bored on the board, he's trouble. He needs to be kept busy.'

'I suspect,' Carpenter said, 'that Gavin Clooney would agree with you.'

'I'll have a word with Celia Hart. She knows the Ayot set-up pretty well. See what she thinks, yes?'

'Will she be subtle?'

'She's ambitious. She wants to go to New York. She'll do what she has to.'

'You know that?'

'What I know about Celia Hart you'll never know, Chip. Just believe me, she's one tough babe.'

'Quite. And after all, Jim Crawford has got what he wanted, hasn't he . . . and in the end we must all, must we not, Owen, lose what we value most?'

Butler's Wharf, London, 13:00

The grey walls of the Tower of London looked sombre today; the river was choppy, flecked with spray as the bitter wind and the currents set wave against wave in a ceaseless, pointless struggle. And Jim Crawford smiled as he opened the scrapbook to the page that held the newspaper picture of John Parker in his dinner suit, smirking in victory, surrounded by his Conservative cronies. Perhaps he was reflecting, now that he had lost his company to the man who he had tried to destroy, that what goes around comes around, and that the bitter taste in his mouth, the taste that would not go away day or night, was the taste of defeat.

And yet, the taste of victory, of winning – what point was there once you had it? The ground under your feet was where you stood, the horizon was where you were going. He pushed the cuttings book to one side and got his notebook from the desk drawer but before he could uncap his pen, the phone rang. He put the pen down and answered.

'Yes?'

'It seems you are to be congratulated,' the voice drawled.

'Am I?'

'Word has it that the shareholders have rushed like lemmings over the Crawford cliffs and now lie at your feet.'

'If you mean, have I won, then, yes. Ayot will, on completion day, own Byfield. And Byfield will be in the way of . . .'

'Actually . . . very little. Old chap.'

Crawford's voice was very quiet, very menacing, when he answered. 'Don't bullshit me, don't ever do that.'

'I'm sorry, old chap, I really am.' Perhaps the drawl was a trifle less confident but there was no regret or apology in the voice. 'That's politics. Had I still been on the wretched committee then I might have done something. I wasn't, so I couldn't.'

'Does this mean there will be no contract with Indonesia?'

'Not as far as the electronics business goes. Those buggers on East Timor put the wind up everybody. No calculation for that sort of thing, not really.'

'So could you tell me what good Byfield is going to be if they aren't going to get awarded this fucking contract?' Other than the swear-word, Crawford betrayed no hint of emotion.

'I presume you'll get whatever good your offer doc promised the shareholders. Really, Jim, if you have any complaints, go and see Robin Cook, he's the grand Pooh-Bah now. These things happen. There'll be other places and other times, don't worry.'

The Weir

After a pause, Crawford said, 'I never worry – that's what I make other people do,' and put the phone down before the other could answer.

So, that was that. No Far East deal. Well, it had always been a chance and he'd always been a chancer. No point in whining about what didn't happen. You did what you had to do:

– you watched as the weir swept your brother away, churning round and round, as if he were in a washing-machine; his cries getting weaker, his struggles more feeble until he looked just like empty clothes through the glassy slick of the water:

– you watched your mother's eyes when they told her and you couldn't read what was there; and you tried to make it better, day after week after month after year; you pushed yourself and it didn't make any difference, not after the first two drinks, and she'd usually had those before breakfast. Even so, you worked and one day she wasn't there anymore but you were still working, because that was what you did. And you discovered that by taking chances – by walking along the very edge of the narrow bridge across the weir – the risk, the thunder of the water falling, the exhilaration of the moment shut everything else out of your mind and it was all right. In fact it was pretty good as long as you never thought of your little brother copying you, teetering along the wet boards, blinking in the spray, his cries for help lost – they had been lost, hadn't they? – in the sound of the waters.

Crawford slid the cuttings book back in front of him, flipped it open, uncapped his pen and drew a circle round Parker's face and a circle round the face of the figure standing beside him, one hand resting easily, arrogantly on Parker's shoulder. Then he ripped the photo out, crushed it into a ball and walked rapidly out onto the balcony, where he threw the paper up into the unforgiving wind, which took it dancing over the water until Crawford lost sight of it or the contentious waves claimed it.

Takeover

Basement Flat, 77 Keeble Street, Victoria, London, 22:55
'He drowned his brother?' Celia said.

'His brother drowned – not quite the same thing.' Hugh looked up from the laptop and stopped typing. 'He was there, at the weir.'

'And are you going to use it?'

'I talked to Angela and we both feel it's legitimate comment; it does help explain the guy, after all.'

'I don't know if it's really that simple, Hugh. His brother drowned; everything he's done since then is some kind of compensation. You just simply can't explain a human being that easily.'

The remains of their Chinese takeaway littered the table – Celia was still picking at bits and pieces as she talked. Hugh had moved across to the desk to polish up his piece on the virtual conclusion of the takeover, though the financial editor would hold it until the completion date.

'I just said it *helps* explain the guy.'

'What if he doesn't like it?'

'What if he doesn't? I can't imagine that caring about other people's feelings ever stopped him doing what he wanted. In fact I know the opposite to be the case.'

Celia snapped down the cardboard top of the braised clam with black bean sauce. 'You know what, Hugh?'

'This is strictly embargoed until the show goes out, right?'

'Sure, absolutely.'

'The old guy, the journalist Harry Burton. After he'd told me about the drowning and we'd had a few more beers, we went back to his place – and believe me, walking the Thames path with five pints of real ale aboard is no joke – and he made supper; an experience which a merciful providence has wiped from my memory . . .'

'You know what I've discovered about journalists?'

'How could I . . . What?'

'They all want to be novelists, which is why we have to suffer

264

these acres of purple prose. Cut the merciful providence and tell me the story!'

Hugh Mead pouted; she'd scored a rather accurate hit. Beyond getting into TV, his most secret dream *was* to be a literary novelist.

'Hugh . . . don't play hurt.'

'OK. After dinner he told me about Crawford's political career. The career Crawford told me never really existed.'

'He was deselected.'

'Not exactly. He was the candidate and there was the business with Andrea, when someone found out, remarkably conveniently, that the two of them had spent the night together in a hotel. He wasn't, by all reports, that popular with certain sections of the local Conservative party. Andrea told me that he had more or less bullied his way into being selected as the candidate. Not that he was a bad choice . . .'

'Just unpopular with certain local interests?'

'Oddly enough, since this was the Thatcher election, he wasn't seen as 'one of us'. He hadn't worked his way up through the local constituency party. He hadn't kissed the right babies or the right arses. So no one was really that unhappy when the sex scandal came out and he was forced to step down.'

'I imagine he was less than happy.'

'I'm not sure how he felt about getting out of his marriage. Anyway, he buggered off and the chosen successor – like the London Mayor really – stepped into the breach and was duly elected to Westminster, where he sits to this day.'

'I have a feeling that I'm missing the key to all this, Hugh.'

'John Parker was the constituency chairman who got Crawford thrown out. Crawford's successor, Patrick Crossly, a long-time party faithful, was also staying at the same hotel as the candidate on the fatal night. Parker and Crossly went way back – they were at school together, both big in local business, both members of the masons, whatever. You know the picture.'

'So Crawford wanted revenge – that was it? This whole deal

was about getting his own back on Parker for something that happened 20 years ago?'

'Not quite. Don't forget Patrick Crossly, who – so George Packenham informed me, when we had a word yesterday – used to sit on one of the committees examining trade links and deals with, among other places, Indonesia. Now, oddly, Crossly has been a sort of unofficial adviser to Crawford's company for the last ten years. Don't ask me why – maybe it was guilt over the betrayal, maybe greed – the human heart is . . . well, all too human.'

'The Tories aren't in, Hugh, in case you hadn't noticed.'

'An easy slip to make nowadays, but Crossly still had contacts on the committee and, what should happen yesterday but that the FO announced that . . . a long-term electronics contract would not be entered into with the Indonesian government. A contract that could, in part, have – allegedly, according to Packenham – been awarded to a British firm with certain expertise.'

'Byfield, in other words?'

'Yup. Shrewd, huh?'

'But bloody dangerous if it ever came out.'

'No proof.'

'It would screw up Crossly's hope of reselection and it wouldn't do much good for Crawford. Are you going to use it?'

'Of course. Packenham is digging for more dirt.'

'What does he get out of it?'

'He's fronting the documentary. I think he wants to ease Paxman out of *Start the Week*, fancies himself as a guru. If he gets anything hard enough, we'll go with it; otherwise, we'll have to pay it carefully.'

Celia sat silently for the longest time – eventually Hugh said, 'Well?'

'I dunno. I like the old bastard, I really do. Don't ask me why. And I'd hate to see him hurt.'

'He'll roll with the punches and come up fighting.'

'I don't know, Hugh, I really don't know. What if he were no longer running Ayot?'

'Oh come on, he'd hardly retire because of this. He's never run away from anything in his life.'

'But if he wasn't there?'

'I guess they'd probably pull it. Yesterday's news.'

'Yesterday's news,' Celia said. She started putting the food containers into the brown paper bag they'd come in. 'I'll get rid of these,' she said, 'if you leave them around they just smell up the house.'

Day +39

friday 10th dec. 18:00

byfield plc, goldhawk mews, london

JOHN PARKER HAD BEEN DRINKING all day and he saw no reason to stop now. He pulled the cork out of the single malt and poured – there was no more than an inch or so left, so he threw it back in one. It didn't really taste but then he wasn't drinking for the taste, hadn't been since the last board meeting. He was drinking so he didn't think anymore – about the loss of Byfield, about the coldness at home between Heather and himself. It was even beginning to affect his relationship with Claire. She had started coming out with the kind of crass embarrassing clichés that would make any cinema-goer squirm in their seat: 'Daddy, why is Mummy crying? Daddy, why don't you smile any more? Daddy, Mummy, what's wrong?' And in the mouth of a child the stupid trite phrases became clean, shiny phrases that re-flected a face made slack by too much whisky, too much self-pity, too much, too far down the road . . .

There had been no more arguments, no shouting; they had, on the evenings he got back before the early hours, existed together in the same space without touching in any way. He was begin-ning to wonder if it would have been kinder to Claire if he'd just moved into an hotel and Heather could have said: Daddy's away on business. Maybe it would come to that.

He picked up the bottle but it was empty. He put it back on the desk, beside the white envelope which bore his official resigna-tion. There was nothing to worry about. The terms were good, he was a rich man now; had all the money he could ever possibly want.

Tim Ericson had said, 'Start again, John, find a little firm and build it up.' But Tim was already busy with the changeover and, for all his concern, hadn't got the time to sit and talk. Dick Worthington, Bill Harper, Angus Howerd were all gone. Only Bryan House, Tom Swift, who stayed down at the Swindon factory, and Beth Stewart were still around.

He knew Beth had been hurt by his attitude at the last meeting and he'd apologised later and she had accepted but there was always going to be something between them now – not just that she was the future and he was the past, it was more the simple fact that he had behaved in a petulant, self-indulgent manner to her. She would never see him – in her own way admire him – in the same way again. Once more, he had let himself down.

Mrs Harrison had taken early retirement and had left the day before – another exquisitely painful moment, though the formality with which they had always treated each other had given them a template which got them through a parting that might so easily have ended in tears – on either part.

He reached out for the bottle – and pulled his hand back. If there was no more whisky, there was no more reason to stay. And there was no reason why he shouldn't do the one thing he still wanted to do. After all, he was retired, no one to please but himself. Lucky old John Parker, eh?

He got unsteadily to his feet, dropped the empty bottle in the waste bin, walked unsteadily over to the coatrack and pulled on the Burberry. The white envelope was still lying there on the table – he picked it up, walked to the door, opened it, switched off the light and went on down the corridor. At Bryan House's office he knocked and went straight in.

'John . . . are you OK?'

'Never better, old man, never better.' He didn't try to smile, that would be too ghastly, but at least he could walk out of *his company* with a straight back.

'Thought you'd better have this, Bryan. Just to make it official.'
He handed the envelope to the non-exec.

'Thanks, John. The accountants will get together with you to
work things out in detail. And you know, if you need office
space or secretarial help for anything – then please do call on
us.'

'I will,' he said. Then added quickly, to forestall any goodbye
speeches that House might have, 'Better be off. Night, Bryan.'

He shut the door and went on down the passage. Beth's office
door was ajar and the room was dark; she wasn't there, which
saved him that, at least. As he walked on to the lifts, some of the
clerical staff started to nod, or say goodbye, but something in his
face stopped them and it was in silence that he walked into the
lift and rode down to reception. The security man nodded – to
him it all meant nothing – even so, House must have primed
him, since he hurried from behind the desk and said, 'Shall I call
you a taxi, Sir?'

'No, I'll walk. Thank you.' And with that, John Parker stepped
out of his kingdom into the cold December air.

No, he wouldn't take a taxi – he wanted to be lost in the
crowds of office and shop workers heading home – busy, tired,
fulfilled, expectant, worried, sad; he wanted just to be one
among millions and lose himself. But the one person you can
never lose *is* yourself. Another stupid cliché, he thought, then
wondered if perhaps Kevin could cure him of this as he had
cured him of other things on that terrible night with Crawford.
And as he walked, lost in the crowd, into the Tube, down the
stairs and onto the train, he thought back to the moment
Crawford had leaned over him and said something about darkness, he couldn't remember exactly what. And he remembered
years before, telling young Mr Crawford that his behaviour was
not up to the standard they expected of their candidate and that
he must resign. Well, here he was, ex-Chairman Parker, going off
to Soho to try and find a young boy – perhaps the only person in
the world whom he could still help, the only person who still

needed him. To be needed. Yes, better than sex, better than friendship, better than love . . . to be needed.

He got off the Tube at Leicester Square and popped in for a quick one before . . . going on. Just a bracer or two or three and then, not even bothering to do up his coat, he stepped out of the pub into the maze of Soho – the narrow streets as noisy and bright and full of obstacles as a pinball machine. But it didn't matter – from the moment he had decided to come here, he had experienced a sense of freedom that had been denied him since that first phone call on the golf course. He was committed now – nothing, not his daughter, nor his wife, nor his reputation would stand in his way. But what if Kevin were not here anymore? He experienced a stab of panic and began to hurry towards the games arcade. What if they'd shut it down? Don't be a fool, he told himself, it'll be there and yes, it was, Venice Amusements, just beyond the glass, the world he had always wanted.

He scanned the faces inside – some intent on playing the machines, some gathered in easy groups, looking about them. Should he go in and ask for Kevin? Why not? What did he have to lose? He felt himself laughing – he felt a touch on his sleeve and turned.

'Dad . . .'

'Paul?' He couldn't work it out – what was his son doing here? 'Paul?'

'I was at Goldhawk Mews, Dad. Tim Ericson rang Mum. He was worried about you. She was frantic. She didn't know what to do. I . . .'

He stood there, a dark figure in a long coat, the gleam of his collar faintly visible at the throat.

'Paul, I was . . . I was . . .'

'It's all right, Dad, it doesn't matter.'

And looking into Paul's eyes he realised that he was right; it didn't matter, it really didn't matter if he started to cry and took hold of his son and hung onto him for dear life.

Completion Day

monday 13th dec.

butler's wharf, london, 20:00

GUESTS HAD STARTED ARRIVING at seven-thirty and by eight the large room overlooking the Thames was heaving with bodies; moving among them were waiters with trays of champagne and canapés. Jim Crawford stood by the door, welcoming arrivals. Andrea was beside him, adding her invaluable civilising touch to the rather gruff hellos Crawford was issuing.

'Owen, you're late, expected you on time.'

'Business first, Jim,' the banker shook hands with Crawford, air-kissed Andrea and passed on into the crowd. He took a glass of champagne from a waiter but refused the canapé – conversation was tricky with both hands full, and he wanted to make a number of contacts tonight. First among them was Beth Stewart, the new arrival on the Ayot main board. Powys pushed across the room to the balcony windows. They were slightly open and he could see Stewart on the illuminated balcony, in deep conversation with an older man. Powys shrugged, not wanting to interrupt anything – first impressions counted and he had a feeling that Miss Stewart was going to become a considerable player. He turned back to the crowd and found himself facing Gavin Clooney, Crawford's mad professor. He nodded politely and started to move away but Clooney held out a restraining hand.

'Mr Powys, I wonder if I might take up just a moment or two of your valuable time?'

Powys was no fool; he could read a situation as well as

anyone, and it was clear to him that Clooney wasn't talking pleasantries.

'Of course, Dr Clooney,' he said, and the two of them wandered over to a comparatively quiet corner.

Out on the balcony, Beth shivered. Her bare shoulders were feeling the chill – still, the view was stunning and well worth the discomfort, and besides, Tim Ericson was only here at her request and, she knew, would be heading home as soon as he could decently take leave of his new boss. He waved his empty glass at Tower Bridge . . . '

'Great view, Beth. What do you think it costs to live here?'

'God knows, Tim. More than you or I will ever make.'

'It's a change from Byfield,' he said. 'I can't imagine John Parker would ever have put on a spread like this. Of course, he would have said he was saving money for the company but . . . what good did it do him in the end?'

'Don't, Tim,' Beth grimaced. 'I'm feeling bad enough already.'

'Oh, come on, didn't I tell you when this started: you'd come through all right?'

'You were there, Tim, at that last meeting.' Every time she closed her eyes Beth could see Parker's angry, hurt, vulnerable face as he said, 'At least have the decency to wait until I'm out of the room before issuing your orders.' On a dozen occasions since then she had been about to share her feelings with Jack but somehow, each time, he was too busy or she wasn't quite sure how he'd respond or even if he'd understand. So nothing had been said and this evening was the first time she'd uttered a word in public.

'Tim, I betrayed him. I sat there and told him it was all over.'

'Someone had to, Beth.'

'It didn't have to be me. You know that Crawford had offered me a position on his board before that?'

'Not for sure, but it was clear enough something had happened. And why not?'

'Because . . . because I hurt him. I could see it, Tim, in his eyes.'

'And what are you worried about, Beth? That you did it or that you *could* do it? Maybe we all discovered a few new things about ourselves during this business. Maybe I feel all that . . .' he turned and looked back into the room, where a swirl of people were in constant motion: expensive dresses and suits, the gleam of gold and silver, champagne sparkling in crystal glasses, smart people being smart, 'isn't what I really want after all. Maybe it will be time for me to go once the integration is finished.'

Beth said, 'I want you to stay on, Tim. I think we need your kind of experience.'

He put a hand on her shoulder. 'That's very nice of you but it isn't true. If I stayed you'd only have to get rid of me. Not that I think you couldn't do it, Beth. You're a lot harder than you give yourself credit or blame for; you're going to learn one hell of a lot in the next few months and I'm going to enjoy reading about you in the business pages.' He smiled and leaned forward and gave her a kiss on the cheek. 'And now I'm going to say my goodbyes to Jim Crawford and go home and read the latest *Angler's Times*. Good night, Beth.'

He turned and walked back inside. Beth hugged herself against the cold. Was he right? Back at that first meeting she'd thought of the takeover as a trip through undiscovered country; what she realised now was that the trip had barely begun.

She picked up her empty glass from the balustrade and went back inside, passing Diane Ellroy, a new colleague, who was talking with the Ayot company secretary, an intense young man whom Beth had not yet had time to get to know.

'Beth, hi! Having a good time?' Diane asked.

'Great, thank you,' Beth nodded, but before she could say any more Gavin Clooney and Owen Powys materialised beside her and steered her away.

'Nice woman, I think she's going to be a real success,' Diane said.

'Never mind her,' Mark said. 'I want to talk about us.'

'There's nothing to say, Mark.'

'I love you, Diane.'

'Don't talk so loud and no, you don't love me. You love the fact that I allowed you to do some of the things you dreamed about. That's not me. It's not even really you.'

Mark started to protest. She silenced him with a look. 'No, listen to me. I'm forty . . . well, forty-ish . . . I've been single all my life. That's one of the reasons I've done so well in business. I intend to do even better. I am who I am, Mark. I need my own space, my own time. I like being alone, I don't like tripping over other people's clothes or other people in my life. I like my friends and . . . I think you are a friend and, I admit, I was stupid to let a friend become a lover. Don't get angry – or do get angry but control it and listen to me. It was just sex. If we pretend it was love, it'll screw us both up and God knows what it'll do to your family.'

'She doesn't . . . Manjit doesn't . . .'

'Oh, come on, Mark, you're not going to tell me that your wife doesn't understand you?'

For a moment it looked as if Mark was going to burst out angrily but he held on and shook his head. 'We've been drifting apart. Manjit, the children . . . we don't seem to make contact any more.'

'It's just a management problem. You'll work it out.'

'Can't you see, Diane, I'm hurting, I'm in pain.'

'Yes, well, it ain't exactly easy for me. It might only be sex but it was great and I wouldn't mind a lot more of it but it ain't gonna be that way. Some things, some people you want an awful lot – you just can't have them and that's what you have to live with.'

'I don't know if I can,' Mark said.

Diane smiled a sweet, sad smile: 'Oh, I think you'll be surprised what you can live with if you have to.'

'Diane Ellroy? We haven't met. Celia Hart, I'm an analyst at Waymouth's.'

Diane took in the young woman wearing a dress so short and tight it might have been sprayed on. 'Oh, yes, you do stuff for Jim?'

'I do. And I wondered if I could have a word with you. Owen Powys mentioned that some people on the board might be thinking about change . . .'

A suspicious look flickered between Diane and Mark. Hart was one of Crawford's people – what was her interest in the coup? Surely not friendly. Was this the first warning shot?

'I don't know if there's any point in talking right now,' Diane said, 'since I really can't confirm . . .'

'Look, Diane, I like Jim Crawford – I also like my career. As it happens, I think that your interests, my likes and my career prospects might actually be heading in the same direction. I want to help him and, oddly, the only way I can do that is by helping you.'

Diane considered. How far should she trust this young woman? Across the room she saw Gavin Clooney peering at her over a smoked salmon and cream cheese canapé. He smiled and nodded and inclined his head towards Celia Hart as if to say, yes, go ahead, by all means, listen.

So Diane did.

Clooney ate the canapé in one mouthful and turned to Peter Allbury. 'Good show you've put on, Peter. Who paid, I wonder?'

Allbury grinned vaguely – he was worrying about one of the pigs which was off-colour – and said, 'Ah, looks like I'm needed. I think Jim is going to make a speech. Excuse me, won't you, Gavin.'

Clooney placed a restraining finger on the impeccably cut shoulder of Allbury's suit. 'If you would, Peter. I think we have a bijou moment before the great man utters. Perhaps you'd join me on the balcony?' Using the same finger he guided the reluctant chairman through the crowd towards the plate glass windows. As they went he caught Diane's eye and indicated that she should join them.

Beth watched and, when Clooney nodded at her, she too followed the group out onto the balcony. This party – and more especially her recent conversation with Clooney – was proving more of an education than even she had expected. Tim's words about betrayal had caused her deep concern. Yes, John Parker was going anyway and, in one sense, it was decent and honest that she should be the one who finally made him see the truth. After all, she was coming out of the whole affair better than anyone else on the board. And this was her reward – a place near the sun, a position on Crawford's board, the chance to aim for the stars. And yet, no sooner had she set foot on the entrepreneur's home turf than she was being recruited by Gavin Clooney for another act of betrayal. Was this really how business worked, an endless round of predator and victim, an evolutionary spiral that cared as much about the individual as did the cosmos about an individual oyster? And if so, was it really what she wanted?

She shivered as she stepped out of the warmth of the room. She was spending more time outside than in – but then, she reflected, the company was better out here – or at least, more lethal. Philip Goodman, the young Sales and Marketing director, was lounging against the balustrade, peering along the river.

He turned and smiled at Beth like a hungry shark: 'Hi, enjoying yourself?'

'Most interesting party I've ever been to,' she said. 'I like the theme.'

'Is there a theme?'

'Renaissance Italy – the Borgias, the poison cup, the knife in the back?'

Behind her, Gavin Clooney chuckled. 'Oh, very good, my dear, yes, yes indeed.'

'I mean it, Mr Clooney.'

'Of course you do,' he said. 'We all mean it. We are very serious people, aren't we, Peter?'

Allbury nodded miserably.

The door behind them slid open and closed and Owen Powys

and Colin Burroughs joined the party. The banker mimed a shiver and said: 'Can we get this over with quickly, I'm freezing my . . .' then, noticing Beth, he finished lamely: 'it's damn chilly.' Burroughs, the clinical Human Resources expert, did not appear to notice the temperature. His jacket was open and he wore only a thin white shirt. 'Well, it's merely a matter of hearing what Gavin has to say. As far as I know we are all in agreement?'

Goodman said: 'For the health of the company, Jim Crawford has to go.'

'You know he'll fight . . .' It seemed for a moment as if Allbury were about to put up his fists like a prizefighter – then all the protest seemed to wheeze out of his body and he slumped. 'It . . . it could be messy. I still don't know if . . .'

Clooney said: 'It's gone beyond that, Peter. The fact that we are here together, the fact that we are a cabal, as it were, means that sooner or later we *will* constitute a threat to Jim Crawford. And he will not be able to countenance that . . .'

'. . . treason?' Allbury supplied.

' "Treason doth never prosper",' Clooney said. ' "And what's the reason? For if it prosper, none dare call it treason." So you see, Peter, all we have to fear is failure. And if we do not, as they say, hang together in this, then Jim Crawford will make damned sure we hang separately.'

'He has to go,' Goodman said. 'It's time. He's done a reasonable job up to now but there's no doubt in anyone's mind here or in the City – right, Owen?'

The banker nodded. 'Absolutely. The bank is . . .' He waved an airy hand as if to say: we're behind you as long as you win.

'It's clear,' Goodman went on, 'that we paid over the odds for Byfield. It was reckless, it was irresponsible . . .'

'Piratical,' Clooney said, 'splendid and, in its way, admirable – but not business, not as we know it.'

'The only question is,' Goodman concluded, 'will he go?'

Typically it was Colin Burroughs who said it like it was: 'If the board votes him out, he's out. That's it.'

'Bad publicity,' Allbury countered. It was obvious he was coming to the end of his defences. However, he did have a point: a messy boardroom battle so soon after the takeover would not help confidence and this would be reflected in the share price.

'He will go,' Diane said. 'To begin with, he'll fight and we should allow him that privilege but when it comes right down to it . . .'

She looked across at Clooney who took up the theme: 'Ms Ellroy and I have talked with someone who has information about certain contacts between Jim and, shall we say, another riparian?'

'Let's push the boat out, Gavin,' Diane said, 'and say something we can all understand. I mean what the fuck is a riparian?'

The interjection punctured the atmosphere of tension which had grown around the group on the balcony and there was an outburst of laughter.

'Well, that's better,' Beth said, 'at least we won't look quite like we're plotting the death of tyrants now.'

Clooney was still smiling as he began again: 'A dweller on the river bank. Ratty and Mole in *The Wind in the Willows*. The point is, if push comes to shove, we have information that will make it virtually certain that Jim will have to go.'

'Virtually?' Beth asked.

'Ah, yes, nothing in this world is certain,' Clooney said. 'But if what our informant has told us – from the best of motives – is indeed true, then even Jim Crawford may find himself facing the inevitable. But that is the future. Now, with the addition of Ms Stewart to our team, we have the numbers to vote Crawford out of his job. As long as we are, each of us, ready to grasp the nettle?'

Beth nodded when he looked at her. Events were moving too fast, she couldn't keep up with herself anymore, or maybe she didn't care to think about it, because if she did, she would have to admit that this was a lot more interesting than travelling into work and spending eight or ten hours pouring over balance sheets. It was an answer to the question she'd asked herself a few minutes earlier: was this what she really wanted? And she only hoped it didn't become a habit, or perhaps an addiction. And she wondered, briefly, if that was how it had started with Jim Crawford.

'I agree, next board meeting we call for a vote of no confidence.' Goodman finished up the accounting. 'And I think it's time we went back inside, otherwise Jim might twig and lock us all out so we freeze before morning.'

This drew a laugh – but it was an uneasy laugh and there was something rather furtive about the group as they drifted back into the warmth, the noise and the general celebrations. The crowd was even thicker than before and Beth noticed the diminutive figure of Bobbi King standing with a tall, louche, sun-tanned man. Bobbi waved: 'Beth, come over. Meet Perry, my ex. We've decided . . .'

'Ladies and gentlemen,' Crawford's voice boomed out over the room, cutting off Bobbi's revelation. 'Thank you for coming. Before you all get too –' Andrea flashed him a warning glance. He grinned, 'Before you get down to the real business of this evening, I'd like to say a few words about the battle we have just fought and won . . .'

END

Business Today

Most of us are not anti-business – we either work in the corporate sector or are dependent upon it. However, there is a tendency to make corporate life unduly complicated, to eliminate any vestiges of fun and to conclude, quite wrongly, that most business problems are unique when they are not.

Successful companies have a number of characteristics in common; they have the ability to choose the right people, to price and position their products correctly, to possess a passion for them, set goals which can be achieved and adjust strategy to meet the changing circumstances. Happy companies build around the successful parts of the business – the building blocks. Unfortunately, too many companies don't know how to grow, only how to control.

A company needs vision and its directors must be creative. It is easy to kill off an idea. The UK, despite some truly notable corporate successes especially in recent years, still holds that there is a stigma to failure and doesn't always differentiate between failure due to incompetence and failure resulting from being bold and having a go. The former, if at board level, is rewarded; the latter is condemned. Yet we should differentiate between the two; nor should we pay our directors to defend the old order, but to challenge it.

Furthermore, successful companies display additional characteristics, often apparently almost seamlessly. They take pride in solving problems themselves rather than in seeking advice from outsiders; in that way the solutions become part of the overall corporate culture. Ayot never quite aspired to that approach, Byfield failed to acknowledge that certain problems even existed.

Of course, success needs to be handled with care. It can make a company, or individual, lazy. Sometimes a company appears to be more successful than it really is because the competition is weak, or because it is comparing itself with internally set yard-sticks, forgetting the fact that the competition is not standing still.

Ordinary companies, rather like Byfield, don't learn from the fast-growing ones, even if the latter can be like shooting stars, here today, gone tomorrow. Few companies know much about the competition in their own sector, and fewer still bother to ask the successful ones why they are successful. Rather unexpect-edly the latter are very willing to explain! We live in a fast-changing world, where competition encourages companies to devour each other, when big names can be the most vulnerable and where sooner than people realise – the unthinkable can happen.

Many companies carry out a conventional exercise in due diligence on a potential purchase but forget to extend the exercise to see whether there would be a cultural fit. It is still commercially feasible to proceed without that fit, but the pur-chaser needs to be aware of the problems and possibly recruit different people later. Crawford has given no hint that he has analysed the takeover of Byfield in that way. Alas, and all too often, the best leave after a successful takeover or, as in the case of Beth, before its completion. Remember, too, when buying a company with a distinctive culture – and probably strong brands as well – it is imperative to appear to manage it at arm's length. Customers will accept the logic and merits of a different culture operating behind the scenes, but they want their product or service, 'their company', merely to be refined or enhanced, not to be tampered with.

Any competitive advantages enjoyed by a company can be quickly lost. The shelf life of most products and ideas is shorter than ever before and many of the means to achieve the original advantage are equally available to the competition. Shorter shelf-life puts up unit costs, which can be brought down by new production techniques that, in turn, merely reduce product costs. Back to square one and no net gain! Access to IT and to so much knowledge on a 24-hour basis is a mixed blessing. Not only is it available to the competition; it can prevent a company seeing the main points clearly and simply.

Some companies fail because overheads rise and rise. It happens so easily. Usually colleagues will argue – the most vocal ones – that an increase in expenditure is necessary before a saving, or increased profits, can be achieved. The latter often fails to materialise.

Ultimately, corporate success is always down to people. Boards tend to deserve the people and teams they get, whether good or bad. A company should always recruit the best it can afford, while being wary of the inherent dishonesty, or gross exaggeration, prevalent in CVs. Few CVs list a single failure.

Not all companies will, by inclination, be entrepreneurial but all must be nimble and keep abreast of change; otherwise they will fall flat, become less profitable, find it harder to recruit or retain the best staff and be subject to either a takeover or even liquidation.

Crawford is a typical modern entrepreneur, acutely aware of his meagre formal education, harbouring an inferiority complex as a result and yet being highly critical of those with the educational advantages that he has overtaken in the corporate stakes. Such people keep wishing to prove themselves; even becoming, on occasion, aggressive. Crawford, though, also re-minds us that few entrepreneurs have a formal education, that they are ideas people and that secondary schools and business schools don't test or develop the skills they need for success – inquisitiveness and tenacity coupled with lateral thinking. The very best Crawfords acknowledge that they make mistakes every day and judge themselves on how they respond to what to them becomes an opportunity.

They will also choose to make things happen, picking a course of action, one of many, and possibly not even the best, and be convinced that the idea is right. They will live the concept 24 hours a day and might even select people who are virtually unemployable to carry out their ideas, but who share the vision and the energy. They are right for that culture.

Directors can gain loyalty, and extra effort, if they are seen to be fighting on behalf of their colleagues or if they delegate in order to develop the talent. So many people, usually directors, think they are indispensable, but they are not. At least, if and when they leave, they should destroy all their papers to give some chance of perpetuating the legend.

Entrepreneurs, like Crawford, are good at ideas but are often poor at detail and they need more conventional people around them in order to control – not stifle – that entrepreneurism, until a time comes when different skills are required and new personnel should be appointed.

Picking winners for the team isn't that easy. Past performance is not always a true indicator of future success. Some are not successful the second time around. The factors may not come together in the same way. The person might be too successful and be less hungry, or have experience of only one company and therefore not be exposed to other corporate cultures and sectors. It is far from certain that the newly created group of Ayot and Byfield will flourish.

In a way, though, the best time to be in a company is when it is having a tough, or uncertain, time. There is more challenge and a steeper learning curve. Both Beth and Diane will, no doubt, look back on these few days of the takeover battle with fascination, even gratitude.

There is a psychology to running a company. First, be neurotic about your customers in order to maintain loyalty and benefit the bottom line. Seek goodwill and attach great value to it. Be cautious about statements about the future, for they can return to haunt you. They are about predictions and are judgements, they are not factual. They may depend upon unpredictable factors, such as how sales might hold up, or how the exchange rate might operate.

Use humour to make unpalatable points. Listen at all levels, including body language. Be cautious and realise that we are all babes in arms outside our selected areas of expertise. However, don't allow yourself to become a hostage to any colleague's technical skills.

Never hang on in case an order might come round the corner. If the situation is that bad, bite the bullet. Nor work at a loss even if it is in the name of goodwill or future business. Concentrate on your major clients, almost be prepared to sacrifice the others. Spend the time where the money is. Your major clients will like this as well. If frightened by your large customers, because of their crucial position to your company, they will force you into a loss-making situation. It is hard, but you must stand up to them.

Realise that people don't work well if only 70 per cent stretched, nor if 110 per cent stretched; they need the right balance. It is a thoroughly rewarding exercise to get people to perform above their known ability. Most of us can achieve more than we realise.

Don't reach decisions either too quickly or too slowly. Walk around the desk, over and over again, working it out, before deciding. Give yourself time to think and understand that younger colleagues are often more impatient. Control the tension, harness it.

Remember that colleagues in middle age, who have held top positions, will want to be statesmen, not be up at 5 a.m., doing 12-hour days, acting like a 35-year-old. The more successful you are, the more sexy you will become. Others will approach you, but just as most political careers end in failure, many business ones do as well. So look after the friends you had before you were quite so successful and especially keep an eye on your wife – or husband – who can change for the worse when you are at the top.

First impressions about companies – as about people – are usually correct, even if every company has skeletons. Most of them, though, are not commercially disadvantageous, even if they can prevent a company wanting to raise its profile – perhaps via sponsorship. Many a good company has kept itself below the corporate parapet because of undue concern about almost non-existent ill will. And if there is bad press coverage, don't flatter yourself that the world will either remember it or bother about it in a month's time. You might, the media and public won't.

The media plays a powerful role in the book and, in the *short term*, press comment can have either an advantageous or detrimental effect. Companies pay their PR firms to gain them publicity – they should pay them more to keep out of the press. If the press says something bad about your company, whether fair or not, it can be very damaging in the short term especially if it appears to come out of the blue. Then the share price can be hit and the directors accused of being negligent.

So managing risk is crucial. There is a need for sophisticated internal audits. The word audit is a misnomer, giving the impression of merely financial considerations. An audit can cover anything, either to see what went wrong or how to prevent the problem – in short, to appraise the effectiveness of internal controls. Sometimes internal audits can hold up decision-making and prove costly – and create yet another new industry, that of regulation, in which only the consultants come out the winners.

Do not think that if a customer is happy with one product he will automatically take another. The additional product has to be one which the customer recognises as a logical one to come from you.

You have to find a carrot to change a customer's behaviour.

It is no use charging for what was free before. Rather you will need to manage change in such a way that the customer is satisfied. The litmus test is to have your customers recommending your firm.

Remember that ultimately, however great the competition, however influential external or even personal factors are on your ability to perform, your competitors will also have doubts and are vulnerable. It is just that they might be disguising them better.

Getting the strategy and the structure of the company right is fundamental. Often companies spend too much time on its formulation, attempting to create the perfect strategy, rather than merely undertaking a thorough exercise, drawing heavily on the input of subsidiaries and being prepared to start implementing it, while constantly reviewing its progress. The strategy will help avoid creating a conglomerate with no logic and little sustainability, especially in bad times. It will highlight where the skills shortages are, may avoid unnecessary acquisitions and encourage organic growth (easier to control and therefore to create additional wealth). Do not be unduly despondent nor surprised if the consensus over vision evident at the strategy stage gives way to tension when things start to go wrong. It is inevitable.

While the first priority of a company is to survive, the strategy will show that mere survival is not enough. If successful and over a long period of time, a firm can become careless and let the structures and controls weaken. A strong strategic culture can avoid this frequent pitfall. Strategy is not a once-a-year exercise, but a continuous, gradual one, considering possible options with good information available. It is not aiming at instant bottom-line success unless you are a company doctor. Ultimately, however good the strategy might be, the company will need to deliver it, make it happen, and so have the right people in place, led by a board which knows how to discuss at length rather than present in detail.

A balanced board, especially one with appropriately appointed non-executive directors (NEDs) – not known personally by the directors, where the chemistry is right and where each is appointed as a generalist and not to rectify a technical imbalance on the board – will help prevent a strategy becoming an ego trip or being too grand and making cash flow even more crucial.

Without a working, effective relationship between the chairman and the chief executive (CEO), nothing else can hold together. The failure of these relationships dominates the story; at Ayot, a weak chairman and strong CEO, at Byfield the reverse. The chairman should run the board, the CEO the company. Effective CEOs are not often shrinking violets, they are optimists to be treated with respect by a chairman who recognises his role as that of coach and mentor, and ultimately grand high executioner. The role of the chairman is to sack the CEO.

It is crucial that the succession planning for the CEO is well worked out and is discussed annually, with no hidden agenda, no embarrassment, taking into account both internal candidates and the prospect of an external one. Never plan to change the chairman and CEO at the same time and it is usually appropriate to appoint the chairman from within the existing ranks of non-executive directors. To parachute one into the chairman's chair usually means that the succession planning has gone wrong.

The chairman should invite all to speak, seeking their judgements and the NEDs should determine what four or five items out of a hundred to be considered in a year are crucial and which ones they can contribute to in a unique way. Having no career in the company, unlike their executive colleagues, they can be bold, have courage, have a go, be the outsider with an insider feel to the company. Their role is crucial and invaluable.

Really effective NEDs, unlike the relatively ineffectual ones in the story – apart from Bryan House – can and should contribute a great deal. While they must never second-guess an executive colleague – the latter will always have far more knowledge of the company – NEDs can insist on putting the right conditions in place at board level. Every company needs leadership – success or failure boils down to one person – and the role of the NED is to ensure that the company has *the* right person in the right position at the right time.

Frequently board papers are over-presented and the company needs a strong NED team to get the true picture. However, they should never become so familiar with the company that the NEDs know the answers to the questions, or think they do and probably before the question is even asked. This is a sign of becoming stale; it is time to move on.

The best NEDs are truly independent – financially and psychologically. They don't need the position for status or for money and so they can walk away from the job. Usually they are in full-time executive positions, unless they are the chairman; otherwise they can become out of date. The NED who holds no executive position will probably sparkle at the first few board meetings, but there is little or nothing to follow. Thereafter, it is mere repetition.

Being an NED should be fun for most of the time and can be a privileged position, with no daily responsibilities. But when the going gets tough the demands can be considerable and the remuneration has not kept abreast with executive salaries despite the increased demands on a NED's time, largely as a result of the escalation of board committees, such as the remuneration, audit and nomination committees. There needs to be a balance here – to pay too much compromises their independence – to pay too little can merely aggravate.

The best NEDs can say 'no' or challenge constructively without appearing disloyal. Not an easy task when one considers that the NED will never know as much as the executive directors. Also when an item reaches the board it has usually got the backing of the CEO and the executive directors.

For the NED, the position should always be a learning exercise. They go to teach but come away learning. It recharges their batteries and gives them exposure to different cultures and

291

sectors, especially important if they have worked mainly for one company as an executive director.

Companies need to spend as much time as possible familiarising the City with their strategy. If the company is not one of the leaders in its sector, the City will spend little time on that company, and the relevant directors mustn't overwhelm the analysts with too much detail. Both Ayot and Byfield failed here. Always try to predict profits realistically or at least achieve results slightly better than City expectations or forecasts.

It is an advantage to know how to influence the City quietly behind the scenes. If the short-term performance is good enough, the City will believe and have patience in the longer-term plans; but if forecasts go array, the City will look hard and unsympathetically at your weaknesses – lack of strategy perhaps or long-term planning. If good news equals events moving in sequence and in the right general direction, then the City is prepared to take notice – less so with isolated events.

Unfortunately, very few directors on the way up to the main board are given any exposure to the City and when they reach the top they are apprehensive and confused by the mystique of the Square Mile.

Professional advisers can be regarded as merely a cruel necessity, burdening any deal with excessive numbers of people and charging high fees. Advisers need to tread carefully, remembering that most have never run a company themselves, and those who run their professional firm are not recognised for their managerial skills. They are often a group of individuals, with a natural temptation to believe that they are virtually self-employed and only coming together for administrative convenience. The better ones, however, acknowledge the challenge facing their clients, recognise that the difference between success and failure can be narrow and that it is not easy to be successful especially over a long period of time.

Perhaps it is wrong to classify women as a separate corporate entity but total equality has not yet been achieved – except perhaps in areas of the City. The glass ceiling will probably crash rather soon now, within five years at most, helped on a little by the wish of directors not to see their daughters penalised when they enter the market place! Women on main boards, who avoid the temptation of reminding their male colleagues that they are pioneers, tend to create more consensus. Alas, before that stage, they will have to overcome the male clubbiness of the board.

We are entering an age where stakeholder considerations are becoming paramount, not just those of the shareholders but of every aspect of business life. Frequently mentioned is the environment. It is quite wrong to label business anti-environment. In many sectors, sustainable economic growth can be achieved only if based on sound scientific costings and, increasingly, the public acts as a watchdog with its instinctive feeling for what is right and wrong when it concerns the environment. If a company meets the consumers' and society's legitimate worries it will win their support, create valuable goodwill and the company's bottom line will benefit. When there is conflict and disagreement the reason is usually not sinister but rather a matter of a conflict of cultures and expectations. Scientists cannot necessarily give black-and-white answers, which businesses and stakeholders (along with politicians) often want and expect.

Business has probably gained a more respectable press in recent years as increasingly people appreciate the benefits of a successful business environment and, in turn, have greater access to it via readily available IT. The younger generation can now set up their own businesses and feel part of the overall corporate scene.

We need to end the culture of envy. Some profits might be excessive, unfair and unwarranted, but they can act as an inspiration and catalyst to others and as a generator of wealth across the economy. Admittedly, it is easy to be somewhat perplexed by the sheer ordinariness of many successful people

– they can't all have married the previous chairman's son or daughter. Such observations should act as a spur, not as a deterrent. When successful yourself try and retain a degree of modesty, even putting the entire corporate scene into perspective. Captains of industry are no more important in real life than academics in their ivory towers, even if society is financed by business success. In fact, the achievements of the academics will probably outlast them all.

There is nothing more salutary, either, than spending years with one company, sacrificing crucial time with the family, not seeing your children grow up, and then seeing that company in due course be taken over or change its name. Your years of service and the place of your achievements will become lost, unknown by the generation who move in on the following Monday morning.

In the final analysis, there are no unique problems in business. They have been faced before and there are no tablets of stone to cover each function, despite the many textbooks and management courses that imply that there are. One of the most interesting factors about corporate life is how many equally successful businessmen and -women contradict each other.

Underneath, however, there are some transferable skills, evergreen and fundamental. Some of those have been incorporated and highlighted in this book.